P9-AQH-378

North Carolina Wesleyan College Library

The Fleming Collection

Given in Memory of
Mr. and Mrs. Robert E. Fleming
and
Mr. Robert E. Fleming, Jr.
by
Mr. and Mrs. John C. Fleming

The Economics
of Planning

The Economics
of Planning

ERIC J. HEIKKILA

CENTER FOR URBAN POLICY RESEARCH
Rutgers, The State University of New Jersey
New Brunswick, New Jersey

330.917
H465e
2000

N.C. WESLEYAN COLLEGE
ELIZABETH BRASWELL PEARSALL LIBRARY

Copyright © 2000 by Rutgers, The State University of New Jersey

Published by the Center for Urban Policy Research
Civic Square • 33 Livingston Avenue
New Brunswick, New Jersey 08901-1982

All rights reserved

Printed in the United States of America

Cover Design: Helene Berinsky

Typesetting by Network Typesetting, Inc., Highland Park, NJ

Library of Congress Cataloging-in-Publication Data

Heikkila, Eric John
    The economics of planning / Eric J. Heikkila.
        p.   cm.
    Includes bibliographical references and index.
    ISBN 0-88285-162-4 (alk. paper)
    1. Urban economics. 2. City planning—Economic aspects.
    3. Regional planning—Economic aspects. I. Title.
    HT321.H388   1999
    330.9173'2—dc21   99-31560
                                                        CIP

About the Author

Eric J. Heikkila is Associate Professor of Policy, Planning, and Development at the University of Southern California. His scholarship, teaching, and professional service lie at the junction of economics and the planning of human settlements. He maintains his Web site at
http://www-rcf.usc.edu/~heikkila/

To the memory of Kustaa Heikkila,
a pioneer in every sense of the word

Acknowledgments

I am deeply grateful to the many cohorts of students who have helped me learn to teach. My wife Sylvia, my children Aarne and Laila, and my father Walter inspire me to do well by them. The collective exhortations of many colleagues who have encouraged me along the way helped to focus my motivation. Robert W. Lake, Arlene Pashman, and Anne Henoch at CUPR Press have been unfailingly generous with their assistance. My thanks to all.

Contents

List of Figures

**1
THINKING TOOLS**

**2
THE ECONOMICS OF LAND USE ZONING**

3
THE ECONOMICS OF HOUSING

4
THE ECONOMICS OF URBAN STRUCTURE

5
PUBLIC GOODS AND PUBLIC CHOICE

6
THE ECONOMICS OF TRAFFIC CONGESTION

7
RETHINKING FISCAL IMPACTS

8
UNDERSTANDING COST–BENEFIT ANALYSIS

9
THE ECONOMICS OF ENTITLEMENTS

List of Tables

7
RETHINKING FISCAL IMPACTS

8
UNDERSTANDING COST–BENEFIT ANALYSIS

9
THE ECONOMICS OF ENTITLEMENTS

Introduction

The Economics of Planning

This book is motivated by and builds on my more than decade-long experience teaching economics to both graduate and undergraduate students of planning. It also reflects my own background as one who is trained formally in economics and works professionally and academically in planning. The wonderful thing about planning is its rich inclusionary approach to social issues. Planners as a profession acknowledge the importance of architecture, community, culture, economics, engineering, environmental sciences, geography, history, politics, quantitative methods, sociology, and many other perspectives on the planning experience. *Planning is broad*. The wonderful thing about economics, especially the neoclassical approach to microeconomics, is its rigorous and axiomatic approach to a certain class of problems using a well-developed paradigm of applied optimization theory. *Economics is disciplined*. At its best, planning draws on the discipline of economics and other specialized fields and provides an integrating framework for these disparate perspectives. At its worst, planning becomes an unsatisfactory mishmash resulting in a superficial dabbling in fields that planning practitioners do not truly understand. To succeed, the broad integrating approach to planning requires sufficient depth to enable it to span the interdisciplinary breadth convincingly.[1]

This situation presents a challenge in teaching economics to planning students. Most accredited planning programs provide some exposure to the economic perspective on planning issues within their core curriculum, and this is often done by way of a single semester course that is taken alongside several others. Because prior training in economics is not generally a prerequisite for admission to a planning degree program, the economics courses found in the core curriculum typically assume no prior knowledge of economics.

Accordingly, the task of such a course is twofold. First, it must provide instruction on the foundation of economic principles, and secondly, it must apply those principles to topics of interest to planners. This is a rather ambitious undertaking if the intended outcome is to produce planners who understand the economic paradigm well enough to hold forth on its merits and demerits credibly. Something more than a "watered down" version of an urban economics text is called for.

Standard urban economics texts are ill-suited to the dual-pronged task of instruction and application because they tend to be written for students of economics who are already well grounded in the economic paradigm. This reflects the general structure of the economics discipline, where all students are steeped in the micro and macro cores at the outset, and where application areas such as urban economics, natural resources economics, international economics, public choice, industrial organization, and location theory all build on this core. This places the instructor of economics courses for planning students in somewhat of a quandary. Should one concentrate on teaching the principles of economic reasoning, or should one focus instead on its applications and hope that students will infer from those applications what the essential elements are? Or, should one try to combine both aspects in a single course, despite the limited exposure students will have to either first principles or meaningful applications?

This book is intended to encourage and support the latter strategy. It does so by infusing first principles of economic reasoning in an exposition of their application to a set of topics that is likely to be of direct interest to planners, including land use zoning, urban structure, housing, traffic congestion, public goods, fiscal impacts, cost–benefit analysis, entitlements, and institutions. Except for the first chapter, which provides a concise introduction to the tools of marginal analysis and present value techniques, the entire book explores how economists approach specific planning topics, but does so without assuming any prior knowledge of or training in economics on the part of the reader. The approach is highly graphical in its orientation, with a minimum of mathematical equations. Those equations that are used are usually introduced as a restatement, in symbolic terms, of what has already been expressed graphically and textually. Thus, for example, an optimality condition such as *marginal benefit equals marginal cost* (MB = MC) is fully motivated and explained within the context of the application at hand, independently of any equations that might also supplement or reemphasize that point further.

Not surprisingly, given the adopted economic perspective of the book, there are a number of recurring themes that provide a unifying framework for the nine main topical areas presented here. One is the distinction between an *equilibrium* and an *optimum* allocation of resources. When the two fail to coincide, we address issues of *market failure*. A related theme is the loss in efficiency, often depicted graphically as a recurring *triangle of inefficiency* associated with suboptimal allocations. Another recurring theme is the lesson that market failure does not necessarily justify intervention, and that intervention may come in many forms and should be tailored to the issue at hand. And finally, the overall approach of the book is an important theme in itself, emphasizing the diverse ways in which a few fundamental ideas can be powerful tools for organizing one's thinking about a broad complex of topics. It recognizes as well that there is a potential downside to casting all planning issues into a single, arguably narrow perspective. Accordingly, the book's emphasis is on illuminating how certain problems look from the economic perspective, rather than on asserting that "here is how things are." The intention is to help train planners who are able to formulate credible answers to the question "How would an economist analyze this issue?" even as they retain a planning perspective.

How to Use this Book

While the primary purpose of this book is formal instruction on the economic foundations of planning and development, it is also written as a kind of handbook for practitioners on the economics of planning and urban development. Although the central themes of the book are amplified and clarified through their repeated presentation in successive chapters, each chapter is also able to stand on its own, so that a practicing planner confronting a particular problem may find it sufficient to consult just that particular chapter of the handbook. I anticipate that the dual functions of textbook and handbook will grow over time as more and more students bring the book out of the classroom and into their professional practices.

In the context of formal instruction, the book is intended for use in a one-semester course at either the graduate or upper undergraduate level. The content can more than adequately fill the time available in a single semester, so one may choose to emphasize certain topics or chapters more than others. In my own classes, I supplement the book with regular assignments that direct the students to find professional reports or newspaper accounts of issues corresponding to each of the chapter topics. The students are asked to make verbal and/or written presentations about those articles, and to use the conceptual framework presented in the book to analyze the specific example the students have brought to light.

Finally, the book is also written as a supplemental text or primer for upper-division undergraduate urban economics classes found within regular economics departments, although the first chapter may be skipped in such courses. The treatment of the material here is, by design and by intent, quite different from what an urban economics text might normally offer, with less detail on formal models and more emphasis on a clear and intuitive presentation of essential concepts. Having a firm grasp of the fundamentals is in fact the true mark of professional competence, and this book serves that end explicitly.

Preview of Topics

Chapter 1 begins with a concise introduction to key technical concepts that arise repeatedly throughout the remainder of the book. The most important of these is the basic framework of marginal analysis, which is explained here without any direct use of the calculus in which it is grounded. A series of diagrams is used to illustrate the relationship of total, average, and marginal value functions to each other and to the concept of constrained and unconstrained optimization. The graphical and narrative presentation emphasizes the sibling nature of the marginal and average value functions as they are derived from their total value antecedents. Additional diagrams explore how the average value counterpart is affected by vertical shifts in the total value function, while the marginal value function is impervious to such shifts, and the implications of this for decision making are expounded upon. Shadow prices, used extensively in the discussion of cost–benefit analysis in chapter 8, are also introduced in chapter 1 in the context of marginal analysis and constrained optimization. Chapter 1 also introduces the concepts of present and future values, and shows how to evaluate assets, liabilities, or projects that generate intertemporal streams of costs, benefits, revenues, and other monetary equivalents.

The first application, appropriately enough for those with a planning orientation, is land use zoning in chapter 2. The chapter focuses on variations of a single diagram that was first introduced in an instructional article by Heikkila (1989), although the presentation has been modified extensively for the purposes of this book. The exposition takes full advantage of the opportunity offered by a fixed supply of land to collapse several diagrams into one, thereby making the cost of one land use explicit in terms of the other(s). Two competing allocations of land use are examined, a market allocation and an alternative zoning allocation. We show that the market allocation will generate the highest aggregate land value, and that the zoning allocation will consistently result in a loss of aggregate value relative to this benchmark, with a market-based triangle of inefficiency to measure the shortfall. However, we also show that market failure may result in a divergence of the optimum allocation from the market allocation, leading to a potential justification of zoning as a means of deriving the maximum social benefit from a land use allocation, with a corresponding benefit-based triangle of inefficiency. We also discuss at length in chapter 2 the relative advantages of price-based versus quantity-based intervention, a topic that planners do not pay enough attention to. In particular, we show that in cases where intervention is justified, taxes and subsidies may sometimes be used to accomplish the same ends as zoning or other quantity-based restrictions, but with less intrusiveness.

Chapter 3 provides an overview of the economics of housing, noting the complexity and confusion that often arise because of the dual role of housing as a stock (of houses) and as a flow (of housing services). As a result, housing issues are linked simultaneously to real estate markets, financial markets, and rental markets. The decision to own or to rent is in part a matter of positioning oneself strategically in relation to these various markets. Price controls on rental markets for housing are discussed in this context. A simple supply-and-demand diagram is used to show how even well-intentioned attempts to enhance the affordability of housing for renters lead predictably to subsidized housing for a lucky few, and to a shortfall of housing for others, with higher prices for would-be renters. The own versus rent decision is also examined in the context of mortgage finance, where the advantages and disadvantages of leveraging are set out with a series of illustrative examples. We show that leverage works to the advantage of the borrower provided that the rate of appreciation of the housing asset in question exceeds the interest rate on the loan. When this condition is not met leverage magnifies the implied loss. Another important aspect of housing that is addressed in chapter 3 is the measurement of housing quantity. Because housing is inherently a multifaceted good, it is intrinsically difficult to measure the amount of housing along a single dimension. We show that under certain conditions housing price becomes a very useful proxy for housing quantity.

Chapter 4 extends the discussion to issues of urban structure. Working first with the standard monocentric model of urban land, we interpret the downward sloping bid-rent function in terms of a trade-off between accessibility and other goods. The parameters of this trade-off vary across economic sectors, with some sectors valuing access more highly on the margin. As a direct consequence, we expect those sectors to bid more for access and to be located more centrally than other sectors. Chapter 4 also examines the importance of technological changes, including improvements in transportation technology, on a steadily flattening land rent gradient with a consequent dispersion of urban land uses away from the center. We also examine the important phenomenon of subcentering, whereby firms achieve many of the agglomeration benefits associated with downtown centers while avoiding some of the more severe congestion effects. The chapter concludes with an economic analysis of the urban sprawl debate, where an adaptation of the basic monocentric model diagram is used to illustrate the key arguments.

Chapter 5 examines another issue that generates more than its share of confusion—that is, the provision of public goods. We begin with a simple diagram that clarifies the dual nature of the term public goods. On the one hand this term is used to refer to goods that are provided by the public sector, while on the other hand it refers to a technical quality that some goods have of nonrivalry in consumption. There is no simple or clear correspondence between these two definitions, and much of the confusion in public discussion about public goods provision may be attributed to this fact. We go on to show that nonrivalry in consumption poses a problem for markets because the optimality conditions no longer correspond with the market equilibrium conditions, so the standard efficiency properties of market allocations no longer apply. This outcome motivates our discussion and diagrams of Charles Tiebout's famous model of local public goods where consumers "vote with their feet," thereby self-selecting themselves into municipalities or clubs that cater to specific preferences and incomes levels, and we show how this process recovers the desired efficiency properties normally associated with market outcomes. A related topic is that of substitutable yet exclusively provided (SEP) goods, including schools, that are provided by both the public sector and the private sector, but where consumers typically opt for one or the other exclusively. We show that this situation can create an incentive for wealthy families to "opt out" of publicly provided services in favor of their private counterparts, and to use their political influence to lobby for reduced public services. These and other issues are discussed in chapter 5 in the context of the privatization debate.

Chapter 6 addresses an issue that is of compelling interest to many: traffic congestion. The series of diagrams that is used here to illustrate the fundamental economic principles of traffic congestion was first presented in an instructional piece by Heikkila (1994). Using these diagrams, we contrast three different perspectives on congestion. From the engineer's perspective, the problem of congestion arises because capacity is too small, so the obvious solution is to build more roads and other forms of transportation infrastructure. From the community activist's perspective, the problem arises because the demand for trips exceeds the given capacity of the road network, so the implied solution calls for a restriction on the number of trips allowed. From the economics perspective, the problem is not congestion per se, but instead arises from the fact that the costs faced by individual drivers differ from the systemwide costs on the margin, so the decisions made by myriad individuals do not result in the system optimum. The solution that follows logically from this perspective is to correct the price signal by setting a toll that varies with the level of congestion. We show, somewhat counterintuitively, that there is such a thing as an "optimum" level of congestion. From this perspective, congestion is the price we pay for a higher aggregate level of mass mobility from a given transportation network. While congestion is undesirable in itself, so too are alternatives to congestion such as restricted access or higher road taxes. From the economic perspective, the real issue is that the equilibrium number of trips will tend to systematically exceed the optimum trip volume, with the consequent loss of efficiency measured by a familiar triangle of inefficiency.

The discussion in chapter 7 on fiscal impacts is adapted from an earlier article by Heikkila and Davis (1997) that argues that the conventional methods for estimating fiscal impacts are inadequate. The basis for this argument is the production relation that links public-sector inputs (such as police, teachers, or roads) to their corresponding public-sector outputs (safety, knowledge, or mobility). This production relation is mediated by the neighborhood context in which it is situated. For example, the level of safety provided by a given level of policing does not depend solely on policing expenditures, but relies also on the socioeconomic profile of the area in which they are deployed. Likewise, the level of traffic congestion depends not only on road capacity, but also on the spatial allocation of employment and entertainment attractors. Urban development by its very nature brings about changes in land use, demographics, and other important characteristics of urban places. When one speaks of the fiscal impacts of urban development, therefore, one is really referring to the manner in which the production relation (or production function, in common economics parlance) is displaced by changes to the urban context. Chapter 7 introduces a service-based impact measure that is based on the changes in public-sector expenditures that would be required to restore service levels to what they were prior to the development whose impact is being gauged. We show that these and related measures of fiscal impact logically require the analyst to develop an empirical understanding of the production relationship itself. Conventional measures of impact fail to do this, and instead use inputs as a proxy for outputs, thereby circumventing the production relationship altogether. Chapter 7 goes on to show how the proposed fiscal impact method can be implemented using tools and knowledge that are already in place.

Chapter 8 moves from fiscal impact evaluation to cost–benefit evaluation. Cost–benefit analysis is a special case of project evaluation in several regards. Project evaluation methods generally constitute several essential phases including project definition, determination of standing, impact identification, and evaluation. Cost–benefit is unique in its use of *shadow prices* as the basis for evaluating impacts; shadow prices here are the same ones discussed in chapter 1 in the context of constrained optimization. The shadow price measures the value of resources on the margin in terms of willingness to pay and opportunity cost, and the discussion in chapter 8 shows how this approach is equivalent to a social benefit optimization problem where the solution is constrained by a finite supply of resources. We further show that this approach yields the same allocation of resources that would emerge from a market allocation in the absence of market failure, and that in this case shadow prices would be equivalent to market prices. From this discussion we are able to conclude that the very undertaking of a cost–benefit study presumes the presence of some kind of market failure, for if that were not the case a favorable cost–benefit outcome is equivalent to a positive profitability assessment, and markets in that case could be relied upon to act upon all worthwhile projects without the prompting of public-sector intervention of any kind. Chapter 8 goes on to review a number of common mistakes made in the conduct of cost–benefit analysis and to delineate cost–benefit analysis from other project evaluation methods such as environmental impact reviews, cost-effectiveness, profitability analysis, and traditional fiscal impact analysis.

Chapter 9 addresses entitlements, a topic with far-reaching implications for planning in general and land use issues in particular. The Coase Theorem, first articulated by Nobel prize winner Ronald Coase, is called upon to clarify the issues involved. Coase's Theorem is concerned with the implications of alternative initial allocations of entitlements (such as the right to devote a parcel of land to a specified set of uses) between competing parties or interests. The theorem points out that if certain conditions are in place, then the final allocation of entitlements will be independent of the initial allocation. In the context of land use, recognizing that zoning is a means of allocating land use entitlements, this would mean that the actual disposition of land uses would be independent of any zoning regulations. The prerequisite conditions Coase refers to are the absence of transactions costs and wealth effects, and these are conditions that Coase argues generally do not hold, so the initial allocation of entitlements does affect final outcomes. Moreover, even when those conditions do hold, we learn in chapter 9 that it does not imply that we are indifferent to the initial allocation of entitlements, because *entitlements are a form of wealth*. Thus, when viewed in this light, zoning is a means of allocating wealth. The Coase Theorem also has important efficiency implications, because the final outcome that would emerge if the Coase conditions held is the one that maximizes total benefit, and a simple diagram helps to illustrate that point, with the familiar triangle of inefficiency showing the loss of benefits arising from suboptimal allocations. An important implication of this is that there is a significant role for planners in creating markets that would promote a more efficient allocation of pollution entitlements or other commodities that are not normally allocated via market mechanisms.

The preceding discussion of entitlements leads easily to chapter 10 and an overview of an emerging field of economics that has important potential for planning. The *new institutional economics* (or neo-institutional economics, as it is sometimes called) is very much in keeping with the Coasian tradition that emphasizes the importance of transactions costs in shaping economic outcomes. The formation of institutions, firms, and organizations from this perspective is a logical economic response to the day-to-day problems faced by individuals who are seeking to function efficiently in a market environment where transactions are costly due to imperfect information, negotiations, search costs, and the like. The nature of the institutions that emerge depends upon the nature of the transactions costs that motivate their creation and adaptation. This leads naturally to a discussion of the conditions that support pure market allocations versus those that favor a more institutional response. To further complicate matters, markets themselves can be seen as a set of institutional arrangements that are used to define and allocate property rights and other entitlements. The evolutionary potential of this arrangement is captured nicely in a set of propositions by Douglass North, another Nobel prize winner who is identified closely with the new institutional economics, and these propositions are also discussed in chapter 10. The discussion clarifies the potential of the richly textured domain of transitional economics for development planners, and more generally, points to the tremendous potential for planners to move to the forefront of the application of markets to suit traditional planning ends.

Note

1. On this point I am persuaded by my friend and colleague Niraj Verma, who argues that interdisciplinary research is about depth, and that the depth versus breadth dichotomy is a false one.

1

Thinking Tools

Introduction

Although this book covers a wide range of topics—from housing economics and traffic congestion to cost-benefit analysis and land use zoning—
a strong unifying theme is provided by the analytical perspective offered by
the microeconomic approach that underlies each chapter. Indeed, it is this
simple yet powerful analytical capacity of microeconomic analysis that explains much of the influence that economics has held over the social science policy domain. It is useful, therefore, before launching into the topical
chapters themselves, to focus specifically on the analytical tools that give
specific form to the microeconomic approach to planning issues. It is encouraging, at least from the perspective of one who is attempting to develop
a working competency in economic logic, to know that there are really just
a few fundamental analytical tools involved. In fact, we may assert that two
techniques dominate above all others. One is applied optimization techniques
using the tools of marginal analysis. The other key technique is that of asset
valuation using the tools of present value calculation. Accordingly, this chapter provides a concise introduction to these techniques and tools, with a pre-
view of how they are applied to the diverse set of topics addressed in the
remainder of the book.

In the next section, "Thinking on the Margin," we examine the relationship between total, average, and marginal. These concepts apply quite broadly
to costs (total, average, and marginal costs), revenues, benefits, profits, and
virtually any other quantifiable phenomenon. The relationship between

1

total and average is, of course, well understood by the lay public, but a bit more training is usually helpful in getting people to "think marginally." While marginal analysis has evolved from its roots in calculus, it is possible to grasp the essence through diagrams such as the ones employed throughout this chapter and the remainder of the book. In "Thinking Optimally" we see that optimal decisions, in the sense commonly used in economics and calculus, rely on marginal analysis because the latter helps us to judge at what point "enough is just enough": Any less would be not enough, any more would be too much, and so the optimum is defined. This approach is used extensively in determining whether net benefits are maximized, costs are minimized, or some other condition is suitably optimized. "Thinking in the Present" introduces the important concept of present value, by which revenues, costs, benefits, or other monetary values are translated from one time period to another, and where "now" is the standard reference point for these intertemporal comparisons. The final section of this chapter, "Thinking as an Asset," explains how present valuation techniques are used to price assets, where an asset is defined in terms of its ability to generate revenues or use value in the future. Those future revenue (or benefit) streams can be translated into present value terms, and this becomes an important basis for determining the current value of the asset. These concepts are fundamental to evaluating the costs and benefits of any investment decisions, as explained in chapter 8, and they are especially useful in clarifying a host of issues relating to housing, as discussed in chapter 3.

Thinking on the Margin

Figures 1.1a, 1.1b, and 1.1c are different representations of what is fundamentally the same relationship. The three figures correspond to the total, average, and marginal value representations, respectively. It may be helpful for the reader to think of these in terms of benefits (total benefits, average benefits, and marginal benefits), but the exposition is intended to be generic, so that it might equally well apply to costs, revenues, profits, productivity, accessibility, density, or any other measurable phenomenon. Likewise, the horizontal axis is termed "n," which is intended as a generic representation of the input or the action against which benefits (or whatever) are measured. For example, the horizontal axis may represent the volume of traffic on a road network, the acreage of urban land devoted to residential use, or the number of employees hired by a local government agency. In point of fact, the relationship in figure 1.1a could be just about any relationship that can be expressed in terms of a continuous x-y graph. To make the exposition as straightforward as possible, the graph drawn in figure 1.1a comprises just a

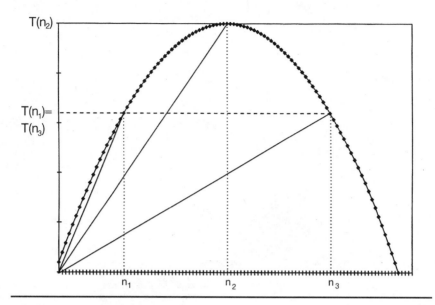

FIGURE 1.1a
The total value function

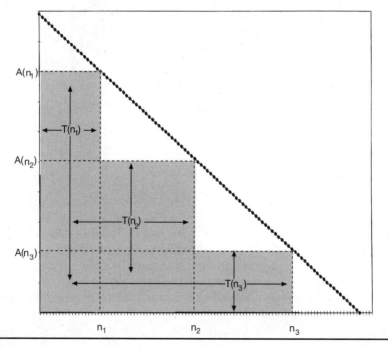

FIGURE 1.1b
The average value function

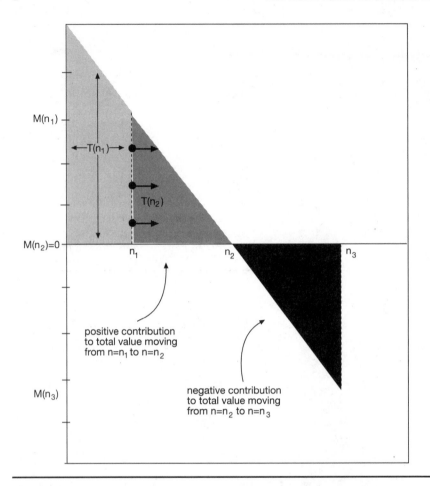

FIGURE 1.1c
The marginal value function

simple curve that rises at first, gradually tapers off, and then falls in symmetrical fashion.[1] A more complicated set of squiggles could equally well be used, but would not necessarily add to the exposition. Likewise, the figures introduced here could be turned on their heads, and one might then think in terms of minimizing rather than maximizing, but the relationship between total, average, and marginal will not change.

If we express the total relationship by the function $T(n)$, then the average is just:

$$A(n) = T(n) / n \tag{1}$$

In terms of figure 1.1a, the average for some value of n can be expressed as the slope of a ray extending from the origin to the corresponding point on the graph. Three such rays are drawn in figure 1.1a, corresponding to points n_1, n_2, and n_3, respectively. Consider the first ray. It intersects the total curve above the point n_1 at a height of $T(n_1)$. Since this ray emanates from the origin, its slope can be quickly calculated as the "rise over the run," which in this case is simply $T(n_1)$ divided by n_1, which as seen from equation 1 above, is just the average value calculated at n_1. In a similar fashion, the average at n_2, n_3, or any point can be obtained as the slope of the corresponding ray from the origin.

Using this approach, we can quickly see that the average value function corresponding to the total value function in figure 1.1a declines progressively from the outset. Certainly, we would expect this to be true where T(n) is itself falling, but it is less clear what we should expect when T(n) is rising. T(n) is rising during the first half of the graph, but of course n is increasing, and it happens that in this particular case, T(n) is not rising in proportion to n, so the denominator in equation 1 is outpacing the numerator,[2] and consequently the average value function is falling. This fact is confirmed in figure 1.1b, which graphs the average value function explicitly. In this particular case, the bow-shaped total value function in figure 1.1a spawns the linear average value function in figure 1.1b, which falls steadily until intersecting the horizontal axis at the same place its total value counterpart does. As we shall see, nonlinear variations of the average value function are possible.[3]

The marginal value function is also defined in terms of the total value function. It is expressed as the change in the total value function arising from the most recent increment in n. That is:

$$M(n) = \Delta T(n) = T(n) - T(n - 1) \tag{2}$$

When these increments in n are small, the marginal value function approximates the slope of the total value curve at any point.[4] One can see from the total value curve in figure 1.1a that positive increments are added in progressively smaller doses as n increases from zero until a point is reached (at n_2) where the increments are no longer positive and then become progressively negative as n continues to grow. This progression is confirmed in figure 1.1c, which graphs the marginal value curve directly. Like the average value curve in figure 1.1b, the marginal value curve in 1.1c declines in linear fashion. Unlike the average value curve, however, the marginal value curve becomes negative at the midpoint n_2 and continues declining beyond that point. As we shall soon see, this can lead to a significant difference between "average thinking" and "marginal thinking" in the context of optimization.

Before turning to optimization, however, it is useful to consider further the relationship between the total, average, and marginal value functions. The total value function is like the "parent" function, while the average and marginal value functions are like two "sibling offspring." In this regard it is interesting to consider how the total value function may be reconstructed from each of its offspring. In the case of the average value function in figure 1.1b, the total value at any point is recovered by calculating the rectangular area defined by the corresponding point on the average value curve. This stands to reason, because the average is defined as the amount that everyone (i.e., every "n") would receive if the total were divided equally among them. Or, rearranging equation 1, we have:

$$A(n) = T(n) / n \rightarrow T(n) = n * A(n) \tag{3}$$

The expression on the right states that the total value can be recovered as the product of n and the average value function $A(n)$. Figure 1.1b depicts the total value rectangles corresponding to n_1, n_2, and n_3, respectively.

The total value function is reconstructed from the marginal value function in a different way. Recall that the marginal value function measures the *incremental addition* to the total value function at each value of n. Beginning with zero, the first increment (n = 1) adds an amount given by the height of the marginal value curve at the outset. The second increment (n = 2) in figure 1.1c adds an amount that is slightly smaller than the first. We may continue adding sections in this manner "slice by slice," just as we might reconstruct a loaf of bread from the individual slices that have been taken from it. At any point such as n_1, for example, the corresponding total value $T(n_1)$ is just given by the cumulative value of the many slices that have been contributed up to that point, as indicated by the lightly shaded area in figure 1.1c. As n increases from n_1, the incremental additions are still positive but progressively less so. This corresponds to the fact that the slope of the total value function in figure 1.1a is positive but diminishing.

At n_2 the total value function reaches its peak at the same moment that the marginal value function hits the horizontal axis. At this point the triangular area to the left of n_2 in figure 1.1b corresponds to the maximum total value depicted by the graph in figure 1.1a. Beyond this point, the total value function begins to decline, which tells us that the incremental additions must be *negative*. In terms of figure 1.1c, as we move to the right of the centerpoint n_2, the area defined by the emerging triangle represents the cumulative amount by which the total value function has been reduced relative to what it was at n_2. By the time we reach n_3, the area within the triangle to the right of n_2 just offsets the area within the triangle lying between n_1 and n_2. This tells us that all of the positive increments that were added to the total value function between n_1 and n_2 were just offset by the negative increments between n_2 and n_3, and so the total value function at n_3 must be the same as it was at n_1, which is indeed the case, as we can see from inspection of figure 1.1a.

The importance of this distinction between marginal and average values, and their relationship to total value, is perhaps best illustrated in the context of our discussion of traffic congestion in chapter 6. There, each individual driver on the roadway at any given time is presumed to share the same experience, and this is described in terms of what is essentially an average cost curve.[5] Accordingly, each driver makes his or her trip decision by evaluating whether his or her benefit (on the margin) exceeds this average cost. However, as is explained in detail in that chapter, the optimal solution calls for reference to be made to marginal rather than the average systemwide cost, and it is the divergence between the two that gives rise to the basic policy dilemma in the context of transportation planning. Our chapter on urban structure also makes use of the distinction between average and marginal values in the context of firms deciding whether to locate in a particular subcenter. Their decisions will be based on the average values experienced by all firms, while optimizing planners will be interested in encouraging behavior based on marginal values.

Thinking Optimally

The discussion in the previous section leads us to the central point of optimizing behavior. To uncover the optimum, one should pay attention to *decisions on the margin*, for it is "at the margin" that one decides whether to add one more or not. This point is illustrated through a comparison once again of figures 1.1b and 1.1c. In reference to optimizing behavior, one often does so in the context of an *objective function*, defined as a total value function that we are trying to maximize (as in the case of total net benefits) or minimize (as in the case of total costs). There is little in the graph of average values in figure 1.1b to indicate at which point the corresponding total value function is maximized. In contrast, the marginal value graph immediately indicates the optimal point n_2 as the value at which the incremental (i.e., marginal) additions are no longer positive.

To use a simple yet compelling example of marginal thinking, suppose that the objective in question pertains to monetary contributions that individuals are making to a local political campaign that you are managing. You are arranging a banquet for contributors where you must bear a fixed cost for each person attending. You must decide which contributors to invite. Suppose that we rank these individuals on a list in an order that corresponds to their relative generosity, with the most generous contributor first, the second-most generous person second, and so on. The first contributor is the

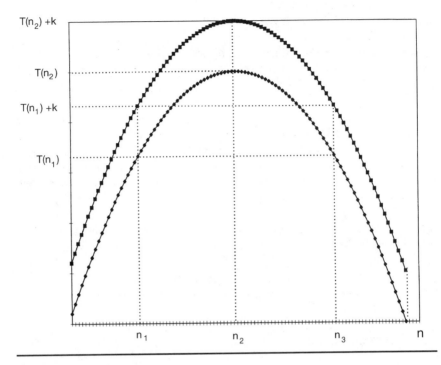

FIGURE 1.2a
Upward shift of total value function

most generous, and her contribution exceeds the fixed per-person cost of the banquet by an amount depicted by the first point on the marginal value graph in figure 1.1c. The second contributor also donates an amount that more than covers the cost of the banquet, but that is slightly less than what the first contributor offered. This process continues, and so long as the individual donations exceed the fixed banquet cost, additional guests are welcome (although clearly some are more welcome than others). At some point, however, as indicated by n_2, the pickings become slimmer and the incoming contributions no longer cover the cost of the banquet. Beyond this point, the campaign is actually losing money by inviting more guests. It should be clear that n_2 is the optimizing point. That is, it is the point that corresponds to the maximum value of contributions net of banquet costs. Notice that "average reasoning" may overlook this optimum, because at n_2 the average net contribution is still quite high (as indicated by the height of the average value curve at n_2 in figure 1.1b), so one might erroneously conclude that more is merrier.

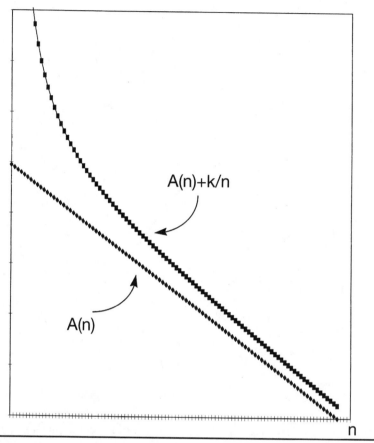

FIGURE 1.2b
Effect of upward shift of total value function on average value function

The distinction between average and marginal thinking is highlighted further in the example illustrated in figures 1.2a through 1.2c, which correspond exactly to the previous figures with the single exception that the total value function has now shifted upward by a constant amount k, as shown in figure 1.2a. Figure 1.2b shows the effect that this shift has on the average value function. For low values of n the effect is quite pronounced, but it quickly tapers off for higher values of n. This stands to reason, because the new total value function can be expressed in symbolic form as equaling the old total plus some constant k:

$$T(n) = T(n) + k \tag{4}$$

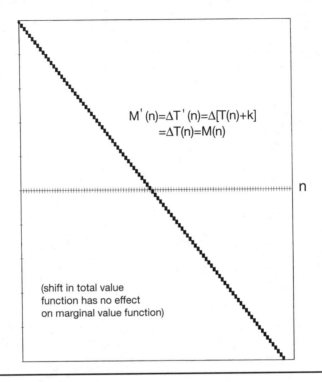

$$M'(n)=\Delta T'(n)=\Delta[T(n)+k]$$
$$=\Delta T(n)=M(n)$$

(shift in total value
function has no effect
on marginal value function)

n

FIGURE 1.2c
Effect of upward shift of total value function on marginal value function

so the new average value function will be the old average plus the constant amount k divided by n:

$$A(n) = T(n)/n = [T(n) + k]/n = T(n)/n + k/n = A(n) + k/n \qquad (5)$$

When n is small, the shift in the total value function must be borne by just a few n, so the effect is relatively large. As n increases, however, the effect of the shift is diluted by the large numbers of n over which it is felt. That is why the new and old average values are far apart initially in figure 1.2b but nearly converge for larger values of n. In fact, the difference between the two average value curves at any point n is just k/n.

Notice, however, that the shift in the total value curve has almost no effect on the marginal value curve in figure 1.2c. The reason for this is that the shift applies uniformly across all values of n, and therefore the difference between any two successive values of n is unaffected. That is, the incremental addition does not change for any value of n, and *that* is what is measured by the marginal value function. Recall that we defined the mar-

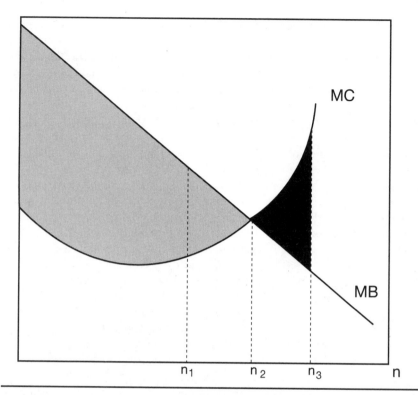

FIGURE 1.3
Marginal benefits net of marginal costs

ginal value function in equation 2 as the incremental change in the total value function. Based on this definition, the additional value of k cancels itself out when we calculate the new marginal value function $M'(n)$:

$$M'(n) = T'(n) - T'(n - 1)$$
$$= [T(n) + k] - [T(n - 1) + k] = T(n) - T(n - 1) = M(n) \qquad (6)$$

The importance of this result is difficult to overstate. As we have already seen, decisions on the margin are the key to optimizing behavior, and this result tells us that a constant shift in the objective function does not affect the optimizing value of the input n. Thus, for example, if the fixed costs of a project are subject to a sudden, unexpected increase, that will not affect the level of activity at which total costs are minimized even though it does affect profits adversely.

The same basic point can be illustrated another way by assuming that the marginal cost is not fixed, but that it varies as shown in figure 1.3, with higher marginal costs initially, decreasing over a range and then rising again. This pattern is typical of the marginal cost curves found in many economics textbooks, and it is based on the assumption that a certain size is needed before one experiences economies of scale, and that beyond a certain point diminishing marginal productivity results in increasing costs on the margin. Continuing with the example of someone hosting a banquet for potential donors, the marginal benefit curve labeled MB shows the political donations of successive contributors as before, except this time the amount of the banquet has not been "deducted" and is instead shown separately as a point of reference.[6] By the same reasoning, we see that all contributors to the left of n_2 are positive net contributors while those to the right of n_2 cost more to host than is warranted by their contributions; so n_2 is still the optimizing point as we have drawn the revised marginal cost curve. The net revenue obtained from the political banquet is now given by the shaded area to the left of n_2. Notice that if the banquet cost were a fixed amount per person, as in the previous example and as indicated by the dashed horizontal cost curve in figure 1.3, the optimum point would not change. It would remain at n_2, the point at which the marginal benefit just fails to compensate for the marginal cost. Net revenues under this scenario would shrink and would correspond to the shaded triangle to the left of n_2 and lying above the horizontal cost line, and so the change in the marginal cost curve as we have drawn it does have an impact on *intramarginal* net revenues (i.e., those revenues that are "inside" the margin of decision) but does not affect the decision on the margin.

If the campaign manager in this example were to make the mistake of inviting too many people to the political banquet, for example to a level n_3 in figure 1.3, then the net revenues generated by the event would fall relative to the optimum by an amount indicated by the shaded triangular area lying between n_2 and n_3. This *triangle of inefficiency* is a recurring theme throughout this book and throughout economics in general. It plays an important part in our discussions of zoning, traffic congestion, housing subsidies, entitlements, and cost–benefit analysis, and it is fundamental to much of economics as it applies to issues of public policy. Economists characterize a policy as inefficient if it can be shown that the same results (such as net benefits) can be obtained at less cost. The triangle of inefficiency is a measure of the loss in net benefits resulting from a suboptimal policy choice with respect to the input or decision variable n.

It is often the case that we are limited in the range of inputs available. More often than not, resource constraints in the form of land availability, skilled labor shortages, budget ceilings, highway capacity, or even time deadlines can limit the range of policy options from which we might reasonably choose. This common dilemma often forces us to think in terms of *constrained optimization*. This concept is illustrated in figure 1.4, where the

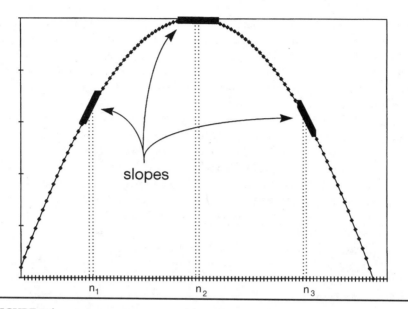

FIGURE 1.4
Constrained optimization

value of the objective function is optimized at n_2 under unconstrained conditions. But what happens if the amount of the resource available is restricted to $n \leq n_1$? In this case the constrained optimum is clearly at n_1, because the value of the objective function at n_1 exceeds anything to the left of n_1, and the more favorable values of n to the right of n_1 are not available to us, so n_1 is the best we can do under the given resource constraints.

Now consider what happens if the resource constraint is set at $n \leq n_3$ instead of $n \leq n_1$. In this case, the constrained optimum coincides with the unconstrained optimum at n_2. Notice that the constraint $n \leq n_3$ places an *upper* bound on the availability of the resource, so we are still free to choose the unconstrained optimum n_2. In cases such as this we say that the constraint is not a *binding* one because, although it does limit the quantity of the resource that is potentially available to us, it does not inhibit our ability to choose as we would in the absence of the constraint. The constraint at n_1, in contrast, is a binding one because its release would enable us to improve system performance. We formalize this notion with the concept of shadow prices, a concept that is at the core of cost–benefit analysis as discussed in chapter 8. The *shadow price* of a resource constraint measures the amount by which the objective function could be improved upon if the resource constraint were relaxed by one (i.e., on the margin). The important point here is that *a shadow price uses the objective function as the basis for evaluating the scarcity of a resource.* This is a very pragmatic or objective-oriented approach to resource evaluation: What can the resource do for us in terms of what we are trying to accomplish? If we are trying to maximize social benefit, then that is the basis for evaluating resource scarcity. If our objective is to minimize costs, then that becomes the resource evaluation basis.

At n_1, for example, we see that adding one more unit of the resource would lead to an improvement because the objective function has been increasing monotonically up to that point and the slope is positive there. Now, suppose we were to release the constraint by one unit, so that we could now move one step to the right, so the constraint is now expressed as $n \leq n_1 + 1$. If we do so the value of the objective function will also increase, from $T(n_1)$ to $T(n_1 + 1)$. This *increase* in the objective function, which is simply measured by its slope at that point, is the shadow price of the resource constraint at n_1. The situation changes by the time we reach n_2, however. At n_2 we have already attained the maximum value of the objective function; consequently, relaxing the constraint by one does not lead to any improvement. Here, too, the improvement in the value of the objective function equals to the slope of the objective function, which in this case is equal to zero. This corresponds to a general rule for unconstrained optimization that suggests that the maximum and minimum points of total value functions will often be located where the slope is zero, because the slope is always zero at the top of a peak or at the bottom of a valley for any smooth total value function.[7]

At n_3, however, unlike at n_1 or n_2, the shadow price of the resource constraint does not correspond to the slope of the objective function at that point. The slope at n_3 is negative while the shadow price is zero. The zero shadow price indicates that an additional unit of the resource at n_3 does not enable us to improve performance in the objective function in any way, nor does it hinder it. More generally, a zero shadow price on a resource constraint tells us that any more of the resource would be a surplus, and that it would have no additional value in terms of the objective function. Shadow pricing is central to an understanding of cost–benefit analysis, because in cost–benefit analysis the costs and benefits of all resource inputs and outputs are evaluated in terms of their shadow prices, where the objective function is some measure of social benefit. As explained in more detail in chapter 8, market prices are perfect substitutes for shadow prices in the absence of market failure, in which case a project is worth doing if the market indicates that it would be profitable to undertake. However, where there is market failure, shadow prices will at least partially diverge from market prices, and so the very conduct of a cost–benefit analysis is predicated upon some notion of market failure.

Thinking in the Present

Another recurring theme found in cost–benefit analysis and many other contexts is that of present value calculations. It is often the case that we are called upon to analyze situations where revenues, costs, benefits, or other monetary equivalents are expressed in different time periods. This is particularly true in the case of durable assets such as real estate or environmental amenities, whose lifetimes extend beyond the present and whose valuation depends critically on an intertemporal assessment of the stream of revenues or benefits that they are expected to generate over their lifetimes. Questions of intergenerational equity also hinge on our ability to make meaningful intertemporal comparisons. In this section we briefly review the basics of present valuation techniques, which are in turn applied in the next section to asset valuation.

The central tenet of present valuation is that we are not or should not be indifferent *now* about a dollar today versus a dollar to be held at some point in the future; they do not have equivalent values. The principal reason for this difference is that money "grows" over time. For example, if we were to place $100 in the bank today at 10 percent guaranteed interest, one year from now it would be worth $110. If we use this same interest rate to "discount backward through time," then we say that $110 one year from now has a worth equivalent to $100 today, or, *the present value of $110 one year from now discounted at 10 percent is $100.* Now suppose that we were to reinvest at 10 percent the $110 in principal plus interest after one year, allowing it to grow for one more year to $121 = $110 + $11. This tells us that $121 two years from now discounted at 10 percent also has a present value of $100. More generally, we note that if we allow the present value (PV = $100) of the principal to grow at a compound interest rate of $i = 10$ percent, its future value (FV) after t years will be given by:

$$FV = \$100 * (1 + i) * (1 + i) *...* (1 + i) \qquad (7)$$
$$= \$100 * (1 + i)^t = PV * (1 + i)^t$$

Equation 7 shows that the compounding effect of interest leads to exponential growth in the principal, as is evidenced by the appearance of time t in the exponent of the term $(1 + i)^t$ rather than as a linear factor such as in the term $(1 + i)*t$. If the interest rate i is positive ($i > 0$), then the future value of our $100 investment grows exponentially as depicted in figure 1.5a. For interest rates of 5 percent, 10 percent, and 15 percent, we see that $100 grows over ten years to become $162.9, $259.4, and $404.6, respectively.

While future values grow exponentially over time, present values *shrink* exponentially as illustrated in figure 1.5b, which shows that $100 received ten years in the future has a present value of $61.4 (using i = 5 percent),

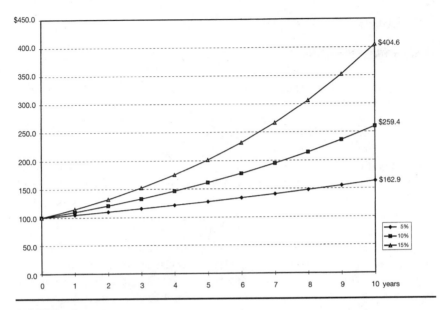

FIGURE 1.5a
Future value of $100 [FV = $100* $(1 + i)^t$]

$38.6 (i = 10 percent), or $24.7 (i = 15 percent), depending on the rate at which that future sum is *discounted.* By inverting the relationship in equation 7 we can express the present value in terms of future values, as follows:

$$FV = PV * (1 + i)^t \qquad\qquad (8)$$
$$\rightarrow \quad PV = FV / (1 + i)^t$$

Notice that there is a logical symmetry in the inverse relationship between present and future values. If we take a sum and "grow it forward" into the future and then "shrink it backward" into the present using the same discount rate i, then we will be left with the original sum. For example, we have already seen that $100 growing for ten years at a rate of i = 15 percent will generate a future value of $404.6. We have also seen that $100 received ten years in the future, when discounted at i = 15 percent, yields a present value of $24.7, or 24.7 percent of its future value. Not surprisingly, 24.7 percent of $404.6 yields $100, and so the reciprocal relationship between present and future valuation is confirmed.

An immediate and practical implication of this for planners concerns contracts that are time denominated. Suppose, for example, that a developer wishes to lease a certain parcel of land from a public authority for thirty years to build an office tower and related facilities. Suppose further that as part of

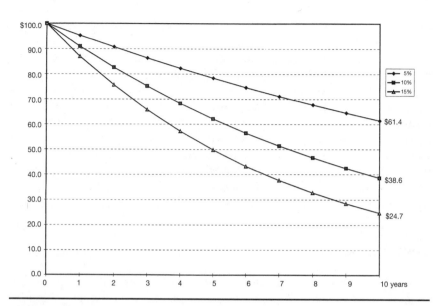

FIGURE 1.5b
Present value of $100   [PV = $100 / (1 + i)^t]

the proposed agreement, she plans to grant full title to those built improvements to the public authority after thirty years' time. All parties agree that after properly accounting for inflation and depreciation, the improvements will have a market value of $10 million at that time. In analyzing whether such a deal is in the interests of the lessor, the analyst needs to know what the *present value* of $10 million is, and then compare that sum with what the developer is offering in terms of compensation (also expressed in present values). It may be surprising to some to learn that, using i = 10 percent, the present value of $10 million thirty years from now is just $573,000, or less than 6 percent of the nominal future value! Put another way, $573,000 earning 10 percent per annum on a compound basis would yield $10 million after thirty years. Clearly, based on an assumed i = 10 percent, it would be better to have $1 million in hand today than $10 million thirty years in the future.

From the discussion above, it is evident that the choice of discount rate is quite critical to these calculations. A deal that looks favorable at i = 5 percent may look poor at i = 10 percent. So what discount rate should one use? The answer depends on several factors, but the most important one is the opportunity cost of capital. The reasoning here is that money held in the present can be used to "grow" money for the future. Thus, if we must wait to receive this money (or investment capital), then we lose the opportunity

to enjoy its productive yield while we wait. That lost opportunity is by definition the *opportunity cost of capital*. The exact discount rate implied by
this consideration depends on a number of factors, including the productivity and riskiness of investments, tax considerations, and the like, but the ability to use capital *now* to create more wealth in the future remains the central
justification for discounting future values. The discussion may be complicated
further by questions of intergenerational equity. For example, some may argue that it is immoral to destroy an irreplaceable amenity like open space in
a crowded urban area, because future generations would lose the opportunity to enjoy it, and that this loss could not be compensated for by any technical consideration such as choice of discount rate. Chapter 8 on cost–benefit
analysis delves further into these issues.

Thinking as an Asset

To understand how present value calculations figure in the evaluation of financial and other assets, consider first the case of a $100 annuity. This is an
asset that generates a lump sum of $100 every year in perpetuity, beginning
one year from now. How much is such an asset worth? On the one hand,
there are an infinite number of future payments, each of them positive, so it
might seem that the annuity would have an infinite value. As we move further into the future, the present value of those future payments may become
quite small, but they will always remain positive, and adding any positive
number an infinite number of times yields an infinite sum. But if the value
of a $100 annuity were infinite, what would be the value of a $10 annuity?
One-tenth of infinity? Something doesn't "add up"!

Another way to approach this problem is to consider the present valuation of each payment, and then add each of these present value components
to produce a total present valuation. This is in fact the correct way to proceed in principle. In the context of figure 1.5b, for example, the present
values of $100 corresponding to i = 15 percent are shown for t = 1 (PV =
$87.0) through t = 10 ($24.7). Table 1.1 reproduces these values and their
counterparts for i = 5 percent and i = 10 percent, extending the range to t
= 30 and noting the ten-, twenty-, and thirty-year subtotals at the bottom.
Based on these figures, we see that a ten-year annuity of $100, with the first
payment arriving one year from now, has a present value of $772 if evalu-
ated at a discount rate of i = 5 percent, $614 using i = 10 percent, and $502
using i = 15 percent. This makes sense, because a higher discount rate dis-
counts the future more heavily. Stated another way, if the opportunity cost
of capital is high, then we are less willing to wait for the future to receive
our $100 payments. In all cases, the ten payments of $100 each have a

TABLE 1.1

Present Values of $100
$PV = \$100/(1 + i)^t$

t	$i = 5\%$	$i = 10\%$	$i = 15\%$
1	$95.2	$90.9	$87.0
2	90.7	82.6	75.6
3	86.4	75.1	65.8
4	82.3	68.3	57.2
5	78.4	62.1	49.7
6	74.6	56.4	43.2
7	71.1	51.3	37.6
8	67.7	46.7	32.7
9	64.5	42.4	28.4
10	61.4	38.6	24.7
11	58.5	35.0	21.5
12	55.7	31.9	18.7
13	53.0	29.0	16.3
14	50.5	26.3	14.1
15	48.1	23.9	12.3
16	45.8	21.8	10.7
17	43.6	19.8	9.3
18	41.6	18.0	8.1
19	39.6	16.4	7.0
20	37.7	14.9	6.1
21	35.9	13.5	5.3
22	34.2	12.3	4.6
23	32.6	11.2	4.0
24	31.0	10.2	3.5
25	29.5	9.2	3.0
26	28.1	8.4	2.6
27	26.8	7.6	2.3
28	25.5	6.9	2.0
29	24.3	6.3	1.7
30	23.1	5.7	1.5
10-year total	$772	$614	$502
20-year total	$1,246	$851	$626
30-year total	$1,537	$943	$657

TABLE 1.2

Cumulative Present Values

	$i = 5\%$	$i = 10\%$	$i = 15\%$
10-year total	$ 772	$ 614	$ 502
20-year total	1,246	851	626
30-year total	1,537	943	657
40-year total	1,716	978	664
50-year total	1,826	991	666
60-year total	1,893	997	667
70-year total	1,934	999	667
80-year total	1,960	1,000	667
90-year total	1,975	1,000	667
100-year total	1,985	1,000	667
V = $100 / i	$ 2,000	$ 1,000	$ 667

present value that is considerably less than the nominal total of $1,000 that would correspond to i = 0 percent, or no discounting whatsoever.

Another notable feature of table 1.1 is the difference in the progression of sums from ten- to twenty- to thirty-year intervals. For i = 5 percent, the thirty-year total is more than double the ten-year total, while for i = 15 percent, the thirty-year total is only one-third larger than the ten-year total. Moreover, there is very little difference at all between the twenty- and thirty-year totals for i = 15 percent, suggesting that adding ten years to the payment horizon has very little consequence in present value terms under those conditions. This idea is confirmed in table 1.2, which extends the present value subtotals decade by decade through a full hundred years. In table 1.2 we see that within sixty years the cumulative present values converge to $667 for i = 15 percent, and that within eighty years the cumulative present values converge to $1,000 for i = 10 percent. For i = 5 percent the cumulative total has still not converged after 100 years, which means that there is still perceptible present value to payments made beyond the 100-year horizon for this lower discount rate. This long-run view with a 100-year horizon is depicted in figure 1.6, where the present value curves for i = 15 percent and i = 10 percent are hugging the horizontal axis well before t = 100, and where even the present value curve for i = 5 percent is near zero by that time.

An interesting graphical interpretation applies based on principles discussed earlier in this chapter regarding the relationship of marginal values to total values. Think of time (t) as the input to a total value function that

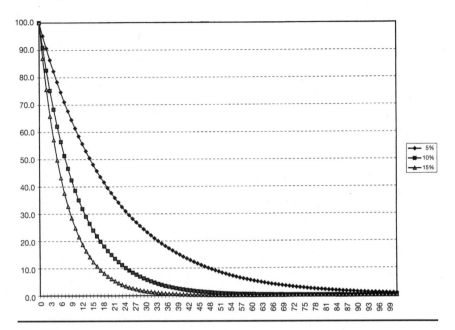

FIGURE 1.6
Long-run present value: marginal view

represents the cumulative present value of an annuity. This total value function is represented in figure 1.7 for i = 5 percent, 10 percent, and 15 percent over a 100-year time horizon. Referring to table 1.1, and using i = 10 percent as our example, we see that the total present value function is $90.9 after one year. After two years, the total value function is $173.5 = $90.9 + $82.6. After three years, the total value function is $244.6 = $173.5 + $75.1, and so on, yielding a total present value of $614 after ten years, $851 after twenty years, and converging to $1,000 within eighty years, as noted earlier. Now, consider the marginal value function associated with this total present value function. We know from our earlier discussion that the marginal value function is the *incremental change* in the total value function. The first year, the incremental change is $90.9, because we begin with nothing and the first payment represents the new total as well as the first increment. The second marginal value is $82.6, because that is the amount by which the total grows, and likewise the third marginal value is $75.1.

It should be apparent by now that the marginal values corresponding to the cumulative total present value function are simply the present valuations of the $100 payments for each successive time period. Thus, the long-run present value graph in figure 1.6 may also be interpreted as the marginal

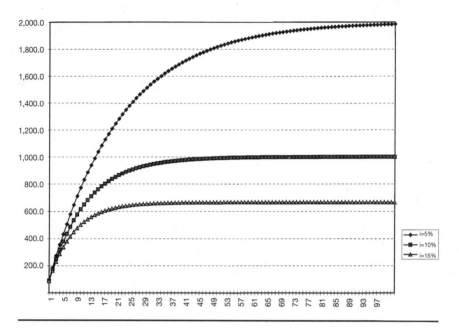

FIGURE 1.7
Long-run present value: cumulative view

value graph corresponding to the total or cumulative present value function in figure 1.7, which in turn represents the value of the annuity in question. Now we are ready to represent the asset value of the annuity in terms of figures 1.6 and 1.7. Remember from our discussion about figure 1.3 that the total value function can be recovered from the marginal value function by taking the area beneath the marginal value function. Thus, the value of the annuity for a given discount rate based on "t" payments can be represented as the area beneath the corresponding present value curve in figure 1.6 or as the height of the cumulative or total present value curve in figure 1.7.

It is apparent from figure 1.7 that the cumulative value functions converge to some limit, but what limit? A useful way to approach this question is to work from the other end: to ask what lump sum would be required *now* to generate a perpetual stream of $100 annual payments. The answer will vary with the interest rate used. For example, if the interest rate is $i = 10$ percent per annum, then a lump sum of $1,000 now would be sufficient, because each year it would generate $100 in interest, which is just enough to cover the annuity payment. On the other hand, a $2,000 lump sum would be needed to generate the same stream of payments if the interest rate were to drop to 5 percent per annum. Finally, a mere $667 would suffice in the case of i = 15 percent. If we let V represent the lump sum needed to generate the annuity of $100 per year, then the relationship that we have just explored can be expressed more generally in symbolic form as:

$$V * I = \$100 \tag{9}$$

or, equivalently

$$V = \$100 / i$$

This equation is nice and easy, but how does it relate to the previous discussion about cumulative present values? The astute reader will have noted that the lump sum equivalents derived from equation 9 are in fact the *same* values to which the cumulative present values converge. Earlier we represented the value of the annuity as the cumulative sum of the present value of each payment. In symbolic form, we had:

$$V = \Sigma_t \$100 / (1 + i)^t \tag{10}$$

where the summation runs from t = 1 through infinity. The expression in equation 10 is what was used to generate the graph in figure 1.7, and the expression to the right of the summation sign was used to generate the graph in figure 1.6. Now, the only remaining puzzle is, how can equations 9 and 10 both be used to calculate the value of the annuity? There is only one way to reconcile these two, and that is for the two expressions to be equivalent, which they in fact are, so:

$$V = \Sigma_t \$100 / (1 + i)^t = \$100 / i \tag{11}$$

It is mathematically very convenient that the somewhat more cumbersome expression in equation 10 should collapse so neatly to the very concise expression in equation 9.[8] It is also convenient in terms of our interpretation. It tells us that the cumulative sum of the present values for each payment extending infinitely into the future converges to the lump sum amount that would be just sufficient to generate that same stream of payments using the given interest or discount rate, and so we have come full circle.

The annuity is a somewhat special case because it represents a regular stream of fixed payments extending ad infinitum into the future. Other assets may not be so regular or neatly defined in terms of the yields that they generate. Nonetheless, the principles articulated in this section apply quite broadly and they provide a very robust basis for evaluating virtually any kind of asset based on the payment or benefit stream it is likely to produce. The cumulative valuation expression in equation 10 can be easily modified to accommodate a more diverse stream of payments rather than the simple $100 annual sum used in our example. As discussed in chapter 3 in the context of housing, the relationship between the value of housing as an asset and the rental equivalent value of the flow of housing services over time is much clarified when viewed from this perspective. And as explained there, the real estate market is where the asset value of housing stock is determined, whereas rental markets are where the value of the flow of housing services are made explicit. Present value techniques such as those presented in this chapter help in our understanding of the economic distinction between these stocks and flows.

Notes

1. For purposes of illustration, figure 1.1a was drawn using the quadratic relationship for the total value function of $T(n) = n*(100 - n)$. Any other relationship might do equally well.

2. $T(n)$ not rising in proportion to n means that an "x percent" increase in n leads to a less-than-x percent increase in $T(n)$.

3. The total value function $T(n) = n*(100 - n)$ described in footnote 1 gives rise to the average value relationship $A(n) = T n)/n = 100 - n$, which happens to be linear.

4. In terms of calculus, the marginal value function is the first derivative of the total value function with respect to n, $M(n) = dT(n)/dn$, which does give the slope of $T(n)$ at any point.

5. The average cost curve in the chapter on traffic congestion is termed an individual cost curve, for reasons that are explained in that chapter.

6. In other words, we have displaced the vertical axis by a fixed amount, and so nothing has changed on the margin. Doing so is slightly more convenient for expository purposes.

7. There are important caveats to this rule. For example, the maximum or minimum points may be at the edges of a function's domain, as in the case of a continually increasing function. Also, if the function is not continuously differentiable, with no discontinuities or sharp breaks or crooks, the rule may not apply. And finally, the converse need not apply. For example, a location of the total value function with a zero slope may correspond to a "local" maximum or minimum. Despite these caveats, the general association between zero slope and optimization is a strong one that does apply quite broadly.

8. We leave it to the interested reader as an exercise to demonstrate the equality asserted in equation 11. Here's a hint: Begin by substituting $r = [1/(1 + i)]$ and show that the expression in equation 10 is equivalent to $\$100*r / (1 - r)$.

2

The Economics of
Land Use Zoning

Introduction

Perhaps no function is more central to what planners do than is land use zoning. Zoning maps apportion the city into distinct zones, each of which has its own set of permitted uses: single-family residential, multifamily residential, commercial, retail, light industrial, heavy industrial, and/or other uses. Rare is the city planning department that does not have a brightly colored land use map on its wall showing what uses are permitted where. Part of the rationale for these maps, or for the designation of land use zones that they depict, is to segregate incompatible land uses. In some cases there is little doubt of the virtuous intent of such exclusionary restrictions—to keep noxious waste-producing factories away from elementary schools, for example. But in other cases zoning can be more controversial, such as when it's used to effectively exclude affordable housing from more well-to-do neighborhoods. These kinds of controversies are best handled within the framework of entitlements, as is done in chapter 9. In this chapter, however, we consider another dimension of land use zoning—that of economic efficiency.

To the economist, land use zoning is seen as an exercise in resource allocation, even if it may not normally be viewed in those terms by planners themselves. One of the most fundamental issues addressed by microeconomics is how to allocate scarce resources in an efficient manner. If the quantity of land is fixed, as it is in most urban settings, then one is forced to

N.C. WESLEYAN COLLEGE
ELIZABETH BRASWELL PEARSALL LIBRARY

make trade-offs. One more acre of land devoted to nonresidential uses, for example, results in one less acre devoted to residential use. From this perspective, zoning maps represent the planners' "solution" to the resource allocation problem. In preparing these plans (as zoning maps are sometimes called), planners must balance a range of considerations, among these economic efficiency. An efficient solution is defined as one that yields the greatest possible output (such as social benefit) for a given amount of input (such as land). An inefficient solution, by this same reasoning, is one that uses more inputs than necessary to achieve a given level of output. While there may be room for legitimate debate about what outputs are important (for example, whose benefits should count?), one would be hard pressed to argue in favor of an *inefficient* solution! After all, if we can receive more benefit from the same amount of land, why not do so?

With this motivation in mind, the next section introduces a simple diagram that illustrates the fundamental precepts of efficiency as applied to land use zoning. The diagram is stripped of all extraneous factors so that the efficiency issue can be examined in its starkest form. It takes advantage of the fixed supply of land within a given jurisdiction, a feature that enables us to represent two competing land uses conveniently on one basic graph in a manner that highlights the efficiency issues involved. We will see that under certain conditions planners may expect the market to generate an allocation of land among competing uses in an efficient or benefit-maximizing manner. In other cases, such as in the case of externalities (effects that are not priced by the market), we may expect that the market solution is inefficient by the same definition. Where markets fail to generate optimal solutions there is the possibility that planning intervention may be warranted. Land use zoning represents a quantity-oriented mode of intervention, where zoning assigns each land use category a set quota of land as indicated by the land use maps referred to above. An alternative mode of intervention is price-based intervention, an option that planners would do well to consider to attain planning ends more effectively.

Two Alternative Allocations: Zoning and Market

Figures 2.1a and 2.1b depict an urban area with a fixed supply of land, S, which can be put to either of two uses. We shall call these uses residential and nonresidential, respectively.[1] The length of the horizontal axis is fixed at S, and any demarcation along this axis denotes a particular allocation of urban land between competing residential and nonresidential uses. For example, the zoning allocation Z delineates the residential uses on the left (Z_r) from the nonresidential uses on the right (Z_n). Note that this representation

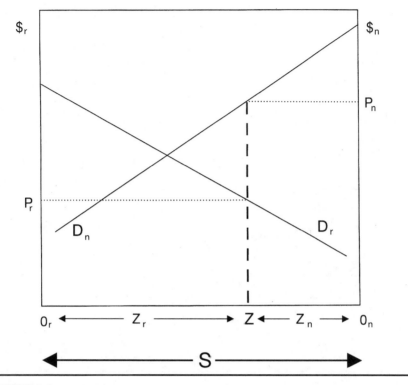

FIGURE 2.1a
Zoning allocation of land between residential and nonresidential uses

simply depicts quantities of land devoted to either use, and does not necessarily imply spatial contiguity within each use category. We shall have occasion to return to this point later.

It is important when speaking about assets of any kind, including land, to distinguish between stock prices and flow prices. The *stock price* is the value of the asset itself, whereas the *flow price* represents the value of the flow of services rendered by the asset. As suggested by its name, the flow price is measured as dollars per unit of time. For example, the flow price of land could be based on its rental value on a yearly or monthly basis. As explained in more detail in chapter 4, there is a close relationship between these two expressions of price, with the asset value reflecting the value of current and future services rendered by the asset, as well as reflecting likely future increases in the value of the asset itself. For the purposes of the discussion in this chapter, the basic ideas expressed in these diagrams could be told with

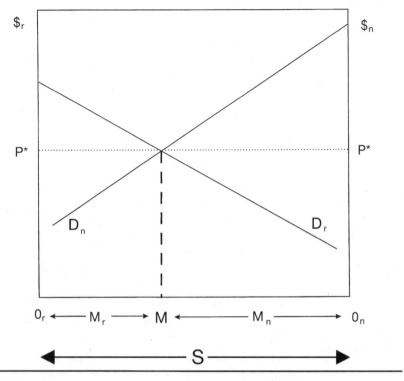

FIGURE 2.1b
Market allocation of land between residential and nonresidential uses

respect to either the stock or flow price in mind. We do so in the context of flow prices.

The vertical axis on the left in figure 2.1b gauges the flow price of residential land, and it is with respect to this axis that the familiar downward-sloping market demand curve, D_r, is drawn. For any given price, the demand schedule tells us how much land will be sought after in the market. It is downward sloping because lower prices correspond to greater demand. The same curve has a different interpretation if read another way. If we begin by selecting a spot along the horizontal (quantity) axis, the height of the curve at that point indicates the marginal benefit to the person who would just be willing to acquire that last bit of land at that price. Based on this interpretation, we may term this same curve the marginal benefit curve for residential land, MB_r. We will have occasion to reexamine and revise this interpretation later in this chapter.

The mirror image of what has just been depicted for residential land applies in the case of nonresidential land, with reference to the vertical axis on the right. Notice that the demand curve for nonresidential land, D_n, is unusual in that it slopes downward to the left rather than to the right. This is not due to any peculiar feature of nonresidential land, but is instead an outcome of the special way that we have constructed the graph so that the quantity of nonresidential land is measured from left to right while residential is from right to left. This is possible in this instance because we are only depicting two types of land use and because the total land supply is assumed to be fixed.[2] It is convenient to juxtapose both demand curves on one graph this way because it allows us to make reference to both curves simultaneously for any given allocation between residential and nonresidential uses as depicted by the corresponding location along the horizontal axis.

With this in mind, let us return our attention to the arbitrary[3] zoning allocation Z. In the context of figure 2.1a, land use zoning has the effect of fixing the total quantities of residential and nonresidential land at Z_r and Z_n, respectively. How does the land market adjust to this fact? Because the quantities of land devoted to either land use cannot be adjusted, any market adjustment must be in terms of prices. As can be readily observed from the graph, the market-clearing prices for residential and nonresidential land corresponding to the zoned allocation Z are P_r and P_n, respectively. Already it is plain to see that planners have a powerful effect through zoning on the market for land. For example, if the zoning allocation had been further to the left, then the price of nonresidential land would be lower while the price of residential land would be higher. *Thus, zoning has a direct impact on the price of land.*

By *market-clearing prices,* we are referring to those prices for which the quantity of land demanded will just be met by the quantity supplied. If the price for residential land is less than P_r, then the market demand for residential land will exceed Z_r. If it is higher than P_r, the demand will fall short of Z_r. Thus, P_r is the only price that is consistent with the fixed supply of residential land. A similar argument applies to P_n, the market-clearing price of nonresidential land. These prices are also *equilibrium prices,* which means there is no tendency for prices to move away from P_r or P_n once they have been attained. Moreover, the equilibria in question are stable in the sense that the prices are self-adjusting. For example, the excess demand resulting from a price lower than P_r will continue to put upward pressure on prices until the equilibrium price of P_r is restored.

The zoning allocation may be contrasted with the market solution, M, in figure 2.1b. Intuition correctly advises us that the market solution occurs where the two market demand curves intersect, thereby equating the market price of land to P^* for either category of use. Thus, no one can earn a profit by buying land that is in one category of use and selling it for another,

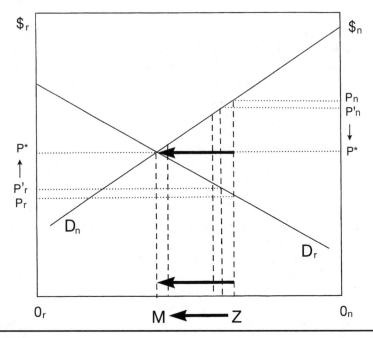

FIGURE 2.2
Market adjustment process

because in each case the value of land on the margin is P*. At this price the demand for residential and for nonresidential land is M_r and M_n, respectively, and so the total quantity of land demanded just manages to exhaust the amount supplied. A simple comparison of figures 2.1a and 2.1b suggests an important difference between the zoning and market allocations: *The market allocation tends to equalize the price of comparable parcels of land across all uses while the zoning allocation will tend to introduce price differentials between comparable parcels of land that are subject to different uses.*

Notice too that the market solution is a stable equilibrium. That is, any movement away from M (for whatever reason) will tend to reverse itself. Suppose, for example, that the initial allocation is at Z as depicted in figure 2.2, but where all zoning constraints have been removed, so that the market is allowed to adjust itself fully. Before long, some bright soul will recognize that this situation creates an opportunity for *arbitrage*: A parcel of residential land can be purchased at P_r, converted to nonresidential use, and sold at price P_n for a net gain of $(P_n - P_r)$. When this transaction is completed, the net result will be one less parcel of residential land and one more parcel of nonresidential land relative to the initial allocation Z. As a direct result, the vertical demarcation line in figure 2.2 will shift one step to the left. When this happens, there will be a slight adjustment in the price of nonresidential land (which will fall) and of residential land (which will rise). After this first transaction is completed, the situation in qualitative terms remains very much as before, with a new price differential $(P'_n - P'_r)$ that continues to encourage conversion of land from nonresidential to residential uses. The magnitude of the differential will be slightly smaller than it was before the first transaction took place (which only confirms that the early bird does indeed get the juiciest worm!), but the basic conversion incentive remains. Eventually, however, as the demarcation line moves steadily to the left in figure 2.2 as a result of market forces, the allocation will converge to the market solution M.[4]

The market equilibrium M with price P^* is a stable one. If the allocation moves away from this equilibrium for any reason, the process just described will bring it back to the price–quantity pair, (P^*, M). Notice too that the adjustment process differed from the one described earlier in the case of the zoning allocation. In the case of zoning, the market adjustment process entails price adjustments only because the quantity of land devoted to either land use category is fixed by the zoning. In the case just described, however, both prices and quantities adjusted in response to the disequilibrium displacement. In the case of zoning, the adjustment process acts on prices until they correspond to the levels indicated by the market demand curves at the specified quantities at Z_r and Z_n. In contrast, the full market solution causes a movement *along* the demand curves until the point of intersection is attained.

Evaluating Alternative Land Use Allocations

It is one thing to note that the zoned solution generally differs from the market solution, but another to judge which allocation is preferable. This, of course, depends upon the criteria we use to evaluate alternative allocations. One possible criterion is to select the allocation that maximizes the aggregate value of land. People who own land often do so, at least in part, as an investment. Such individuals are typically eager to see that the value of their asset (the land) is kept high, and this concern is often reflected in local government decisions pertaining to land use matters.

The market value of any single parcel of land is given simply by reference to the demand curve for the use in question. We have seen that this value responds to changes in the quantity of land available, with the market price falling as land of a given category becomes more abundant, as indicated by

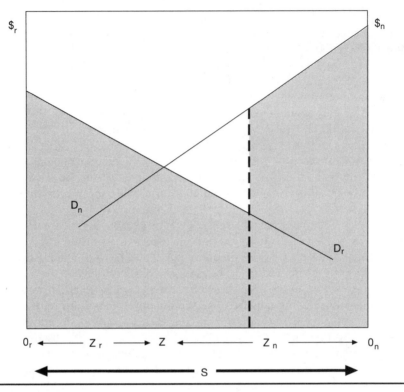

FIGURE 2.3a
Aggregate value of land under zoning allocation

the downward-sloping demand curve. Stated another way, *the marginal value of land decreases with quantity.* The demand curve has a dual interpretation as a marginal valuation curve, or as a marginal benefit curve where the benefit in question is from the perspective of the person whose demand is registered in the demand curve. Chapter 2 tells us that the *area* beneath a marginal valuation (or benefit) curve is a measure of aggregate value (or benefit). Thus, in figure 2.3a, the area beneath the residential demand curve to the left of the zoning allocation Z measures the aggregate value of residential land when the allocation of land between competing uses is as denoted by Z. Likewise, the aggregate value of nonresidential land corresponding to the allocation Z is given by the area beneath the nonresidential demand curve to the right of Z. By similar reasoning, the aggregate value of residential (nonresidential) land corresponding to the market allocation M is given by the area beneath the residential (nonresidential) demand curve to the left (right) of M in figure 2.3b.

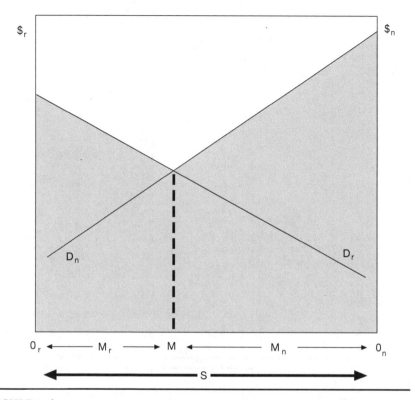

FIGURE 2.3b
Aggregate value of land under market allocation

It is useful at this point to distinguish between the aggregate value of land as defined above and the market value of land as depicted in figure 2.4. The market value of land for a given land use category is calculated as the price of land times the quantity of land. In effect, the market valuation of land applies the *marginal value* of land across the board, as though it were an average price. We see this method used from time to time in the popular press, where the total value of land (for example, in the downtown area) is calculated by taking recent sales prices for a given category of land use and multiplying that by the amount of land in the same use category. By comparing figure 2.4 with figure 2.3a it should be evident that the market value of land understates the aggregate value because it fails to account for the rising marginal valuation of land as quantities become more scarce.

It is now possible to compare the aggregate value of land directly for the two land use allocations, M and Z. In figure 2.5 we note that there are six distinct areas that are delineated by the two demand curves and by the

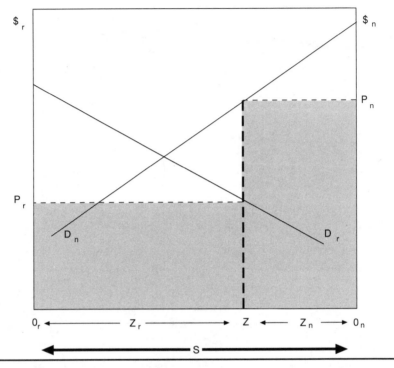

FIGURE 2.4
Market value of land under zoning allocation

vertical supply curves corresponding to the allocations M and Z. Making reference to figure 2.5, we can compute the aggregate value for each scenario as in table 2.1:

TABLE 2.1

Comparing the Aggregate Value of Land
Under Alternative Land Use Allocations

Land Use Allocation	Aggregate Value of Residential Land	Aggregate Value of Nonresidential Land	Aggregate Value of All Land
Z—Zoning Allocation	= [1] + [2] + [4]	= [5] + [6]	= [1] + [2] + [4] + [5] + [6]
M—Market Allocation	= [1] + [2]	= [3] + [4] + [5] + [6]	= [1] + [2] + [3] + [4] + [5] + [6]
D = M - Z	= -[4]	= [3] + [4]	= [3]

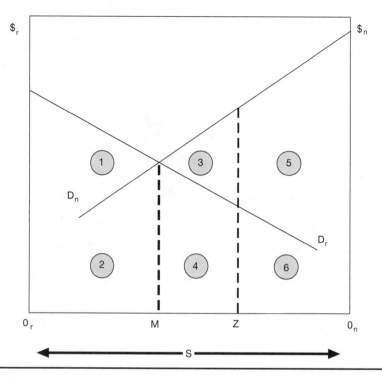

FIGURE 2.5
Zoning allocation of land between residential and nonresidential uses

Under both the market and the zoning allocations, the areas denoted by [1] and [2] contribute to residential land value while [5] and [6] contribute to nonresidential land value. For the zoning allocation Z, the area denoted by [4] contributes to residential land value, but this is converted to the nonresidential side of the ledger for the market allocation M. Most significantly, the triangular area marked [3] does not contribute at all under the zoning allocation, whereas it does constitute part of the nonresidential value under the market allocation. Thus, the aggregate value for all land under the market allocation M exceeds aggregate value for the zoning allocation Z by the amount depicted in the triangular area [3], which corresponds also to the darkly shaded triangular area in figure 2.6. We term this area the triangle of inefficiency, as it measures the aggregate loss in value associated with the zoning allocation Z relative to the market allocation M.

Notice that this result holds generally, and not just for the specific configuration drawn in this particular version of the diagram. Some reflection on these diagrams leads to the conclusion that the market allocation is always

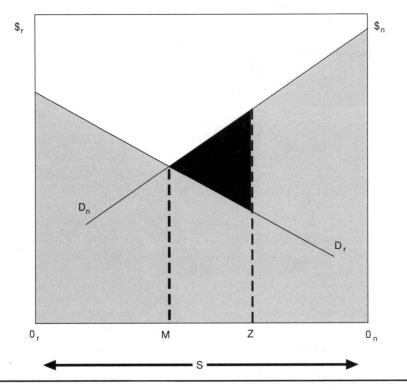

FIGURE 2.6
Triangle of inefficiency

the one that generates the maximum possible aggregate value of land as measured by the market demand curves. This is a powerful result and is one of the reasons that economists tend to be so enthusiastic about markets. Markets "automatically" uncover the land use allocation that maximizes the aggregate market value of land. This is not surprising in light of the adjustment process described earlier whereby entrepreneurs convert land from residential to nonresidential use in response to the price differential $[P_n - P_r]$ as depicted in figure 2.2. In fact, if we add up the net profits made by these entrepreneurs, the total is precisely equal to the triangle of inefficiency. Thus, the market demand curves not only measure the marginal valuation of land to its owners, they are also instrumental to the mechanism by which the value-maximizing land use allocation is uncovered.

Thus far it would appear that the market allocation M is inherently superior to the zoning allocation Z, at least with respect to the aggregate value criterion as specified here. Indeed, it would appear to call into question the rationale for the zoning allocation which, as we have seen, will always have a triangle of inefficiency, such as the one depicted in figure 2.6, associated with it. Only when the zoning allocation coincides with the market allocation will there be no triangle of inefficiency, and of course where the two allocations coincide the use of zoning is redundant. However, it would be premature to jump to this conclusion, because it is predicated upon the assumption that the marginal valuation provided by the market demand curves is the appropriate measure of aggregate value. As we shall see, there are many cases where this assumption does not hold.

Market Failure

The term market failure applies to any situation where the market outcome does not produce the maximum social benefit. Recall that the market demand curves provide the marginal valuation of each parcel of land *from the owner's perspective*. This should be apparent because the market demand curve registers willingness to pay, and as explained in chapter 8, willingness to pay is the standard measure of individual benefit in cost–benefit analysis. If the owner of the good is the only one who is affected by its consumption, then the owner's benefit is equal to the overall social benefit. However, it is not rare to encounter situations where the benefits or costs of the use of a good extend beyond the owner of the good in question. This is particularly so in the case of land use, as is evidenced by all the attention given to land use issues in public hearings on parcel-specific rezoning issues. In many such cases the general public is quite affected by visual distractions, traffic noise, "undesirable elements," noxious fumes, quality-of-life issues, or other environmental impacts that are not encapsulated in the market price of the parcel in question. These and similar effects are not internalized in or reflected by market prices and so they are termed *externalities*. They are effects that are external to market prices.

Our analysis of the relative benefits of the market and zoning allocations must be modified to account for externalities. We do so in figure 2.7a, where a marginal benefit curve has been introduced for nonresidential land. Notice that this curve (denoted MB_n) lies beneath the market demand curve for nonresidential land. The vertical displacement of the two curves is a measure of the externality cost imposed by nonresidential land use in this example. Thus, while the owner may be willing to pay (and hence may benefit) an amount that is indicated by the demand curve D_n for nonresidential land, the benefit on the margin of nonresidential land use must be discounted by an amount that reflects the externality costs imposed on others by nonresidential uses in this example. As before, aggregate benefit is measured by the

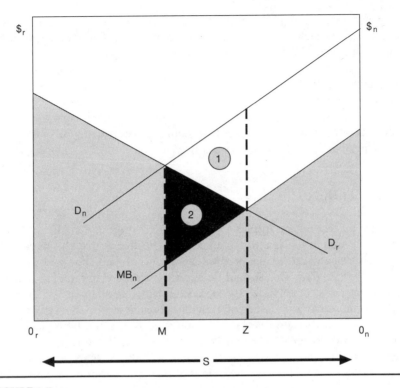

FIGURE 2.7a
Negative externalities and aggregate benefit

area beneath the marginal benefit curve, but in this case the relevant marginal benefit curve does not coincide with the market demand curve.

With this in mind we may once again compare the total benefits corresponding to the alternative land use allocations M and Z. In this example the aggregate benefit from residential land use remains unchanged and is still given by the area beneath the market demand curve D_r to the left of M or of Z, depending on which allocation is being evaluated. However, the aggregate benefit of nonresidential land use is now given by the area beneath the MB_n curve, which is less than what is implied by the nonresidential demand curve D_n. Using the same technique as was used earlier, we can see from figure 2.7a that the tables have been reversed: Aggregate benefits are now maximized at the zoning allocation Z rather than at the market allocation M. Moreover, the difference in aggregate benefit between these two allocations is given by the triangular area denoted by [2] in figure 2.7a. Thus, the triangle of inefficiency has moved from its original location at [1] to its new location at [2]. We refer to these as the *market-based* and the *benefit-based* triangles of inefficiency, respectively. Where there is no market failure, the MB curves and the D curves are one and the same, so these two specifications of the triangle of inefficiency coincide.

The result just reported on is significant. Aggregate benefit is now maximized by the zoning allocation Z rather than by the market allocation M. Moreover, the new triangle of inefficiency [2] now measures the loss in aggregate benefit corresponding to the market allocation relative to the zoning solution. This turns the previous result on its head and provides a potential justification for intervention by planners into the land use market. The market develops the "highest and best use" of properties from the owners' perspectives, but this may not coincide with the land use allocation that maximizes social benefit. However tempting it may be, as planners we must resist the temptation to leap in at this point with cries of "market failure!" as a justification for wanton intervention in land use markets by way of zoning. Atkinson and Stiglitz (1980) tell the story of a king who held a contest between two violin players. After hearing the first player, the king immediately awarded the prize to the second—without having heard him play! The point, of course, is that market failure does not preclude the possibility of even worse regulatory failure. We shall return to this important point a bit later on in this chapter.

Figure 2.7b provides an alternative view of how externalities may cause the zoning allocation Z to be favored over the market allocation M. This time, however, the externality is a positive one and it is presumed to affect residential uses rather than nonresidential uses. As before, the externality is represented by a divergence of the marginal benefit curve MB from the market demand curve. As depicted in figure 2.7b, the marginal benefit curve MB_r lies above D_r. Not surprisingly, this positive externality in favor of residential land uses causes the optimum (i.e., the social benefit–maximizing allocation) to shift to the right, from M to Z. And as in the previous example, we observe that a second triangle of inefficiency has been introduced, so the market-based [1] and benefit-based [2] triangles of inefficiency no longer coincide. Thus, we see that the externality that might cause us to favor the zoning allocation Z over the market allocation M need not be a negative one. Positive externalities, too, are a kind of market failure and may form the basis for a rationale for intervention. In fact, we do see this kind of claim made often in the context of, for example, homeownership and social stability.

In the discussion of market failure thus far, particularly with reference to figures 2.7a and 2.7b, we have used an example of negative externalities associated with nonresidential land uses and of positive externalities linked to residential land uses. One should not conclude from these examples that all nonresidential uses generate negative externalities and that all residential uses

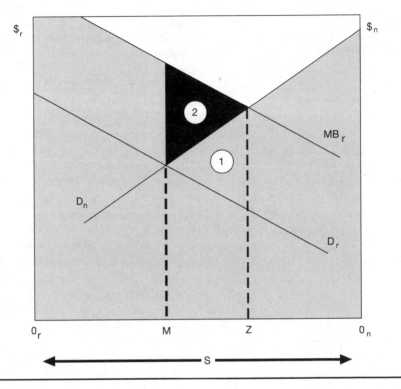

FIGURE 2.7b
Positive externalities and aggregate benefit

generate positive ones. In fact, the positive externalities associated with job creation are widely recognized, and many local governments have economic development departments whose primary mission is to encourage productive nonresidential uses of land within their jurisdictions.

Price-Based Intervention

Let us suppose that, based on evidence of significant externalities, it is clear to all concerned that the zoning allocation Z in figure 2.7a is the single allocation of land uses that maximizes social benefit. Does it follow that zoning is called for? Not necessarily. There are two aspects of markets on which economists are inclined to focus: price and quantity. Land use zoning is a kind of quantity-based intervention because it places restrictions directly on the quantity of land available for each land use category. In particular, it re-

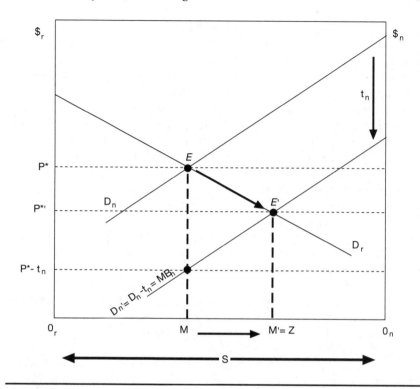

FIGURE 2.8a
Taxing a negative externality

stricts the quantity of residential and nonresidential land to equal Z_r and Z_n, respectively. Prices are left to adjust accordingly, as described earlier in this chapter.

An alternative mode of intervention is via the price dimension. This is very commonly done in other contexts through the use of taxes and subsidies, but it is a practice that planners have thus far been slow to adapt to land use issues. To see how price-based intervention works, consider figure 2.8a, which builds on the discussion pertaining to figure 2.7a. In figure 2.8a the demand curve for residential land has not changed, but there are now *two* demand curves drawn for nonresidential land. One of these is the original market demand curve D_n, while the second one is the demand curve that results after an annual tax, t_n, has been applied to nonresidential land use. The resultant after-tax demand curve is labeled D_n' and is vertically displaced from the original D_n by an amount equal to the tax.

To see why the demand curve shifts downward as a result of the tax, it is useful to recall our previous discussion about the dual interpretation of the market demand curve. On the one hand (when translating from price into quantity) it tells us how much land of a given category is sought after at any given price. A dual interpretation (when translating from quantity into price) is that at any given quantity, the curve registers the benefit on the margin of owning the specified parcel of land. If the owner is subject to a tax, t_n, on that parcel, then the marginal benefit drops commensurately. This is true for any spot along the horizontal axis; the result is a downward shift in the market demand curve by an amount equal to the tax, t_n, assessed on each parcel of nonresidential land.

The downward shift of the market demand curve for nonresidential land in figure 2.8a causes a displacement of the equilibrium from the original point of intersection (denoted by E in figure 2.8a) to the new point of intersection (E') for the residential and nonresidential market demand curves. This causes the market allocation of land use to shift from the original point M to a new allocation M'. Not surprisingly, the market responds to a tax on non-residential land by shifting its allocation of land in favor of residential uses. If the tax is set correctly, the new market demand curve for nonresidential use D_n will correspond precisely to the marginal benefit curve MB_n, and therefore the new market allocation M' will correspond to the zoning allocation Z, as is the case depicted in figure 2.8a.

And what about the new market equilibrium price for land, P*'? Will it fall by an amount equal to the tax? As seen from figure 2.8a, the answer is clearly no. Because the market demand curve for nonresidential use shifts downward by t_n, the price ($P^* - t_n$) must correspond to the new demand curve at the original market allocation M. However, as we have seen, the market equilibrium will have shifted as a result of the tax, and so the new market land use allocation M' lies to the right of the original one. This corresponds to a movement along the demand curve, and so there is a partial price adjustment. The new equilibrium price P*' is less than the original equilibrium price P* but is greater than ($P^* - t_n$). What has happened is that the market has responded to the reduced attractiveness of nonresidential land (arising from the imposition of a tax) by shifting its land use allocation in favor of residential land. This causes nonresidential land to become more scarce, increasing its value on the margin *relative to what it would have been* had that quantity adjustment not been allowed. At the same time, the shift in favor of residential land use causes the value of residential land to fall on the margin (because the demand curve is downward sloping), and so the new equilibrium price is less than it was originally. This combination of factors assures us that $P^* > P^{*'} > (P^* - t_n)$.

A similar line of reasoning applies in the case of a subsidy, as illustrated in figure 2.8b. A subsidy is a kind of "negative tax," which in the case

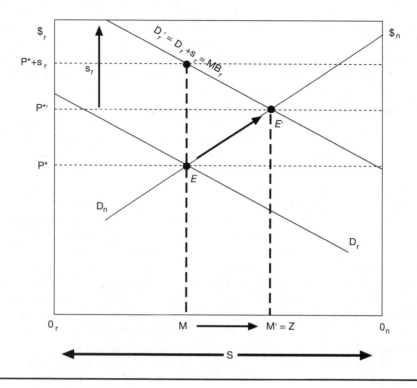

FIGURE 2.8b
Subsidizing a positive externality

described here is used to support or encourage residential land uses. An important example of this is mortgage interest deductibility which, as explained in chapter 3, provides a tax subsidy to homeowners. This increases the attractiveness of homeownership, which in turn causes an upward shift in the market demand curve for residential land by an amount s, equal to the effective subsidy on residential land. This in turn causes the market allocation of land use to shift in favor of residential land, from M to M', with a corresponding increase in the equilibrium price from P^* to $P^{*'}$, where $P^* < P^{*'} < (P^* + s_r)$.

Price-Based versus Quantity-Based Intervention

The question remains whether price or quantity intervention in urban land markets is preferable from an economic perspective. As one might expect, the answer is not quite that simple, and there are persuasive arguments to be considered from either perspective. Relevant considerations include the relative information requirements of these two modes of intervention, the desirability of spatial contiguity of land uses, and issues of fairness or political process. There are also issues of institutional inertia, political palatability, and professional training to consider.

Zoning decisions may at times appear rather arbitrary, but so too can tax regulations, subsidies, or development fees. An arbitrary decision in this sense is one that is not rooted in some systematic analysis of the conditions that might warrant such intervention. This calls into question the information requirements that might inform such an investigation by planners who are contemplating the possibility of an intervention into land markets in their jurisdictions. This brings us back to a consideration of figures 2.7a and 2.7b, which are the bases for preferring the land use allocation Z over the original market allocation M. These diagrams remind us that the rationale for possible intervention lies in the divergence of the true marginal benefit curve MB from the market demand curve D for whichever land use category is being considered. Knowing that there is a divergence tells us that the benefit-maximizing allocation is likely to diverge from the market allocation, but that knowledge is not enough to tell us *where* the benefit-maximizing location is. To infer the proper location of Z, the planner must know the location of MB, because Z is determined by the intersection of MB with the opposing demand curve. This is a rather onerous requirement. Few practicing planners would claim to divine the shape of marginal benefit curves corresponding to various land use allocations.

The information requirement for price-based intervention is less onerous. Here the planner needs only to know the extent of the cost (or benefit) associated with the externality so that the correct tax (or subsidy) can be calculated. This is still a challenging task, but it is less so than in the case of quantity-based intervention, where one not only must know the vertical displacement caused by the externality, but also the shape of the marginal benefit curve over a sufficiently wide range of allocations to determine where the benefit-maximizing location is. For price-based intervention, however, the market is left to uncover the new allocation (as in figures 2.8a and 2.8b) once the correct tax or subsidy has been specified. Moreover, as market conditions change, the market continues to adjust itself, while zoning intervention requires recalculation of the optimum allocation each time there is a fundamental change in market conditions.

As we have seen, price intervention has the potential advantage of allowing market allocations to evolve over time in response to changing market conditions. Built form, however, is durable and costly to alter to any great extent. Hence, decisions of the past may display considerable inertia whether quotas are in place or not. And if land uses are allowed to evolve in response to price signals, an additional element of uncertainty is thereby introduced into urban land markets. Moreover, zoning is often undertaken with an explicitly spatial or geographical frame of reference. Many of the advantages of price intervention mean very little unless there is careful reasoning behind the manner in which these fees or subsidies vary across the map. It is also very difficult to capture the interactive effects of land use externalities. For example, the externality costs imposed by nonresidential land may depend on what the surrounding land uses are. It may become very cumbersome and difficult to design a set of taxes or subsidies that properly accounts for such interactive effects.

Another issue is one of fairness and political process. Earlier in this chapter we examined the arbitrage process by which the market would move from the zoning allocation Z to the market allocation M, if it were allowed to do so, as illustrated in figure 2.2. When zoning regulations are in place that arbitrage process is stymied and the allocation is "stuck" at Z, leaving the price differential in figure 2.2 unexploited. This potential gain is sorely tempting, and local newspapers in virtually every city are replete with stories about individuals who have interests in a particular parcel of land and who are alleged to have made unseemly if not illegal contributions to the political campaigns of the local elected officials who are charged with approving or denying applications to rezone specific parcels of land from one use category to another. The situation is depicted quite clearly in figure 2.2, where the price differential $(P_n - P_r)$ is the potential gain to be realized from such a rezoning. The same impulse that drives the market (or more precisely, individuals operating within a market context) to move from allocation Z to M is in place regardless, but the outlet for that impulse differs when zoning regulations apply.

Similar arguments may be made regarding taxes and subsidies, for they too cater to specific interests (for example, homeowners who receive mortgage interest tax subsidies) who may be tempted to appeal in dubious ways to the political decision makers who enact legislation or bylaws that determine the scope and extent of those taxes and subsidies. Indeed, lobbying of political decision makers is nothing new and certainly is not confined to land use zoning. From this perspective, seeking a rezoning on a specific parcel is akin to seeking special exemption from a tax that applies broadly to owners of a particular class of land. This line of reasoning suggests that the issue of undue or unfair influence over the political decision-making process is not specific to zoning regulations or to taxes and subsidies, but is instead more broadly applicable to a general class of circumstances where public officials hold discretionary powers over legislation that impacts specific individuals in favorable or unfavorable ways, and where this situation may open the way to influence peddling. Further treatment of these issues would take us beyond the scope of this book, but these issues should not be overlooked completely by planners nor by economists. Zoning has one political advantage over price-based intervention—it has at least the superficial appearance of being a "no cost" solution to the land use allocation problem. Unlike taxes or subsidies, the implementation of zoning does not require monetary transactions in the form of payments to or from the public coffers, and so no budget allocation is required for its implementation.

In point of fact, it is an absolute fallacy to assert that zoning is costless, a fallacy that is predicated on confusion between an accounting view of costs and an economic view of costs. The key difference, as explained in chapter 8 on cost–benefit analysis, is that economists do not limit their calculation of costs or benefits to only those transactions that show up on an accounting ledger. In all of the diagrams discussed in this chapter that represent a triangle of inefficiency, the associated costs are *real*. They represent real opportunities to create something of value, opportunities that are lost or forgone because of misallocations. The area depicted by the triangle of inefficiency is a measure of the real loss in wealth (or benefits) that society might enjoy collectively or might allocate to specific individuals or groups for their enjoyment. That loss may be less tangible when represented as a triangle on a diagram in a textbook, but it is no less real than any transaction that is recorded in an accounting ledger. From this perspective, this so-called advantage of zoning is really a disadvantage because its apparent costlessness is in fact misleading, even if not intentionally so.

Institutional and professional inertia present another challenge to planners in the adoption of price-based intervention in land markets. The simple reality is that planning departments everywhere are already fully committed to quantity-based intervention via zoning. The institutions and mechanisms that are responsible for designing, enacting, and enforcing land use regulations via quantity-based interventions may not be readily adaptable to new methods based on price-based interventions. The same can be said for planners themselves. Most planners are not sufficiently well versed in the fundamental economic analysis of land use zoning that they would recognize the potential limitations arising from a solely quantity-based approach to intervention in land markets. Of course, that is why books such as this are written! Throughout this book the expressed point of view is that we planners have an opportunity to enlarge our repertoire by including within it aspects of economic analysis. This does not imply doing away with zoning, but instead, supplementing it with price-based methods.

A final observation is appropriate regarding the trade-off between quantity-based modes of intervention in land markets (such as zoning) and price-based modes (such as taxes or subsidies). Even if the situation we are faced with is accurately depicted by figures 2.7a and/or 2.7b, it does not necessarily follow that intervention is called for at all. In light of the many costs associated with intervention of any kind, one might reasonably conclude that the burden of loss implied by the triangle of inefficiency is less than the burden or cost implied by the very act of intervention. One such cost is of course the maintenance of a regulatory staff that draws its salary from the public purse. Additionally, as we have already seen, the information requirements for intervention are quite onerous; it may not be reasonable to expect that planners have sufficient information or knowledge to intervene wisely, and so the welfare or benefit gains from intervention may be more illusory than real. And finally, some might also argue that the infringement of freedom and the intrusion into the public domain inherent in government intervention represent a significant cost to social welfare. Based on these considerations, the range of choices may best be cast as quantity-based intervention, price-based intervention, and nonintervention.

Notes

1. The discussion in this chapter applies equally well to three or more competing uses. The diagrams, however, are much easier to handle in two dimensions.

2. If the supply of land were not fixed, then it would have the effect of "expanding" or "shrinking" the length of the horizontal axis on our graph.

3. The zoning allocation Z is "arbitrary" in the sense that it could be any point on the horizontal axis, without reference to the market demand curves. It is arbitrary with respect to the market. This does not in any way imply that the zoning decision was made "arbitrarily."

4. If there are transactions costs associated with land conversion (such as real estate broker commissions or permitting fees), then the solution may stop short of the point of intersection.

3

The Economics of Housing

Introduction

The housing supply-and-demand diagram in figure 3.1 is deceptively simple. After all, what could be more innocent than an equilibrium price ($\$^*$) and quantity ($Q^*$) level of housing determined by the point of intersection of a downward-sloping demand curve and an upward-sloping supply curve? Indeed, this supply-and-demand diagram is the very crucible upon which economic analysis is founded. So, what is the problem? In the case of housing, there are two fundamental issues that one must address. First, housing can be thought of both as a *stock* and as a *flow*, so we must distinguish between the characteristics of a physical asset and those of the accommodation services that can be derived from it. Second, *housing is a multifaceted good,* and this fact complicates our measurement of housing quantity. These two issues are discussed at length later in this chapter, and that discussion will introduce topics such as asset pricing, financial leverage, and hedonic regression.

Having raised some cautionary notes about issues lurking behind the diagram in figure 3.1, we may now proceed to make some use of it. In doing so we set aside for the moment detailed questions about how the quantity of housing was defined or measured, or about whether the diagram is referring to housing stocks or the flow of services derived therefrom. For our immediate purposes it suffices to define quantity in terms of square feet of

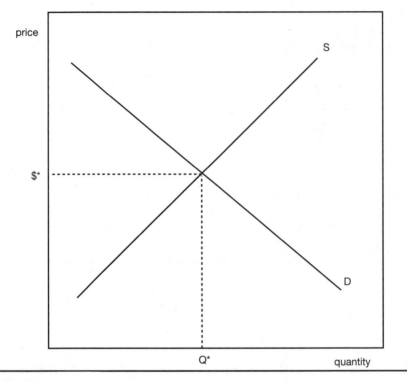

FIGURE 3.1
Supply of, and demand for, housing

livable built space, where all prices are calculated in terms of monthly rents on a square-foot basis. The product of price and quantity therefore measures the flow of payments in dollars per month, because:

$$\text{Price} * \text{Quantity} = [\$ / \text{sq ft} / \text{month}] * [\text{sq ft}] = [\$ / \text{month}] \quad (1)$$

We will assume that the time frame here is sufficient to allow a fair bit of adjustment to occur in response to changes in market conditions. As rental rates fall, we would expect that tenants in this rental market would begin to utilize more living space, so the demand curve is downward sloping. Landlords, on the other hand, would respond to higher rents by offering more space to let, or even by building more accommodation space if time allows, so the supply curve is upward sloping.

Rent Controls and Finder's Fees

In figure 3.2, rent controls are imposed upon the rental market described by figure 3.1. The price ceiling is denoted by the thick-dashed horizontal line at $\$^D$. Rent controls are motivated by a *prima facie* desire to make housing more affordable by suppressing rents to a level that is below the market equilibrium described by $\$^*$. Typically the mechanism for implementing rent controls is legislation that limits the ability of landlords to increase rents in response to changing market conditions. For example, it may be that the demand curve has shifted outward over time from D_0 to D_1 in response to growing population or incomes. In this case the former equilibrium price of $\$^D$ is below the new market equilibrium at $\$^*$. If landlords are not permitted to respond to this change in market conditions, effectively a price ceiling has been imposed.

Whatever the specific form of the regulation, the result of rent controls

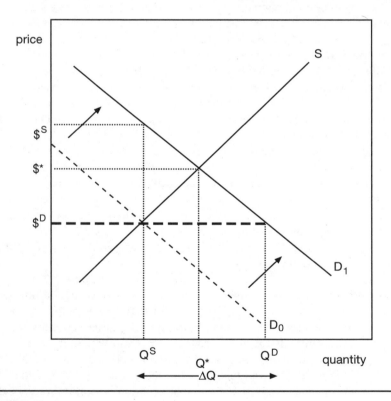

FIGURE 3.2
Imposing rent controls

is an excess of demand relative to available supply. Relative to the equilibrium quantity Q^*, we can see that excess demand is described by $\Delta Q^D =$
$[Q^D - Q^*]$ while the shortfall in supply is $\Delta Q^S = [Q^* - Q^S]$. The *total gap* between supply and demand is then given by $\Delta Q = \Delta Q^D + \Delta Q^S$. Rent controls
may be effective in keeping prices low for those who are able to secure a
rental unit, but the gap defined by ΔQ represents a queue (visible or not) of
individuals who are left wanting rental accommodation at the posted price
but who are unable to find it. Queues are a normal response to price ceilings. If scarce resources cannot be allocated and rationed through a price
mechanism, then the impact of excess demand must be absorbed by the
quantity dimension. Visions of babushkas in long queues on the streets of
Moscow during the Soviet era are not entirely misleading or inappropriate.
Bread was cheap in the Soviet Union—if one could find any. One must be
cautious about associating rent controls with a draconian Soviet-style form
of government, and that is surely not the intention here. Nonetheless, the
underlying economic phenomenon is the same in these two cases: Price ceilings result in a gap between the amount supplied and the amount demanded
at due imposed price. Those left standing in the gap effectively form a queue
of people waiting for additional units to be made available.

   This brings us to the issue of finder's fees. It usually does not take long
before someone in a slow-moving queue begins to think of ways to jump to
the front of the line. Isn't that why we learn to provide generous tips to the
maitre d'hotel at a fancy restaurant in hopes of securing quick access to one
of the choicest tables? The same principle applies in the market for rental
housing. The "underground market" rental rate of $\$^S$ that prevails in this mar-
ket can be gleaned by reference to the demand curve where only Q^S units
are available. As scarce units become available at the margin defined by Q^S,
there is potential for someone to collect a finder's fee equivalent to $\Delta\$ =$
$[\$^S - \$^D]$.[1] The exact fee may differ because it may be costly to find that
individual who is most willing to pay; besides, it is illegal to circumvent the
rent controls, and so there may be a fine line between finder's fees and illegal charges in lieu of rents.

   There is a certain irony to the situation depicted in figure 3.2. Rent controls were imposed in response to the perception that the equilibrium price
of $\$^*$ is somehow too high or otherwise unjust. The result is that we are left
with three basic classes of renters. To the left of Q^S there are those tenants
who benefit as intended from the rent controls and who enjoy rents of $\$^D$.
In the gap defined by ΔQ we have those who seek accommodation at this
rent but cannot find it. And finally, at the margin defined by Q^S, there are
tenants who pay as much as $\$^S$ for rental accommodation, more than they
would have in the absence of rent controls. Ultimately, housing affordability
is best achieved by encouraging additional supply so that the supply curve

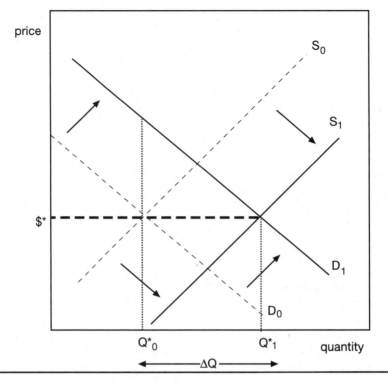

FIGURE 3.3
Supply response to increased demand

shifts to the right as in figure 3.3. This can be accomplished by removing or limiting unproductive[2] land use controls and other restrictions on supply. Rent controls have precisely the opposite effect. By inhibiting supply they drive up the effective price on the margin.

Housing Stocks and Flows

Physically, housing is a stock. From a financial perspective, that stock is viewed as an asset, i.e., a good that retains value over time. The value of an asset is ultimately rooted in its ability to generate a flow of valued services from one period to the next. In the case of housing, we look for a flow of accommodation services over time. We don't consume our houses per se, but we do derive benefits such as shelter, location, and even prestige on an ongoing basis from our housing stock. Whereas the value of a *stock* is mea-

TABLE 3.1

Assets and Corresponding Dividends

Type of Asset	Nature of Dividends
Housing	Accommodation services, shelter, location, prestige
Automobiles	Mobility services, "cruising" services, social signaling
Home appliances	Use of the appliance
Factory	Flow of manufactured output
Stocks	Dividend payments based on profits
Bank accounts	Interest payments
Bonds	Yields
Precious art	Aesthetic value, prestige
Precious jewelry	Adornment value, aesthetic value, prestige
Heavy machinery	Use of machinery

sured in *dollars* (sales price of a condominium), the value of a *flow* is measured in *dollars per unit time* (monthly rent). Debates over housing affordability are often muddled by a failure to delineate stock prices from flow prices.

Assets generate a flow of value in two fundamental ways, through *use value* and through *speculative value*. In financial terms these correspond to *dividends* and *capital gains*, respectively. As the term suggests, use value is rooted in the way we make use of the stock itself. In contrast, the speculative value of an asset is based on our expectations about how the price of the asset is likely to increase or decrease over time. Investors may be willing to hold assets that yield very little in the way of tangible dividends if they believe that the market value of the asset will continue to increase. This is often the case with owners of gold or other precious metals. Likewise, the owner of an asset whose market value is declining may be willing to continue to hold on to it if he or she is able to derive sufficient use value from it. Most of us who own automobiles fall into this category.

As noted, dividends are derived from *use of the thing itself* and so are intrinsically tied to the nature of the asset under consideration. To clarify this point, table 3.1 explores the nature of dividends for a sampling of assets.

In all cases the nature of the dividend component is rooted in the nature of the asset and how we use it. In some cases, the value of the dividends is enumerated in dollars. For example, the dividend payments one receives as a shareholder have a definitive dollar value. In other cases the value of the dividend is made explicit through markets. For example, rental markets for housing or for heavy machinery provide an explicit evaluation of the value

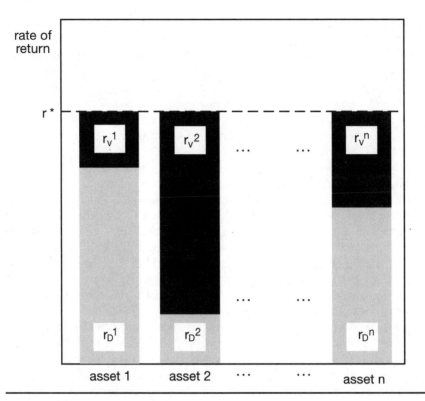

FIGURE 3.4
Equilibrium rate of return on assets

associated with use of those assets. In other cases the use value is more implicit, as in the case of precious art.

Some investors specialize in specific asset markets, either because they have an affinity for those assets (collectors) or because they have developed specialized knowledge about them. For a "pure" investor, however, all assets are measured against a single criterion—their total rate of return based on both dividends and capital gains. The pure investor will shift investment funds back and forth between competing assets based on perceived differentials in their total rates of return. The net effect of all this is to produce a single benchmark rate of return, call it r^*, that is common to all assets on a risk-adjusted basis.[3] Expressed in mathematical form, the equilibrium rate of return for any asset is given by:

$$r^* = (r_V + r_D) \qquad (2)$$

where r_V refers to the rate of increase in the value of an asset (i.e., the rate of capital gains) and r_D denotes the rate of return derived from dividends. Or, for those for whom mathematical symbols are an obstacle rather than an aid to understanding, we have the symbolic representation in figure 3.4. Whether it be expressed mathematically, symbolically, or in narrative form, the message is the same: The rate of capital gains may vary from asset to asset, and so too may the dividend rate, but they must always sum to the same benchmark rate of return r^* if financial markets are to be in equilibrium. Otherwise, markets will continue to adjust until an equilibrium is established.

While it is clearly a simplification to speak about a single worldwide rate of return, the reality is surprisingly close. Worldwide differentials in interest rates can be largely explained by reference to differing rates (or expected rates) of inflation, exchange-rate appreciation, or risk associated with different assets in different countries. Financial capital is sufficiently mobile that assets yielding lower rates of return will quickly be abandoned for those with higher rates of return. The net effect will be to drive down the price of one asset while driving up the price of the other until equilibrium is restored. For our purposes, therefore, it is reasonable to treat the benchmark rate of return to assets r^* as a given.

Let's consider a specific example, where we take the benchmark rate of return r^* to be 4 percent per annum. Figure 3.5 illustrates a situation where the rental market has established a value of $1,000 per month for the accommodation services derived from a typical housing unit in a specific neighborhood. Houses of this type have been selling reliably in recent months for about $300,000. Based on this information the dividend rate, r_D, can be quickly computed to be 4 percent per year:

$$r_D = \frac{(12\,\text{months}\,/\,\text{year})\,^*\,(\$1,000\,/\,\text{month})}{\$300,000} \tag{3}$$

$$= \frac{\$12,000\,/\,\text{year}}{\$300,000}$$

$$= 4\%\ \text{per year}$$

If the benchmark rate of return for assets is 4 percent per annum, then we can infer that there is a general expectation on the part of investors that housing prices in the area will remain stable. In this case we have

$r_D = 4\%$—rate of return from accommodation services provided by housing stock

$r_V = 0\%$—rate of capital gains on housing stocks

and so

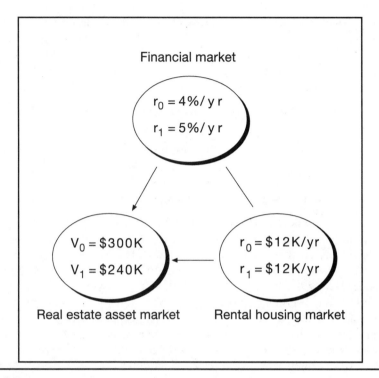

Financial market

$r_0 = 4\%/yr$

$r_1 = 5\%/yr$

$V_0 = \$300K$

$V_1 = \$240K$

$r_0 = \$12K/yr$

$r_1 = \$12K/yr$

Real estate asset market   Rental housing market

FIGURE 3.5
Effect of interest rate changes on value of rental housing assets

$$r^* = (r_V + r_D) = 4\% \tag{4}$$

and the equilibrium condition from equation 2 is satisfied.

If the underlying market conditions should change, something will have to "give." What will it be? That depends on the nature of the change. For example, suppose that the benchmark rate of return r^* increases to 5 percent per annum. This might occur because the Federal Reserve Board decides to adopt a "tighter" monetary policy and so Treasury bills now yield 5 percent.[4] Now investors will expect to receive a 5 percent return and will shift their funds to T-bills if need be. The proper way to describe this from an economic perspective is that the *opportunity cost of capital* is 5 percent.

If nothing has changed in the rental market for housing, the use value of these housing assets remains $12,000 per year. Setting aside for the moment the possibility of capital gains, this implies that investors will not be willing to hold on to these housing assets unless their price falls to $240,000—the amount for which $12,000 per year represents a 5 percent annual return.

Notice that this implies a capital loss of $60,000 for the investor who was caught holding the bag when the benchmark rate of return suddenly changed. Small wonder that Wall Street hangs on every utterance of the Federal Reserve Board chairman! After equilibrium is restored in this case we have the following situation:

r_D = 5%—rate of return from accommodation services provided by housing stock

r_V = 0%—rate of capital gains on housing stocks

and so

$$r^* = (r_V + r_D) = 5\% \tag{5}$$

Speculative expectations about future housing prices can also have an important impact on current prices. For example, let's modify the previous example slightly so that the benchmark rate of return is still 5 percent, but that—for whatever reason—there is a general expectation that the price of housing *next year* will be $261,000. In this case we can show that the equilibrium price of housing *this year* is $260,000. None of our assumptions here have directly affected the rental market for housing, so we may continue to assume that the dividend from rental income remains at $12,000 per year. If housing is worth $260,000 this year and $261,000 next year, then investor income from capital gains over the year is $1,000 for a total return of $13,000 (= $12,000 + $1,000). Note that $13,000 is 5 percent (= r^*) of $260,000, so the equilibrium condition continues to hold, where in this case:

r_D = ($12,000 / $260,000) = 4.6%

r_V = ($1,000 / $260,000) = 0.4%

and so, as before,

$$r^* = (r_V + r_D) = 5\% \tag{6}$$

The examples presented above are simplified in order to clarify the central ideas. In reality, the housing market is marred by uncertainty, confusion, transactions costs, inflation, and shifting expectations. All of these factors complicate the situation, although they do not alter the underlying economic principles in any fundamental way.

Owning versus Renting

Consider for a moment the situation depicted in figure 3.6. Here we have two individuals, A and B, who own identical houses that they rent out to

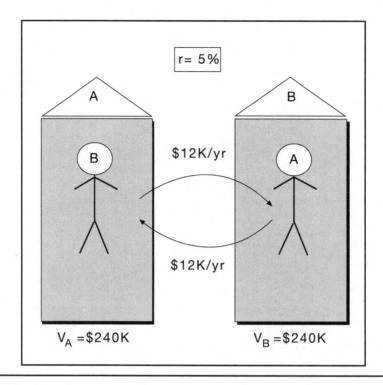

FIGURE 3.6
Renter-occupied housing

each other. Each house has a market value of $240,000, and draws $1,000 per month net rental income. At $12,000 per year, the rental income that each owner receives is just equal to the benchmark rate of return of 5 percent per year, and so the presumption is that there is no expectation of capital gains. As tenants, each individual is paying a fair market rent for housing accommodation services. As investors, each is receiving a fair rate of return on their investments.

Now, what happens if A and B trade places, so that each one lives in their own home as depicted in figure 3.7? From an economic perspective, nothing has changed. As investors, both are still receiving a 5 percent return on their investment, but this time it is in the form of *rent not paid*. In other words, because they live in their own homes, they are not required to write out checks to themselves to cover each month's rent, and so this savings is itself the return on their housing investments. From their standpoint as tenants, they are still receiving the same level of accommodation services (because the houses are identical), and they are "paying" for this with forgone

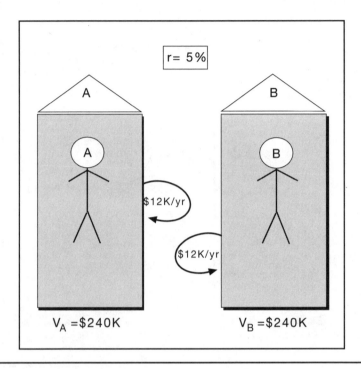

FIGURE 3.7
Owner-occupied housing

rent. By living in the housing units themselves, both landlords are giving up the opportunity to receive monthly rent payments from some other tenant, and so $1,000 per month is the opportunity cost associated with living in their own homes.

While this example may be helpful in illustrating the economic principles behind homeownership, it leaves some questions unanswered. Most importantly, our gut instincts tell us that the two situations depicted in figures 3.6 and 3.7 are fundamentally different. If they are identical from an economics perspective, then perhaps the economic point of view is lacking in some important respects. In fact, there are some important differences between the two situations. For example, few tenants are likely to look after their homes with the same care shown by the owners themselves. More generally, the owner–tenant relationship is surely different when owner and tenant are one and the same! Moreover, the situations in figures 3.6 and 3.7 are viewed differently from the perspective of tax authorities in most countries, so there may be different tax implications arising from these two configurations.

TABLE 3.2

Tax Advantages of Homeownership

	Individuals A and B rent to each other (figure 3.6)	*A and B "rent" to themselves as owner-occupiers (figure 3.7)*	*A and B deduct mortgage interest expenses (figure 3.7 adapted)*
Total Housing Investment	$240,000	$240,000	$240,000
Down Payment	$140,000	$140,000	$140,000
Mortgage or Business Debt Amount	$100,000	$100,000	$100,000
Interest Paid*	$2,500	$2,500	$2,500
Taxable Income from Rental Payments (Imputed or Otherwise)	$12,000	$12,000	$0
Taxable Income from Other Sources (Assumed)	$30,500	$30,500	$30,500
Gross Taxable Income	$42,500	$42,500	$30,500
Deduction for Mortgages or Business Debt Interest (from above)	$2,500	$2,500	$2,500
Net Taxable Income	$40,000	$40,000	$28,000
Tax Due (at 30%)	$12,000	$12,000	$8,400

Note: * The mortgage interest will vary over time as the debt is repaid. Initially, interest is generated by the entire $100,000 mortgage debt. Using a 5 percent mortgage interest rate, this comes to roughly $5,000 for the first year, depending upon the length of the loan. As the loan is almost paid off, the interest on the debt approaches zero. The figure used here is a midpoint between these two extremes.

In the first situation, the one described by figure 3.6, the investor and the tenant are at "arm's length," and their relationship is "strictly business." The owner of each housing unit is expected to declare the rent they receive as part of their investment income for the year. However, against this income they are allowed to deduct basic expenses associated with their business, including maintenance and interest payments on business loans. This arrangement is fairly standard for most countries with well-established market economies. Now, if we were to transfer the same arrangement to the situation in figure 3.7, we would expect each owner to continue to declare an *implicit income* of $1,000 per month, which is the *imputed rent* they receive from themselves each month as a dividend or return on their investment as homeowners. They should be entitled to deduct basic expenses against this income as they would with any other business arrangement. If the tax laws were set up in this manner, the economic equivalence between figures 3.6

and 3.7 would be maintained, and this is the arrangement that most economists would argue in favor of. However, in the United States and some other
countries the tax laws do not treat the two situations equivalently. Instead,
the owner–occupiers in figure 3.7 *are permitted* to deduct interest payments
on their home loans but they are *not required* to declare the imputed rental
income they receive from themselves as homeowners.

This tax arrangement strongly favors the configuration shown in figure
3.7 and was indeed designed to encourage people to own their own homes.
By allowing mortgage interest payments to be deducted without having to
declare the offsetting income, the tax authority is in effect providing a subsidy for owner-occupied housing at the expense of rental housing. To clarify
this point, consider the summary calculations in table 3.2, where the tax rate
on taxable income is assumed to be 30 percent and where three distinct cases
are considered. The first two cases correspond to figures 3.6 and 3.7, respectively, where it is assumed that the tax law is neutral between them. The
third case corresponds more directly to the situation in the United States today where mortgage interest is deductible but where the imputed rental income from homeownership need not be declared. As expected, the taxable
income profiles in the first two cases are identical. Rental income of $12,000
per year supplements $30,500 assumed income from other sources, for a
gross taxable income of $42,500. From this amount, $2,500 in debt repayment is deducted as an income expense, leaving a net taxable income of
$40,000 and a tax bill of $12,000. In the third case, gross taxable income is
just $30,500 because the $12,000 imputed rental income is not included in
the calculation of taxable income. The same interest deduction of $2,500 is
allowed, however, leaving a net taxable income of only $28,000 and a tax
bill of $8,400. The net result of the tax code, therefore, is a subsidy to home-
owner occupiers of $3,600 relative to what they would have to pay for com-
parable rental housing. Now, you may well ask, what is wrong with
subsidizing homeownership? After all, while *houses* may be viewed as investments, to the people who live in them they are not merely houses, they
are *homes*. Moreover, homeownership is strongly identified in the public
mind with civic virtues such as stability and fostering a stake in one's community. The answer, of course, is that the subsidy must come from the same
general public that receives it. At first glance this would appear to be a
zero-sum game, with the cost of the subsidy being equal to the benefit. Unfortunately, this is not the case. In fact it is generally the case that the cost
of providing a subsidy *exceeds* the benefits derived from its receipt. To understand this point, consider figure 3.8 which shows the effect of a price
subsidy where the downward-sloping demand curve may also be interpreted
as a marginal benefit curve.

Initially we have an equilibrium price and quantity level defined by $* and

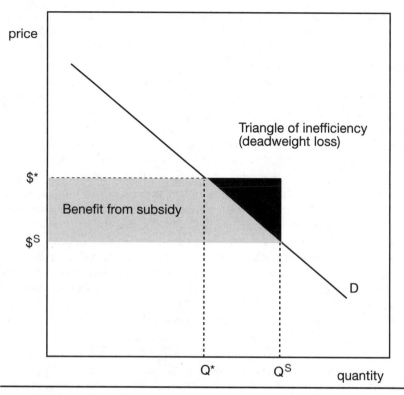

FIGURE 3.8
Deadweight loss from a subsidy

Q*, respectively. When the mortgage interest–based subsidy is introduced, the price of owner-occupied housing accommodation services falls to some amount $\$^S$, as a result of which the amount of housing services consumed increases to Q^S. With a little thought we can see that the increase in benefits derived by homeowner occupiers as a result of the subsidy is denoted by the lightly shaded area beneath the marginal benefit curve and between the two price levels. This can be compared directly to the cost of providing the subsidy. The subsidy amount is given by the vertical distance between the two price levels, and this subsidy is applied to *all* owner-occupied housing. This results in an aggregate subsidy payment represented by the rectangle of width Q^S and height equal to the vertical distance between the two price levels. Thus, we can see that the portion of the subsidy rectangle that falls outside the marginal benefit curve represents a *deadweight loss*. Subsidies are paid but no comparable benefits are obtained. This triangle of inefficiency is similar in principle to the ones we have seen in other chapters. In this case the deadweight loss arises because the homeowners on the margin, i.e., those between Q^* and Q^S, are induced to increase their demand because of lower prices. However, if they were given a choice they would clearly prefer to have the cash equivalent. The net result is that the benefit received by these "induced" homeowners is less than the cost of the subsidy provided to them by the taxpaying public (that's us, folks). Now, if this policy is so inefficient, why doesn't the Internal Revenue Service include imputed rental income in its calculation of taxable income? The answer, of course, is that any proposal that smacks of increasing taxable income, and hence taxes on income, is wildly unpopular with the general public. The basic problem is that this same public does not understand, or does not choose to believe, that they are the same ones who are paying the subsidy.

A final note on homeownership. Anyone who purchases a house is—whether they recognize it or not—making an investment decision. Some people choose to live in their investments; these are individuals who base their selection of a house on investment criteria, including an eye to possible capital gains and tax benefits. Most homeowners, however, invest in the places they choose to live in. As noted earlier, houses are also homes, and the decision about where to live is based on many factors, including quality of schools, neighborhood character, location, and a host of other intangibles. Economic issues certainly factor in, but that is not the same as saying that the decision is treated purely as an economic one. Accordingly, the discussion here is intended to promote a better general understanding of what the economic implications are of the housing decisions we do make.

Mortgage Financing

What do the words "mortgage," "amortize," "mortuary," and "mortify" all have in common? The somewhat gruesome answer is that they are all etymologically rooted in death, *le mort* in French. In the case of a standard mortgage loan, it is the debt itself that is being amortized, or killed off through monthly payments of a constant amount for a fixed period of time. Table 3.3 and figure 3.9 illustrate the principle involved. In this example, the home buyer has taken out a $100,000 loan to be repaid with 12 percent interest over fifteen years with a constant series of monthly payments of $1,200.17 each. A 12 percent interest rate applied to a $100,000 principal generates interest payments of $12,000 per year, or $1,000 per month. If the constant mortgage payment were only $1,000 per month, the principal would never be repaid, therefore we know that the constant monthly mortgage payment must exceed $1,000 if the principal is to be paid within fifteen years.

TABLE 3.3

Mortgage Principal and Interest
Interest Rate = 12% per year
Loan Period = 15 years

	Beginning Period Principal	*Total Payment*	*Interest Payment*	*Principal Payment*	*End of Period Principal*
1	$100,000.00	$1,200.17	$1,000.00	$200.17	$99,799.83
2	$99,799.83	$1,200.17	$998.00	$202.17	$99,597.66
3	$99,597.66	$1,200.17	$995.98	$204.19	$99,393.47
4	$99,393.47	$1,200.17	$993.93	$206.23	$99,187.24
5	$99,187.24	$1,200.17	$991.87	$208.30	$98,978.94
6	$98,978.94	$1,200.17	$989.79	$210.38	$98,768.56
7	$98,768.56	$1,200.17	$987.69	$212.48	$98,556.08
8	$98,556.08	$1,200.17	$985.56	$214.61	$98,341.47
9	$98,341.47	$1,200.17	$983.41	$216.75	$98,124.72
10	$98,124.72	$1,200.17	$981.25	$218.92	$97,905.80
11	$97,905.80	$1,200.17	$979.06	$221.11	$97,684.69
12	$97,684.69	$1,200.17	$976.85	$223.32	$97,461.37
...	...	...	...	...	...
...	...	...	...	...	...
169	$ 13,507.98	$1,200.17	$135.08	$1,065.09	$12,442.90
170	$ 12,442.90	$1,200.17	$124.43	$1,075.74	$11,367.16
171	$ 11,367.16	$1,200.17	$113.67	$1,086.50	$10,280.66
172	$ 10,280.66	$1,200.17	$102.81	$1,097.36	$9,183.30
173	$9,183.30	$1,200.17	$91.83	$1,108.34	$8,074.96
174	$8,074.96	$1,200.17	$80.75	$1,119.42	$6,955.55
175	$6,955.55	$1,200.17	$69.56	$1,130.61	$5,824.93
176	$5,824.93	$1,200.17	$58.25	$1,141.92	$4,683.01
177	$4,683.01	$1,200.17	$46.83	$1,153.34	$3,529.68
178	$3,529.68	$1,200.17	$35.30	$1,164.87	$2,364.81
179	$2,364.81	$1,200.17	$23.65	$1,176.52	$1,188.29
180	$1,188.29	$1,200.17	$11.88	$1,188.29	$0.00

So what is the payment amount that will just pay off the principal, with interest, in fifteen years? One guess, an incorrect one, is obtained by dividing the $100,000 principal into 180 (= 15*12) equal pieces of $555.55 each and adding this amount to the $1,000 needed to repay the principal, for a total monthly payment of $1,555.55. The problem with this approach is that it neglects the fact that the principal will be steadily dwindling, and so the interest payment required will likewise diminish over the repayment period.[5]

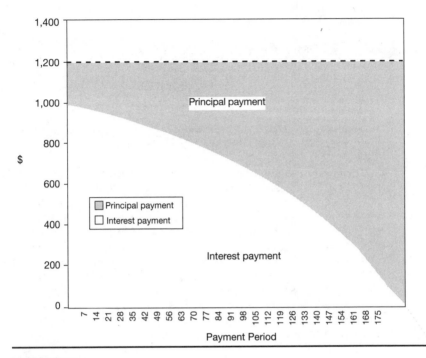

FIGURE 3.9
Mortgage principal and interest

The $1,200.17 payment shown in table 3.3 is the constant payment amount that just manages to pay off the principal after 180 monthly installments. In the initial payment period, $1,200.17 is $200.17 more than required to repay the $1,000 monthly interest bill generated by the $100,000 outstanding principal. As a direct result, the principal due in the second period is about $99,800. The monthly interest payment generated by this reduced principal is $998, or $2 less than in the previous period, which means that there is $2 extra to be used for principal repayment. And so the cycle continues: Each period's principal repayment eats away at the principal, which in turn generates a smaller interest bill, thereby allowing for more aggressive repayment of the principal. This is illustrated clearly in figure 3.9, which shows how principal repayment consumes an increasing share of the $1,200.17 monthly payment over time. The bottom rows of table 3.3 detail the payments made during the final year of the loan. By this time the lion's share of the $1,200.17 monthly payments goes directly to repayment of the principal, where the latter is too small to generate a substantial interest bill. By the miracle of modern finance, the principal at the beginning of the final period is just sufficient to generate an interest bill that, when subtracted from the $1,200.17

constant payment, leaves just enough to repay the remaining principal, and so the loan has been fully amortized. It's dead. *C'est mort!*

Leverage as a Double-Edged Sword

A question that arises in the context of mortgages and housing investments concerns how much debt one should assume when purchasing a home. In part, the answer depends on how poor or wealthy you are. If your level of wealth is quite modest, it may not be possible to purchase a home without borrowing money. In part, the answer also depends on the tax code. As we have already discussed, the tax system in the United States and some other countries provides a subsidy to those who purchase a home using mortgaged debt. However, another important consideration is the effect that debt has on the rate of return to one's investment. *Leveraging* is the use of debt to magnify this rate of return. As we shall see, its effectiveness depends critically upon the supposition that housing prices will rise more rapidly than the interest rate on one's debt. If this condition is not met, it is the potential loss that is magnified, and hence we say that leverage is a double-edged sword—it can cut both ways!

We begin with the definition of some basic terms: value (V), equity (E), and debt (D). Debt, as some of us know only too well, is money that one borrows and must pay back, usually with interest. For our purposes, the value of an asset is taken to be the price it could fetch in the corresponding asset market. Equity is defined in terms of these first two concepts. For any asset in some time period denoted by *t*, the three terms are linked together through the following identity:

$$E_t \equiv V_t - D_t \tag{7}$$

Note that this relationship is not merely an equation—it is an *identity*. This means that equity in any period t is *defined* as the residual value of an asset after paying off any debt that may encumber it. Equity doesn't just happen to be equal to (V-D), it is defined thus. In the case of a homeowner, her equity in the home is the amount of money that she would walk away with if she were to sell her home today and use the proceeds to pay off any outstanding debts that are "attached" to that asset.[6]

An example may help to illustrate this point while also preparing a foundation for understanding the principle of leveraged investments. Consider an investor who has $100,000 in cash, pure equity. To keep the numbers easy, we will assume that houses in the neighborhood are selling for that same amount, $100,000 each. If the investor purchases one of these houses today and sells it one year later for $108,000, then the rate of return to investor's equity is clearly 8 percent, which is also the rate of appreciation in the value of the housing asset. More formally, letting t = 0 and t = 1 denote the initial and subsequent years, respectively, we have:

Leverage Factor; L = 1	Value	Debt	Equity
t = 0	$100K	0	$100K
t = 1	$108K	0	$108K
rate of increase	$r_V = 8\%$	$r_D = NA$	$r_E = 8\%$

In this case the relationship between value and equity is straightforward because no debt is involved, and so we say that the leverage factor is one, L = 1, where L is defined as the ratio of V to E, that is, L = V/E.

Now, let's assume that this same investor chooses to purchase two homes rather than one, although there is still only $100,000 in initial equity to work with. In this case she must borrow $100,000 to bridge the gap, where we assume that the rate of interest on debt is 5 percent. Now we have a leverage factor of two, and the situation may be summarized as follows:

Leverage Factor; L =2	Value	Debt	Equity
t = 0	$200K	$100K	$100K
t = 1	$216K	$105K	$111K
rate of increase	$r_V = 8\%$	$r_D = 5\%$	$r_E = 11\%$

Note that leveraging in this instance has brought about an increase in the rate of return to equity, from 8 percent in the previous example to 11 percent here. The reason for this is the positive differential between the rate of appreciation of housing assets (8 percent) and the rate of interest on debt (5 percent). By borrowing $100,000 the investor creates a debt of that amount. The debt thereupon begins to grow steadily at a 5 percent rate. Offsetting this debt is the housing asset that the investor purchased with the $100,000 loan. Depending on how the market evolves, this asset also has the potential to grow in value, and in this example it does so at 8 percent. Thus, at the end of the year the investor is able to use the $108,000 from the sale of her housing unit to pay off the $105,000 debt and still have $3,000 left over to augment her equity. As a direct result, the end-of-year equity is now $111 rather than $108; the investor has clearly profited through leveraging.

Emboldened by this finding, our investor now decides to purchase three houses with the initial $100,000 in equity. The situation can now be summarized as follows:

Leverage Factor; L = 3	Value	Debt	Equity
t = 0	$300K	$200K	$100K
t = 1	$324K	$210K	$114K
rate of increase	$r_V = 8\%$	$r_D = 5\%$	$r_E = 14\%$

The return to equity has again risen by 3 percent, and is now at 14 percent. From these examples we may infer the following relationship between the rate of return to equity, the rate of appreciation in the value of housing assets, and the interest rate on debt:

$$r_E = r_V + (L - 1) * [r_V - r_D] \tag{8}$$

This expression says that the rate of return to equity is the same as the rate of appreciation in the housing market if no leveraging takes place (i.e., if L = 1), but that it increases by the differential $[r_V - r_D]$ each time the leverage factor is increased by one. To test this just a bit more, let's try a leverage factor of ten:

Leverage Factor; L = 10	Value	Debt	Equity
t = 0	$1,000K	$900K	$100K
t = 1	$1,080K	$945K	$135K
rate of increase	$r_V = 8\%$	$r_D = 5\%$	$r_E = 35\%$

and indeed,

$$35\% = 8\% + (10 - 1) * [8\% - 5\%] = 8\% + 9 * 3\% = 8\% + 27\%$$

which is just what the formula predicts.

So far all of this looks very attractive from an investment standpoint. It stands to reason that *if housing assets are increasing in value at a faster rate than debt is growing*, then it will pay to take on debt to purchase more housing. The italicized premise of the preceding conditional statement can be expressed algebraically as follows:

$$[r_V - r_D] > 0 \tag{9}$$

The opposing side of our double-edged sword comes into play when this condition is reversed. Suppose, for example, that the housing market does not live up to the investor's expectations, so housing assets increase by only 2 percent over the year ($r_V = 2\%$). For the sake of completeness, let's see how this affects some of the cases we reviewed above.

First, with no debt:

Leverage Factor; L = 1	Value	Debt	Equity
t = 0	$100K	0	$100K
t = 1	$102K	0	$102K
rate of increase	r_V = 2%	NA	r_E = 2%

As before, having no debt leads to a rate of return to equity that is equal to the rate of appreciation in the market for housing assets, which in this case is 2 percent. With zero debt one's equity is by definition the value of one's asset, and so it comes as no surprise that equity increases at the same rate as the market value of the asset.

Next, with a leverage factor of two:

Leverage Factor; L = 2	Value	Debt	Equity
t = 0	$200K	$100K	$100K
t = 1	$204K	$105K	$ 99K
rate of increase	r_V = 2%	r_D = 5%	r_E = -1%

As before, the rate of return to equity increases by the differential $[r_V - r_D]$, which in this case is negative, and so r_E drops by 3 percent.

And finally, a leverage factor of ten:

Leverage Factor; L = 10	Value	Debt	Equity
t = 0	$1,000K	$900K	$100K
t = 1	$1,020K	$945K	$75K
rate of increase	r_V = 2%	r_D = 5%	r_E = -25%

We can verify that this case also satisfies the general formula set out earlier:

$$r_E = r_V + (L - 1) * [r_V - r_D]$$

since

$$-25\% = 2\% + (10 - 1) * [2\% - 5\%] = 2\% + 9 * (-3\%)$$

Note that leverage can lead to an acute *negative* rate of return to investor equity even though the market value of the housing assets that the investor purchases are themselves growing at a positive rate. The reason, of course, is that the investor's debt is growing more quickly, and so the larger the debt burden the investor assumes, the more quickly does his equity dissipate.

Measuring Housing Quantity

As noted in the introduction, housing is a multifaceted good. This fact makes it difficult to measure housing quantity along a single dimension, and so we find different measures used on different occasions, depending upon purpose. For example, municipal housing surveys may count the number of individual housing units in their jurisdiction, where a housing unit is defined as a distinct dwelling designed for a single household. From this aggregate perspective, one home equals one housing unit. A slight modification of this method is to group homes into categories based on housing type, such as single-family dwellings, condominiums, or apartments.

From a more microperspective, however, we know that not all homes are created equal. The most obvious feature delineating one house from another is size or floor space area, which in the United States is typically measured in square feet.[7] But even if we simply consider the physical dimension of housing units themselves, square feet is not the only consideration when we think about "how much" accommodation services we are able to derive from them. Quality of construction, design, and configuration are all important. Moreover, as most homeowners will attest, many of the most important aspects of a decision to purchase a home center on "nonhousing" considerations such as quality of schools, local crime rates, urban services, location, and neighborhood amenities. If all of these factors are inputs to our collective housing decisions—and they most certainly are—then surely they should also enter into any calculation of how much housing (or housing services) we are consuming. The challenge is to somehow reduce these multifaceted considerations into a single defensible index of housing quantity.

In principle, it is clear what is needed. We want a summary index of housing quantity, Q, that somehow "weights" each of the housing (or near-housing) characteristics discussed above in an appropriate manner. In symbolic form, we have:

$$Q = \Sigma \, w_i \, x_i \tag{10}$$

where w_i represents weights for a set of characteristics indexed by the subscript i and where x_i measures the quantity of those characteristics. Measuring characteristics, while not a trivial task, is straightforward in principle. We can measure square feet of living space or lot size. We can count the number of bedrooms or bathrooms. We can indicate the presence of a pool (= 1) or not (= 0), and we can do the same with any number of other special features that might add to or detract from the value of a home. We can calculate the distance in miles or minutes to the downtown or to other major employment or commercial centers. We can even gather data on local crime rates or standardized test scores for students from neighborhood schools.

While some of these measures may be imperfect, they are the same kinds of data that find their way into the subliminal calculations of most home buyers.

The real challenge is to find a set of weights that is defensible on some logical and/or empirical basis. In the example used earlier in this chapter we implicitly set $w_i = 1$ for i = "floor space," and $w_j = 0$ for j = "all other." That is, we used floor space alone as our single measure of housing quantity. Now, how could we verify or justify that or any other choice? Ideally, we would like to apply the same weights that households do (albeit implicitly or at least informally), and so it would be best if we could measure directly the weights that they use. One possibility is to survey householders who have recently purchased homes. The downside of this strategy is that it can be costly to construct a sample that will yield statistically significant results. Moreover, individuals may have difficulty or be reluctant or unable to specify what weights they used or would use in purchasing a home.

As strange as it may seem (or perhaps not!), an alternative strategy that is used widely by real estate economists is based on good old-fashioned *hedonism*, which the dictionary *(Concise Oxford English Dictionary,* Clarendon Press, 1990) defines as "belief in pleasure as the highest good and mankind's proper aim" and which is rooted in the ancient Greek word for pleasure. From hedonism comes the adjective *hedonic. Hedonic regression analysis* entails the application of statistical techniques to housing sales data to discern which characteristics of houses appear to be most highly correlated with the market value of homes. The underlying premise is that people are willing to pay more, on average, for those characteristics that give them the greatest pleasure.

It is beyond the purview of this book to provide instruction on hedonic regression analysis. As used by the most skillful practitioners of the art, it is a technique that draws on advanced statistical and economic theory as a basis for interpreting variations in a sample of housing prices in terms of the corresponding variations in related housing characteristics. A highly simplified presentation is offered here in order to illustrate the basic idea. Table 3.4 provides a small sample of data similar in content to what might be obtained from a multiple listings service or some other agency that maintains data on real estate transactions. In addition to the sales price, there are data fields that describe characteristics of the property itself. Locational attributes such as street address, zip code, census tract, school district, or even municipality can provide the investigator with a key for accessing other data about the general area in which the housing unit is located. For example, census data can help us to describe the socioeconomic characteristics of the neighborhood whereas locational coordinates can help us to calculate the distance to major employment or commercial centers in the area. The data

TABLE 3.4

Sample Data on Housing Sales

#	Address	Sales price	Bedrooms	Den	Pool	House (sq. ft.)	Lot (sq. ft.)
1	12 W. Adams St.	$180,000	3	1	0	1,986	10,500
2	37 E. Bartok Ave.	$168,000	2	1	1	2,002	11,800
3	97 N. Chopin Dr.	$212,000	4	0	0	1,920	9,800
4	88 S. Dvorak Cr.	$240,500	4	1	0	2,198	11,200
5	75 W. Epstein Way	$177,000	3	1	0	1,868	8,604
6	46 E. Fantasia Dr.	$175,900	3	0	0	1,799	10,977
7	39 N. Goodwin Pl.	$230,000	5	1	1	2,404	11,200
8	55 S. Harmony Dr.	$197,000	4	1	0	1,966	10,800
9	20 W. Innis Way	$203,500	4	1	1	2,079	10,888
10	18 E. Jalabak Dr.	$188,888	3	1	0	1,897	9,308
11	43 N. Kreisler St.	$192,000	4	0	1	2,070	8,007
12	80 S. Layla Pl.	$244,000	4	1	1	2,401	14,351
13	62 W. Mahler Ave.	$189,900	3	1	0	2,055	12,808
14	94 E. Newhart Dr.	$220,000	5	1	1	2,433	9,806
15	67 N. Ouvert Pl.	$232,900	4	1	1	2,237	13,090
16	59 S. Puccini Blvd.	$168,000	3	1	0	1,712	9,456
17	86 W. Queen St.	$208,900	5	1	0	2,323	10,080
18	77 E. Rouan Dr.	$198,000	4	0	0	2,101	9,705

sets that researchers work with may contain data for tens of thousands of transactions, so computers are essential to the task. Geographic information systems (GIS) are often used to organize the data, especially where one needs to cross-reference locational coordinates with areal boundaries.[8]

Hedonic regression analysis is typically applied to data that are similar to those shown in table 3.4. There are two kinds of input to the procedure. One is the general form of the relationship as specified in equation 10. This limits the procedure to a certain class of relationships linking housing characteristics with housing prices. The other form of input is the data set itself. Hedonic regression analysis uses these data to determine which set of weights when applied to the general relationship specified in equation 10 yields the "best fit" between the observed data and those that are predicted by the specified relationship. The core output from the regression analysis comprises a set of specific numerical weights (or estimated parameter coefficients) that are rooted in observed data and which can be used in place of the "w's" in equation 10.

For the sample of data in table 3.4, the weights that emerge from a simple

TABLE 3.5

Results from Hedonic Regression Analysis

Variable	Corresponding weight ("beta")
BEDROOMS	16,848
DEN	-2,567
POOL	28.09
HOUSE SIZE	6.28
LOT SIZE	-1,925
Intercept	15,944

Predicted and actual sales prices:

#	Predicted	Actual
1	$185,648	$180,000
2	$175,488	$168,000
3	$198,813	$212,000
4	$212,847	$240,500
5	$170,426	$177,000
6	$185,957	$175,900
7	$233,556	$230,000
8	$203,818	$197,000
9	$205,620	$203,500
10	$175,662	$188,888
11	$189,841	$192,000
12	$236,412	$244,000
13	$202,080	$189,900
14	$225,617	$220,000
15	$223,887	$232,900
16	$171,395	$168,000
17	$226,172	$208,900
18	$203,300	$198,000

regression analysis are given in table 3.5 and can be used to generate a *predicted value* for the sales price of any house based on its square footage and other housing characteristics. These predicted sales values for our sample of data are compared to the actual ones in table 3.5 where we observe that the regression model sometimes overpredicts, sometimes underpredicts, but on average corresponds with the actual sales value. The reason that the predicted and actual sales prices do not correspond exactly is that the former is constrained to a linear relationship linking sales price to housing characteristics while the latter is determined in a more quixotic fashion, with each transaction having its own peculiar history. The use of hedonic regression analysis is more palatable the smaller the size of the discrepancies between actual and predicted sales values.

The predicted sales price is a suitable measure of housing quantity, Q. At first glance this statement may seem untenable. After all, how could we use predicted *price* as a measure of *quantity*? The answer may best be given by way of example. When you go to the store you might specify quantity indirectly by asking for "a dollar's worth of peanuts." The analogy applies here to housing. We summarize the multifaceted features of a housing unit, including size, location, and neighborbood attributes, by folding them into a single index that measures *the amount one would expect to pay to acquire such a house.* Thus, one might examine the characteristics of the first house in tables 3.4 and 3.5 and determine that, on balance, those characteristics combine to form "xxx,xxx dollars' worth of housing."

With this definition of quantity in mind, we may reconsider our interpretation of price. It is useful in this regard to recognize that expenditure combines both price and quantity in the following way:

$$\text{Expenditure} = \text{Price} * \text{Quantity} \tag{11}$$

From which it follows that

$$\text{Price} = \text{Expenditure} / \text{Quantity} \tag{12}$$

Returning to table 3.5, and recognizing that housing expenditure is defined as the amount one actually spends on housing, we can calculate price by dividing actual sales price (expenditure) by predicted sales price (quantity). Doing so yields a price that hovers around unity and that on average equals exactly unity. What this tells us is that, on average, we pay one dollar for each "dollar's worth" or "hedonic unit" of housing.

One question remains. If "price" is approximately one dollar per hedonic unit of housing, then why is $xxx,xxx referred to as the sales price of the home? Isn't this confusing? It needn't be. If we consider again the relationship between expenditure, price, and quantity given by equation 11, we see that price and expenditure are the same when quantity equals one. Thus, when people equate sales price to expenditure, as is often done, they are implicitly setting quantity equal to "one house," and so price is calculated on a *per-house* basis. But as we have seen here, the measurement of housing quantity is a more complex task, and should account for the multifaceted nature of housing. Doing so by means of the method discussed above leads to the measurement of housing quantity in terms of hedonic units, where on average one hedonic unit is one dollar's worth of housing. In some cases people pay more than this, while in others they pay less. The graph in figure 3.10 illustrates this for the data from table 3.5, where predicted price

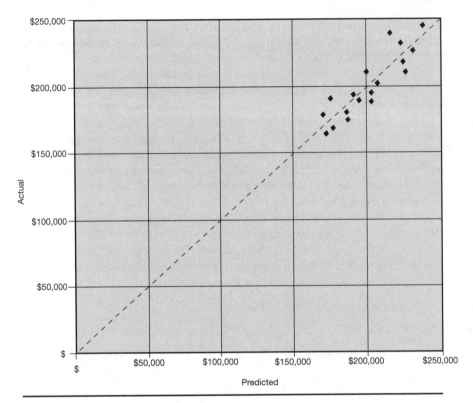

FIGURE 3.10
Actual versus predicted sales prices

is compared with the corresponding actual sales price. Those data points that lie below the 45° line represent "bargains" for the purchasers because the actual price paid is less than what our data and hedonic method would predict based on the characteristics of those houses. Those observations that lie above the 45° line, on the other hand, represent skillful negotiation on the part of the sellers.[9]

To summarize this discussion of housing quantity, we recognized that housing can be measured along a whole range of characteristics, and we determined that housing characteristics ought to be weighted in terms of their relative importance. The hedonic regression procedure does this by using the sales price of houses as an indication of value or importance, and it analyzes variation in housing price in terms of the corresponding variation in housing characteristics. Those characteristics that appear to be more highly correlated with housing prices are the ones that will be given greater weight in the hedonic index, where the latter is a quantity measure of the "dollars' worth" of housing that corresponds to a given set of characteristics.

Notes

1. A finder's fee is most likely to be in the form of a lump sum payment, whereas the quantity shown in the figure is expressed in terms of dollars per square foot per month. Later in this chapter we discuss how to convert a stream of payments to a lump sum value.

2. Land use controls may be "productive" in the sense that they help to create valuable amenities that might otherwise be lost, as discussed in chapter 2.

3. Investors will not hold assets whose anticipated returns are suspect unless they are induced to do so by a risk premium. The single rate of return r^* is the one that emerges after adjustments have been made to accommodate this risk factor.

4. The rates set by the Federal Reserve Board are in fact widely used as a benchmark for investors.

5. In fact, $1,555.55 would pay off the principal in the ninth year, rather than after fifteen years.

6. Note that the equity one has in one's home may be further obligated or encumbered by other outstanding debts (for example, student loans) that are unrelated to the purchase of the house itself.

7. In many other countries, particularly those in Europe, square meters are the basic units of measurement for floor space area. In much of East Asia the traditional unit of measurement is derived from the number of tatami mats that would be required to fill the space.

8. For applications of GIS to urban planning, the interested reader is referred to W. E. Huxhold, *An Introduction to Urban Geographic Information Systems*, Oxford University Press, 1991.

9. One should be careful about pushing this interpretation too hard because deviations of predicted from actual sales values may also point to flaws in the method used to generate predicted values.

4

The Economics of Urban Structure

Planners and Urban Structure

Ownership of land is a kind of entitlement (see chapter 9), and indeed ownership is established in most advanced market economies through some form of publicly registered land title. Typically, the owner of a parcel of land is entitled, within the parameters of land use regulations, to determine what kind of land use the site will be devoted to, whether residential, commercial, industrial, or other. *The cumulative effect of all such land use decisions by all property owners is the resultant pattern of land uses that defines urban structure.* In an urban area with a well-developed real estate market, interested parties will bid for parcels of land based on the net benefits they expect to gain through the perogatives of ownership.

Urban planners affect real estate market outcomes in two ways. First, planners enact zoning bylaws and other land use regulations that define the limits placed on the entitlements of landowners. This is a very direct effect that planners have on the use and therefore on the value of land. Second, planners intervene in various ways to shape the overall urban context. It is with reference to this urban context that individuals base their own valuations of the entitlements attached to the ownership of land. While less direct, this can be equally important in determining the value of a parcel. This set of relationships is illustrated in figure 4.1, where bundles of entitlements for a specific property are evaluated with reference to a specific urban context,

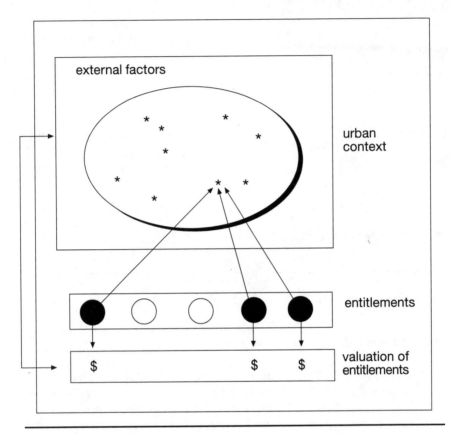

FIGURE 4.1
Factors shaping land use decisions

which is itself embedded within a larger context of external factors ranging from population growth to demographics to interest rates.

The net result of a property owner's valuation of these bundles of entitlements determines how the owner will utilize that particular parcel of land. The myriad decisions made by similar property owners throughout time contribute to an evolving urban context, which in turn affects the evaluation of future entitlements. What we find is a complex spatial interplay between the value of land and how land is used, with each aspect influencing the other. The net result of this interplay is manifest in many ways in urban areas throughout the world. While each city is unique, there are also broad similarities that apply, and in this chapter we shall explore the economic foundations of those fundamental similarities and their implications for planners.

Valuing Access in a Monocentric Urban Area

"Location, location, location." Who does not know this to be the answer to the question, *"What are the three most important determinants of real estate values?"* But location is clearly relative. Knowing the longitude and latitude coordinates of a parcel of land is not sufficient for us to determine the value of that parcel. Its value is derived from its location relative to other locations, which are themselves similarly valued. More precisely, the value of any one parcel is based on its accessibility to the activities or amenities found at many other sites. Location is contextual, and hence so are land values.

Early economic models of urban areas are termed *monocentric* because they focus on accessibility to one central location, usually termed the central business district (CBD). In such models, distance to the CBD is a key determinant of the value of land, with land values dropping off steadily in all directions as one moves further from the CBD toward the outer limits of the urban area. While it is clear that urban areas are more complex than what is implied by a simple monocentric formulation, it is nonetheless useful to analyze the sources of land values in a simpler model before adding complications attributable to multiple centers. In all cases the fundamental basis for land value is *access*. Location is important insofar as it affects accessibility.

"Time is money" is another truism, one that in the urban context is rooted in a recognition of the opportunity costs associated with time spent commuting or otherwise overcoming the "friction" associated with distance. Consider the simplest case of an urban area with one central business district and with a population of identical households composed of individuals who would all like to reduce their commuting distance by living in identical neighborhoods closer to work. Clearly, not everyone can live in those preferred locations nearer to the CBD; some must be persuaded to opt for more remote locations. For residential real estate markets to be in equilibrium, land prices must adjust to the point that all households are equally content at all locations throughout the urban area, with the lower prices in more remote locations just compensating for the burden of greater distance. Thus, the implicit trade-off between time and money is reflected in the land rent profile. Locations closer to the CBD will command a higher rental than those farther away, and land values will reflect those land rent differentials.[1] If this condition did not hold, people would rush to acquire land that yielded larger benefits than what is reflected by market prices, and market prices would adjust upward for those sites experiencing excess demand until equilibrium was restored.

We can quickly add variations to this basic model of land price equilibrium in a monocentric urban area with identical households. In figure 4.2

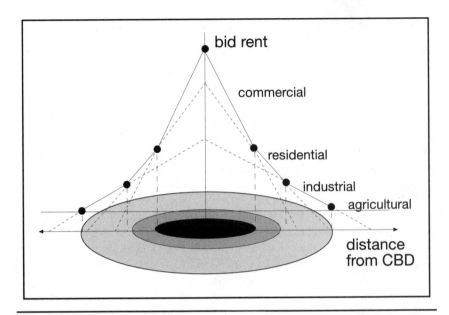

FIGURE 4.2
Bid-rent curves for urban land

we repeat the analysis for several categories of land use. The curve labeled "residential" shows the equilibrium price of land that households would be willing to pay at varying locations. As just discussed, the market-clearing[2] equilibrium price must fall as we move further away from the CBD; otherwise no one would be willing to purchase land at more remote locations. This curve is often referred to as the households' bid-rent curve, because it shows the maximum amount of rent (or prices, in the context of our diagram) that households would be willing to bid in order to live there. As shown in figure 4.2, there are similar bid-rent curves corresponding to commercial, industrial, or other types of land uses. The same basic logic applies. In the initial analysis all households were identical, so they each shared the same perception regarding the trade-off between accessibility and value. However, it stands to reason that the value–accessibility trade-off will differ for different types of land use. For example, business offices are likely to place higher value on ready access to the downtown because of the advantages of face-to-face communications for transacting business, and this is shown in figure 4.2 where the bid-rent curve for commercial activities is higher than the residential bid-rent curve at locations nearer the downtown. At the other extreme, industrial uses are shown in figure 4.2 to place the least value on accessibility.

The net result of the bid-rent curves depicted in figure 4.2 is a land use pattern that features successive "rings" of land use, with commercial land uses in the inner ring and residential and industrial rings further out. There are several aspects of this model that deserve comment. First, the reference to commercial, residential, and industrial uses is for purposes of illustration. The exact ordering of the true bid-rent curves by land use category will vary depending on technologies, preferences, and other factors contributing to the trade-off between distance and value. Second, we can accommodate different types of households in this model by creating a land use category corresponding to each household type, so it is easy to relax the assumption of identical households. Third, the spatial extent of the urban area occurs at the point where the maximum bid-rent value for urban land uses no longer exceeds the value of land in nonurban uses, where that default alternative is often referred to in urban economic models as agricultural use.

Finally, note that the steepest bid-rent curves are also the ones that have the highest values nearest to the CBD. The steepness of the slope, or the "gradient" as it is usually referred to, tells us how much more valuable it is to be a bit closer to the CBD. A steeper bid-rent curve implies a sharper or more dramatic loss in value as one moves away by one more mile (or kilometer, or whatever unit of distance one chooses to work with). In an urban area with multiple land uses the steeper curves must be the ones whose bid rents are highest nearer to the CBD. Figure 4.3 illustrates this point, using two categories of land use, called commercial and residential. For commercial land uses three alternative bid-rent curves are depicted, each with the same slope, and hence each with the same trade-off between changes in accessibility and changes in value. For the inner bid-rent curve for commercial land uses in figure 4.3, the rent bid is nowhere near sufficient to displace residential uses; this would result in no commercial uses at all. The outer bid-rent curve for commercial land uses results in the opposite extreme, with no residential uses anywhere. It is possible for either situation to arise, but the implication is that one or the other land use is not represented at all in that urban area. Only in the middle case are both land uses manifest, with the more steeply sloped bid-rent curve for commercial use dominant near the CBD. It then declines quickly to the point of intersection with the residential bid-rent curve, which in turn is dominant beyond that point of intersection.

It is also possible for the gradients (slopes) of the bid-rent curves to vary significantly over distances, depending on technologies and preferences, with multiple rings associated with a single type of land use as represented in figure 4.4. For example, businesses may prefer proximity to the CBD in order to facilitate face-to-face communications. Alternatively, they may choose to invest in electronic mail, fax, voice mail, and other telecommunications that

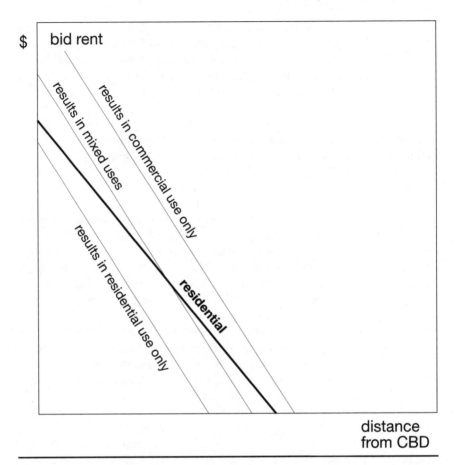

FIGURE 4.3
Alternative commercial bid-rent curves

enable businesses to function without intensive face-to-face interactions. In the latter case, businesses may be willing to locate in peripheral locations and enjoy the lower land rents as compensation for the loss of face-to-face communications and for the telecommunications investment costs. Industrial land uses may have a choice between rail and road networks for transporting their goods, and these choices may point to a preference for locations either near a central rail depot or on the periphery with good freeway access. Likewise, households may enjoy either the stimulation of a central urban location or the tranquility of a semirural setting more than a poor compromise in the middle. In each of these examples it is the nature of household preferences or the nature of a firm's production technologies that de-

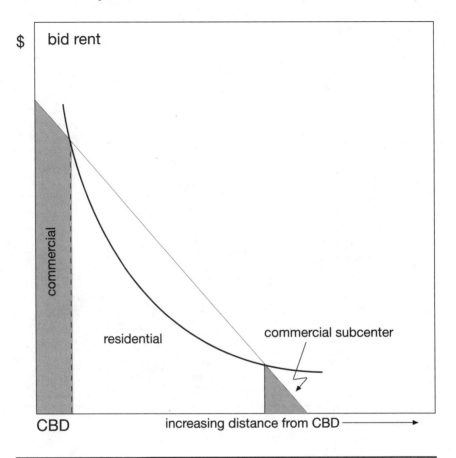

FIGURE 4.4
Nonlinear bid-rent curves

termines how much value is placed on an extra bit of accessibility, and how that value varies with distance.

Economic analysis suggests that there will be a secondary effect resulting from these land rent differentials. With land closer to the CBD being more expensive, there will be a tendency to use less of it relative to other labor or capital inputs. For example, where land prices are high it may make sense to build a parking garage to conserve the amount of land devoted to automobile storage, but that would not be economical in more remote locations where land rents are much lower. Similarly, it would be lavishly extravagant to build a ranch-style home with a large backyard in a central-city location with high land costs. These examples illustrate a fundamental principle of

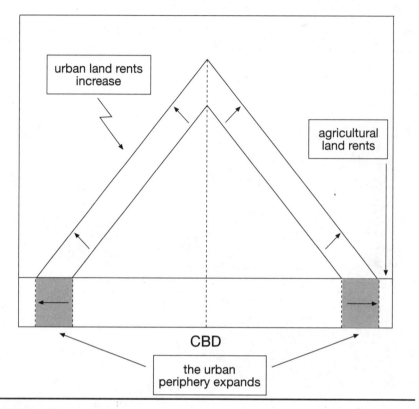

FIGURE 4.5
Land rents respond to population growth

economic analysis known as the *substitution principle.* In this context, the
substitution principle simply states that households and firms alike will tend
to substitute away from those inputs whose relative prices are higher in favor of those whose relative prices are lower. The implication for urban land
use is that more expensive land near the center (in a monocentric model)
will be used more intensively, so that each unit of land will have more capital (such as buildings) and more labor used with it. That is why we find
high-rise buildings teeming with people in many central cities and lower densities toward the periphery.

How do we expect this land rent gradient to evolve over time in response
to population growth, technological innovations, or other significant changes
that might affect urban form? Imagine first the case of population growth,
where we need not assume that there is any change in people's locational
preferences—there are now just more people who share those same prefer-

ences. This means that the trade-off between price and accessibility is unchanged from before, and so the slope of the land rent curve will not be altered. However, land within a given distance of the center has now become more scarce relative to demand. Of course the supply of land has not diminished, but now there are more people bidding for it. If land prices remain the same as they were, the market will not clear because there will be people left over who still have unmet demand. The only way for the market to clear is for land prices to increase. If land prices increase while the slope of the bid-rent curve remains the same, then we know that the height of the bid-rent curve is raised uniformly at all locations, as in figure 4.5.

Notice that this will increase the areal extent of the urban area because urban land rents at the old urban–rural boundary will now exceed agricultural rents, so there is an incentive to convert agricultural land to urban uses. This conversion will continue outward until urban land rents at the margin are once again equal to agricultural land rents. This "pure" upward shift in land rents (i.e., no change in slope) may be thought of as an upward shift in demand. The bid-rent curve is not itself a demand curve—the latter shows how much land is demanded at a given rental price—but its upward shift is a direct response to an upward or outward shift in the demand for land, in this case due to population change. We might expect a similar response to increased per capita income even if population remains constant. As household incomes rise, we may expect that people will purchase more of most goods as their budgets expand. Indeed, economists' definition of a *normal* good is precisely that; it is a good for which demand increases with income.[3] There is little reason to doubt that land is a normal good by this same criterion, so if incomes rise there will be unmet demand for land at the old prices. By a similar reasoning, we can deduce that land rents will rise as in the previous example. In monetary terms, aggregate income is the product of population and per capita income. Many cities in developing countries experience a "double-whammy" effect as both population and per capita incomes rise dramatically in response to rapid economic development in those cities; land rents then rise and the urban perimeter expands in dramatic fashion.

Technological change has a different effect on the urban land rent profile, with its primary impact being on the gradient (slope) rather than on the height of the bid-rent curve. Consider the advent of the automobile, or more recently, telecommunications advances such as fax, e-mail, and the like. These technological innovations have the effect of reducing the "friction" associated with distance. Before the innovation is introduced the original gradient reflects the old trade-off between distance and value. Closer locations are more valuable because they save us time. That same principle holds after the technological innovation, but the trade-off is different now. It is now possible to bridge further distances in less time, so a location further away

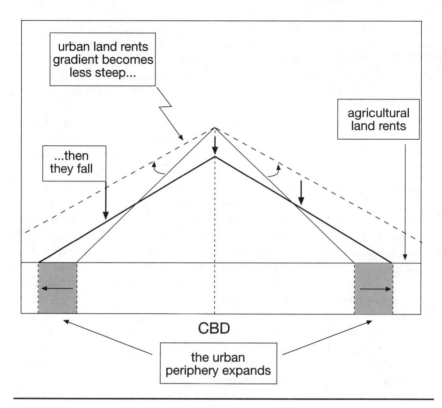

FIGURE 4.6
Land rents respond to technological change

is no longer discounted as heavily ("Only fifteen minutes by car!"). This translates into flatter bid-rent curves, as shown by the heavier lines in figure 4.6.

Now, let us suppose that rents in the center remain unchanged. Together with flatter bid-rent curves, this implies that land rents rise everywhere else, as depicted by the dashed lines in figure 4.6. The total area beneath these "uplifted wings" is in direct proportion to the total land rent for the urban area, and we can see that this increases dramatically if rents at the center do not drop. That will only happen if the population as a whole believes that land has become more valuable and thus decides to spend a larger proportion of aggregate income on land. While not inconceivable, it is more likely that as a first approximation total land rents will remain unchanged. The heavier lines correspond to this case, where the gradients (slopes) are smaller, but the total area beneath the bid-rent curve remains unchanged. Notice that here too the spatial extent of the urban area increases. This time the increase

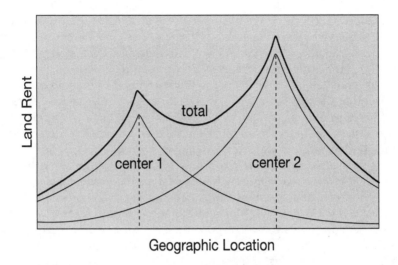

FIGURE 4.7
Land rents in a polycentric urban area

in demand for urban land is brought about by a change in relative prices. In effect, urban land has become less expensive because it is now easier to access (acquire). People naturally respond to that change by buying more of it, and so the city grows. Combining all three examples, we can readily understand why cities enjoying rapidly rising incomes, growing populations, and an influx of technological changes undergo dramatic changes manifested in rising land prices and expanding urban areas.

Polycentric Models of Urban Space

A more generalized notion of accessibility makes reference to many potential destinations rather than to a single destination (such as the CBD) alone. It is important to make this generalization if we want models that can explain adequately the structure of modern urban areas where the central business district typically contains less than 10 percent of all metropolitan employment, and where there are often several urban centers within one metropolitan area that act as central business districts.

Figure 4.7 provides a cross-sectional representation of how the aggregate land rent surface may respond to the presence of two subcenters, located at x_1 and x_2, respectively. Each subcenter exerts an influence on land rents similar to what one finds in a monocentric urban area. The aggregate land rent at any location x is then taken to be the sum of all such influences at x. Of course what we observe when we look at land rents in an urban area is only the aggregate surface; we cannot see the individual components directly. However, numerous empirical studies have used regression analysis to disentangle and identify the effects of multiple centers. These studies strongly confirm that the aggregate rent surfaces for cities in the United States and elsewhere are best understood as the outcome of an underlying polycentric urban structure. The latter is often described in terms of one older historic central business district together with newer *subcenters.*

The subcentering phenomenon is best understood as the result of a "struggle" between two opposing forces: agglomeration and congestion. The top section of figure 4.8 shows total benefits and total costs as measured against the number of firms (N) co-locating in a central business district. The bottom section shows the corresponding marginal benefit and cost curves which, as explained in chapter 2, correspond to the slopes of the total benefit and total cost curves, respectively. As the CBD begins to grow in size, total benefits in figure 4.8 rise quickly at first, as indicated by the relatively steep slope of the total benefit curve. This steep rise in benefits reflects the positive *agglomeration effects* that firms derive from close proximity to one another. When firms are clustered together there is a higher density of potential clients and suppliers within easy distance, and vital information flows are greatly facilitated by face-to-face communications. As the number of firms in the CBD increases, total benefits continue to increase, but at a decreasing rate, as seen by the gradually diminishing slope of the total benefit curve and, hence, by the declining marginal benefit curve. As N increases, there is more redundancy in the potential benefits provided by the agglomeration of more and more firms. So long as firms' basic supply needs are being met competitively, and so long as they are receiving essential information flows in a timely fashion, the benefits derived from the co-location of additional firms are less valuable on the margin. The benefits that firms provide to each other become increasingly redundant, therefore marginal benefits decline even as total benefits continue to increase (albeit at a decreasing rate).

The total cost curve in the top section of figure 4.8 also increases with the number of firms, but at an *increasing* rate due to congestion effects. The bottom section shows that marginal costs are increasing steadily. As discussed in chapter 5, there is less rivalry at lower densities in the consumption (use) of roads, public space, and other goods, but as the number of firms increases, so too does the extent of the rivalry in consumption. This phenomenon is also described in detail in chapter 6 in the context of traffic congestion. Both agglomeration and congestion effects are *externalities* because the benefits or costs engendered by other firms are not captured by market prices. There is no direct market feedback encouraging firms to locate in

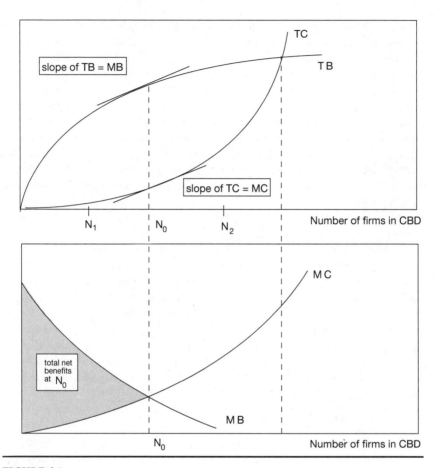

FIGURE 4.8
Agglomeration and congestion effects in the CBD

the CBD because of the agglomeration benefits they confer on others. Like-wise, firms receive no price signals from the market that indicate to them the congestion costs they are imposing on others. Of course these conges-tion and agglomeration effects do show up in land prices as firms are will-ing to bid more to locate near agglomeration effects. Note, however, that a higher land price will *discourage* more firms from locating in the CBD, so land prices in this example do not send out signals that specifically encour-age firms to bring their agglomeration benefits to town. Each firm considers the benefits or costs it experiences due to the presence of other firms but does not consider its effect on others when making its decision about whether or not to locate in the CBD.

The principles of marginal analysis that recur throughout this book apply equally well to the situation depicted in figure 4.8. In particular, we can see that *total benefits net of costs* are maximized when $N = N_0$ firms are located in the CBD. At this point the marginal benefit of more firms is just sufficient to compensate for the marginal cost. Below this point, marginal benefits are higher than marginal costs; total net benefits can be increased by adding more firms to the CBD. Beyond N_0, marginal benefits no longer compensate for marginal costs; therefore more firms will bring about a reduction in net benefits. Based on this reasoning, it would be more (net) beneficial to have two centers with N_0 firms located in each of them rather than a single center with $2*N_0$ firms. In the same fashion, more net benefits are derived from three centers with N_0 located in each of them rather than a single center with $3*N_0$ centers, and so on. *This is a basic motivation for the emergence of subcenters within a metropolitan area.*

Our analysis thus far of the optimal size of a central business district has been from a planner's perspective that takes into consideration total benefits and costs for all firms. What does the situation look like from the perspective of individual firms, each of which shares equally in the agglomeration benefits and congestion costs associated with a central business district address? Because they share equally in these costs and benefits, it is the *average* cost and benefit that are relevent for the individual firm's decision about where to locate. At any point N (i.e., for any subcenter with N firms), the total benefit at N is experienced equally by N firms, yielding an average benefit of:

$$AB = TB / N \tag{1}$$

This average benefit is represented graphically by the slope of a line drawn from the origin to the total benefit curve at the designated point.[4] Average cost is calculated in a similar fashion but with reference to the total cost curve, so that:

$$AC = TC / N \tag{2}$$

Careful scrutiny of figure 4.8 reveals that *average benefit* declines steadily with larger values of N whereas *average cost* rises steadily. This means that firms will be attracted to smaller subcenters in order to enjoy the higher average benefits and lower average costs there. Of course, as more firms flock to the smaller subcenters, these subcenters will become larger. From this we can conclude that for the situation depicted in figure 4.8 there is a kind of "leveling action" whereby firms relocate from larger centers to smaller ones and where this process continues until all subcenters are of the same size. Furthermore, this outcome will coincide with the optimum subcenter size N_0 (where marginal benefits equal marginal costs) only if the number

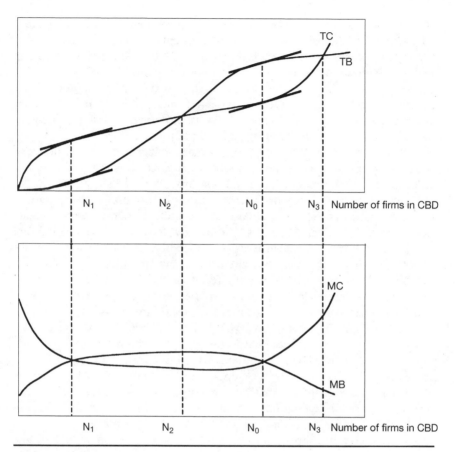

FIGURE 4.9
Modified view of agglomeration and congestion effects in the CBD

of subcenters is just right. Too many subcenters will result in subcenters that are too small; too few will yield subcenters that are larger than desired.

In the preceding discussion we took for granted some fixed number of subcenters that compete for firms. But in fact subcenters may emerge as a result of firms' location decisions. For the conditions described by figure 4.8, we have seen that firms are attracted to smaller subcenters. Taken to its logical extreme, we would expect the situation in figure 4.8 to result in a highly diffused urban structure with each firm forming its own center. Common sense tells us that there is a minimum threshold below which the agglomeration benefits of subcenters do not take hold. In figure 4.9 we modify the shape of the total benefit and total cost curves to reflect this reality. The shape of both curves beyond N_2 is similar to the situation depicted in figure 4.8, with declining marginal benefits and rising marginal costs. However, the total benefit curve in figure 4.9 is no longer concave with steadily declining marginal benefits. Instead, for smaller values of N, the benefits of agglomeration begin to kick in gradually at first, and then more rapidly as the subcenter reaches critical mass. Likewise, total costs in figure 4.9 rise quickly at first for smaller subcenters that are not large enough to enjoy economies of scale in the provision of infrastructure and other basic services.

As before, total benefits net of costs are maximized at N_0 where marginal benefits are just sufficient to compensate for marginal costs. The astute reader will notice that the marginality condition MB = MC is also satisfied at N_1, but it is clear that N_1 does not correspond to the optimum city-center size because total costs exceed total costs at N_1, while at N_0 the reverse is true. Additionally, it is clear that firms will be attracted only to subcenters that are larger than N_2 and smaller than N_3. Subcenters smaller than N_2 are not of sufficient mass to generate agglomeration benefits that compensate for the heavy infrastructure and other fixed costs of maintaining a viable subcenter. Subcenters larger than N_3 experience congestion costs so severe that they swamp any agglomeration benefits the firms might otherwise enjoy. Only within the interval $[N_2, N_3]$ do average benefits exceed average costs; thus firms will be attracted to only these locations. At the planner's optimum, N_0, average benefits do exceed average costs. It is possible that some other value of N nearby will support an even wider divergence of benefits from costs so that firms may be more attracted to some value of N other than N_0.[5] Notwithstanding that fact, it is apparent from inspection that the equilibrium level of N in figure 4.9 is "fairly close" to the optimum level, and that it therefore approximates the kind of result that economists are most fond of—where incentives at the microlevel are compatible with optimal outcomes at the societal level.

It is useful at this point to recapitulate the significant points that emerge from the preceding discussion. We have seen that the optimal size of urban subcenters can depend on the relative strength of agglomeration benefits versus congestion costs. In both figures 4.8 and 4.9, that optimum (labeled N_0 in both cases) occurs where the marginal benefits from additional size just compensate for the marginal costs. We have also seen that this optimum point may not correspond closely to the equilibrium size of subcenters, defined as the size subcenter firms themselves are most attracted to. The reason for this divergence is that firms base their location decisions on the *average* benefits and costs encountered at subcenters while the planner's optimum is derived by examining *marginal* benefits and costs. There is more justification for planning intervention where the divergence between equilibrium and optimum subcenter size is large. The extent of the divergence depends on the precise nature of the agglomeration and congestion effects. In figure 4.8 the divergence is large, whereas in figure 4.9 it is much less serious.

Where Do Subcenters Come From?

Several questions remain. First, what is the mechanism by which subcenters emerge? Second, where will these subcenters locate? And finally, why do cities vary with respect to the number and size of subcenters they comprise? In addition to all of these questions, we also want to know what the potential role for planners might be in bringing about more beneficial outcomes. Regarding the first question, we saw in figure 4.8 that average net benefits were largest for the smallest subcenters, so there was no incentive for firms to cluster together to form centers. Or, if the number of centers was predetermined (for example, if land use regulations prohibited certain classes of firms from locating outside designated subcenter districts), then firms would tend to relocate away from larger centers in favor of smaller ones, and equilibrium would not be obtained until all of the subcenters were of equal size. If the planners were to choose the number of subcenter districts correctly, this equilibrium size could correspond closely to the optimum size N_0.

In the case of figure 4.9, we encounter a different problem. As noted previously, no firms will be attracted to subcenters smaller than N_2 because the agglomeration benefits for such centers are too small to compensate for the relatively large infrastructure costs. The problem is that no new subcenters can emerge spontaneously in figure 4.9, because in order to generate a subcenter larger than N_2 one must first pass through prior stages with fewer firms. Stated another way, large subcenters do not appear magically; they grow from smaller ones. The situation in figure 4.9 discourages the development of smaller subcenters that might grow into larger ones later on. This suggests a potentially positive way for planners to intervene through incentives and other strategies designed to bring emerging centers past the critical threshold at N_2. The danger, of course, is that planners may inadvertently squander large sums of public money attempting to foster the development of subcenters that are not truly viable. The potential gains or losses are large, and it can be a difficult call. The best strategy is to develop a sound understanding of the particulars of any given situation and make judgments accordingly.

The question of where subcenters will arise is a difficult one to answer a priori. In hindsight one can usually point to particular locational advantages or historical incidents that triggered an urban agglomeration at one location rather than another, but it is much more difficult to do so in advance.[6] We can say that accessibility remains a key consideration and that the potentiality of a location is likely to be highly correlated with any reasonable measure of accessibility. And of course land use regulations and other public-sector interventions can be instrumental in determining whether centers emerge (or do not emerge) in specified locations. Access to potential clients/customers or suppliers is an especially important consideration, and this has long been recognized in models of urban structure. *Central place theory,* in particular, sees urban space as being organized in terms of hierarchical market catchment areas.

Another question we raised is why cities have different numbers of subcenters of varying size and character. The reasons are multifaceted but focus primarily on the nature of the agglomeration and congestion effects depicted in figures 4.8 and 4.9. The shape and position of the total cost and total benefit curves are affected by factors as diverse as natural resources and amenities, public-sector investments, historicial antecedents, the mobility of firms, the labor market, transportation and communications technology, and geographical considerations. Moreover, firms in different sectors will respond differently to the same set of conditions. One thing is clear, however, from studying many of the largest cities in the world, and that is that it is increasingly common to find metropolitan areas with several active and viable subcenters with distinctive characters. In megacities in particular —those with populations of 10 million or more—it is apparent that subcentering is a natural if not inevitable response to the opposing forces of agglomeration and congestion. Firms that are located in any one of the subcenters of a megalopolis are positioned to enjoy many of the agglomeration benefits that accrue to a city of that size while avoiding the more acute congestion problems that would arise if there were only one urban center within those metropolitan regions.

The Urban Sprawl Debate

One aspect of urban structure that has received a great deal of attention from both planners and regular citizens is *sprawl*, a term that refers to low-density suburban development that encroaches, often in "leapfrogging" fashion, upon agricultural land on the urban periphery. Urban sprawl is roundly denounced by its many vocal opponents on several grounds: (i) it leads to a loss of precious agricultural land, (ii) its low-density character is inefficient from the perspective of infrastructure and basic service provision, and (iii) it results in an unimaginative, stifling suburban form that is sadly lacking in urban amenities. Based on this reasoning, many planners view it as their duty to enact land use regulations that limit urban sprawl. Let us examine each of these charges in turn.

There is no doubt that the outward expansion of an urban area leads to a loss of agricultural or other nonurban land use activities. Essentially, the supply of land is fixed, and more land devoted to urban uses necessarily implies that less land is available for nonurban uses. Moreover, in many cases it is prime agricultural land that is the first to be converted, thereby compounding the overall sense of loss. Of course it would be unbalanced in the extreme to only look at what is lost without considering what has been gained. Certainly land is valuable as a factor input for agricultural uses, but it is also valuable as an input for urban uses. The discussion pertaining to figures 4.6 and 4.7 earlier in this chapter indicates that urban expansion occurs because of a growing demand for urban land, and we know that demand reflects benefit. The reason someone is willing to pay more for land in one use compared to another is because the perceived benefits are higher. Chapter 2 discusses in detail the manner in which markets allocate scarce land resources between competing uses so as to maximize the total market value of land. The example used there is residential versus nonresidential, but those same arguments apply equally well to the urban-rural land use debate. A reduced supply of agricultural land should be reflected in higher food prices. If the demand for food is relatively elastic,[7] then we can expect a significant shift in consumption patterns away from agricultural produce in favor of other items competing for household budget shares. If, as is more likely, the demand for food is relatively inelastic, we can expect that food consumption will remain fairly stable, and higher prices will result in increased returns to agriculture; this will enable farmers to compete more aggressively in land markets along the urban periphery. Thus, from a strict market perspective, we would expect that the vaunted value of agricultural land uses would be supported by a strong, relatively inelastic demand for agricultural produce.

There are special considerations that may apply in the case of agriculture and its competition for land along the urban periphery. In some countries, Japan being a notable example, preserving agricultural land is seen as a means of avoiding an undue dependency on foreign countries for essential food supplies. This is a case where market failure may occur because markets for agricultural produce are unlikely to factor in to food prices any considerations of national security. An economist's instinct is to try to correct any such market failure by incorporating the relevant price signals into market prices. Tariffs on imported produce or subsidies in support of domestic produce would work in this direction and would allow land markets to function independently of any considerations of national food security or the like. However, trade barriers of this type are frowned upon by the World Trade Organization and other international bodies seeking to promote free trade, so many governments resort to more roundabout measures, including land use controls, to protect agricultural land.

One method that has been employed, most notably in the Seoul metropolitan region, is the designation of a protected greenbelt area around the urban periphery wherein no urban development may occur. The consequences of a greenbelt policy for land rents are illustrated in figure 4.10. The initial bid-rent curve for urban land is denoted by R_0, and D_0 marks the initial urban–rural boundary where the urban bid-rent curve just meets the value of land in agricultural use, R_A. Let us suppose that a greenbelt policy is imposed at this time, so that no urban development can take place from D_0 outward to some point D_1. As the urban area grows, the bid-rent curve eventually reaches some level R_1; this would normally cause urbanization to encroach into the rural area, but the greenbelt policy disallows that. The result is that the interval $[0, D_0]$ over which urban land is supplied is inadequate to meet demand at the prices implied by R_1, so the price of urban land must rise in order for the market to clear, and a new bid-rent curve is established at R_2. Notice that at this price level, urbanization will leapfrog over the greenbelt and take root on the far side.

The efficiency implications of the resultant land use pattern can be viewed from two perspectives. One is the increased rent given by the vertical distance $R_2 - R_1$. This increase in rent does not represent extra benefit nor does it measure inefficiency per se; it is simply a higher scarcity premium on urban land. Inefficiency arises from a *misallocation* of land; the interval $[O, D_0]$ is still devoted to urban use, so it is not being misallocated. The misallocation, from a market perspective, occurs over the interval $[D_0, D_1]$. A more direct measure of inefficiency is given by the triangle wedged between R_1 and R_0 within the interval $[D_0, D_1]$. This is directly comparable to the triangle of inefficiency seen in chapter 2, which resulted from zoning restrictions on land. It is a measure of the inefficiency of misallocating agricultural land for urban uses. Countering these inefficiencies, there may be some amenity benefits (positive externalities) generated by the greenbelt itself. These amenities are a public good in the technical, nonrival sense of the term as discussed in chapter 5. It is conceivable but by no means assured that the amenity benefits generated by the greenbelt may outweigh the countervailing inefficiency costs.

In many settings agricultural land is depicted as being a precious link to a way of life that is portrayed in nostalgic and even moralistic terms. From this perspective, the argument that urban sprawl is "immoral" is only a half-step away. Similar arguments are made regarding environmental treasures and other nonurban uses. Of course there is nothing to prevent anyone in a market context from purchasing land to devote to agricultural or other

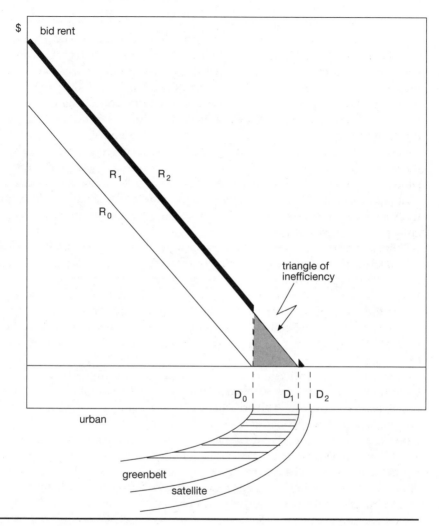

FIGURE 4.10
Greenbelt preservation

nonurban uses, nor is anyone compelled by reasons other than opportunity cost to sell agricultural land to those who would use it for other purposes. Land ownership consists of a bundle of entitlements, and as explained in detail in chapter 9, entitlements are a form of wealth, so the struggle to restrict land to agricultural uses can be understood as an attempt to transfer entitlement wealth from the owners of agricultural land to those who prefer to see such land remain nonurban.[8]

Arguments against urban sprawl are fortified by a view that the conversion of land from rural to urban use is irreversible, that once gone, agricultural land is "lost forever." While not wholly irreversible, there is clearly a very large transaction cost barrier that does make it impractical to convert urban land back to nonurban use. Indeed, this is indicative of a more general problem arising from durable capital in any form, and certainly in urban form. Massive buildings or freeways built from concrete and steel impose themselves emphatically on the landscape, with life spans measured in decades or even centuries. They encapsulate their developers' best guesses at the time regarding future conditions, but unlike economic goods with much shorter life spans, their quantities cannot be adjusted rapidly in response to changes in demand or other variable market conditions. Once a building or freeway is in place, it is likely to remain so for a long time. Subsequent unanticipated changes in demand will result in windfall gains or losses to the owners at the time. These are important aspects of durable products that any investor should be cognizant of, but they are not necessarily arguments against urban sprawl per se. The developer, as much as anyone (except perhaps his lender), is the one bearing the greatest burden of risk of developing on the urban periphery prematurely. Developing too late also has its risks, because it gives one's competitors an opportunity to line up their market shares early. Many a developer has gone bust by coming in just at the end of a boom cycle.

A second major criticism of urban sprawl is that its low-density leapfrog pattern of development is inefficient from the perspective of infrastructure-based service provision. The argument is that a higher-density form of development could be serviced at lower cost to taxpayers. There are two related issues here; one is the extent to which the marginal cost of service provision is (or is not) reflected in the cost of the final "product," and the second is one of objectives. These two issues are joined in households' decisions about what kind of development they may choose to live in. Chapter 7 on fiscal impacts explains in detail how to evaluate the impacts of a development on service provision. Essentially, a service-based impact is defined as the minimal cost required to maintain existing service standards. We show that a sound knowledge of the underlying production process by which services are produced is required in order to calculate reasonable estimates of these impacts. Opponents of urban sprawl argue that the fiscal impacts of sprawl are higher than what might reasonably be justified. The key, from our perspective, is whether those impacts are reflected in the price of the housing and other developments that result from sprawl. If they are, then the market is given an opportunity to do what it does best—facilitate trade-offs using price signals. Finally, it is useful to examine the premise that sprawl results in lower-density development. In the long run, a leapfrogging development pattern may result in higher densities overall as infill gradually occurs (Peiser and Heikkila 1992).

A related issue is what the ultimate objectives of development are. Infrastructure is a means to an end, not an end in itself. The same principle applies quite generally. In constructing a building, one doesn't necessarily configure the rooms strictly on the basis of keeping costs at a minimum, although costs are certainly a major consideration. If it costs more to configure the rooms to suit the tastes of the end user, the relevant question is whether the benefits to the user outweigh the costs. The surest way to get an answer to that question is to price the alternatives so that they reflect the underlying cost structure. If the user is willing to pay a premium, we may conclude with assurance that the extra benefit does indeed outweigh the additional cost, so net benefits are increased by proceeding with construction. The same argument applies to sprawl. The issue is not whether the cost of infrastructure provision rises, although that is an important consideration. Instead, the issue is whether the entire "package" of benefits and costs embodied in sprawl development is an improvement over the relevant alternatives. So long as the relevant costs are properly incorporated in end prices, the end user is the best judge of whether benefits exceed costs. Indeed, if keeping infrastructure costs at a minimum is the sole objective, we would be best advised not to allow any development at all. That solution may not do much to help our housing problem, but it certainly keeps costs at a minimum.

The third major criticism of sprawl is that it results in boring, unimaginative forms of suburbia that stifle creativity and constrain lifestyle choices. That may or may not be true, but in either case similar criticisms can be leveled at television programming, fast-food outlets (which are by no means confined to suburbia), and many other aspects of consumer culture. Should these forms of consumer culture be banned along with sprawled suburban development? There is certainly a pervasive tendency to appeal to the "lowest common denominator," and that tendency is strongly reinforced by economies of scale in production—it is easier to keep the price of burgers to 59 cents each if one is measuring production volume in the billions. The housing industry is also characterized by significant economies of scale, and that creates an incentive to build self-contained planned unit developments or new towns on the urban periphery. That incentive is compounded by the attractions of working with a "clean slate" where the developer is relatively unencumbered by the unwanted legacy of earlier developments that may now be out of fashion or otherwise unmarketable. The real issue is one of so-called consumer sovereignty. The typical developer is not seeking to impose her tastes on some unwitting consumer—her business motives are to earn a profit by building homes for less money than people are willing to pay for them.

If no one is willing to pay a sufficient price for suburban sprawl, we may be assured that she will not continue to build them. The real estate developer is an *agent* of final consumer demand, and it is both trite and simplistic to assign blame for tasteless sprawl to the developer, just as it would be to blame fast-food chains for the fact that we appear to gobble up their burgers as quickly as they can produce them. If one doesn't like fast food, one is not obliged to eat it, nor is one obliged to live in sprawled suburban development, yet there we are. To adapt a well-known phrase: "We have met the purveyors of bad taste, and they is us."

Notes

1. "Land rent" refers to the value per unit of time (for example, annual rental per square foot of land) of occupying a particular site. The value of land reflects the capitalized value of those land rents, as discussed in this chapter, and in chapters 2 and 3, in the context of present value and housing, respectively.

2. The market-clearing price is that price at which demand just equals supply.

3. By the same definition, an *inferior* good—potato gruel, perhaps—is one for which demand falls as incomes rise.

4. One way to grasp this point is to recall that the slope of a curve is given by "the rise over the run." In this case, TC is "the rise" while N is "the run."

5. The most attractive subcenter from an individual firm's perspective is one with the greatest positive divergence between average benefits and average costs. Recall that the average benefit (cost) at any point is just the slope of the line connecting the origin to the total benefit (cost) curve at that same point. Then, the greatest average net benefit will be found at a subcenter of size N with the greatest angle between the average benefit and average cost connecting lines.

6. If that were not so, I might well be speculating in real estate rather than writing textbooks.

7. We say that the demand for a good is *elastic* (*inelastic*) if a percentage change in price leads to a larger (smaller) percentage change in the quantity demanded.

8. There may well be individuals who fall into both camps: owners of agricultural land who desire to see that land remain in agricultural use. There is no contradiction between the two, but there are clear implications for which group at large holds the relevant entitlements.

5

Public Goods and Public Choice

Introduction

A recurring debate within the planning community concerns the provision of public goods. A contributing factor to the longevity and vociferousness of this debate, no doubt, is the confusion that reigns in many quarters over just what is meant by the term *public goods*. As is explained in the next section of this chapter, there are two dimensions of "publicness." On the one hand, there are all manner of goods that are provided by the public sector. On the other hand, there are goods that are nonrival in consumption (a term that will be explained in detail in the next section) and which are therefore intrinsically public in the technical sense of the term.

Confusion arises because goods that are public in the technical sense may or may not be provided by the public sector, and conversely, goods that are provided by the public sector may or may not be public goods in the technical sense of the term. It is unfortunate that the term public goods is often used either way, so that statements about public goods are readily misinterpreted or misconstrued. Accordingly, the first aim of this chapter is to clarify what is meant by the term public goods in different contexts. Doing so enables us to address a number of important issues concerning the debate over public goods, including optimal provision of nonrival goods, privatization issues, and neighborhood character as a special case of local public goods.

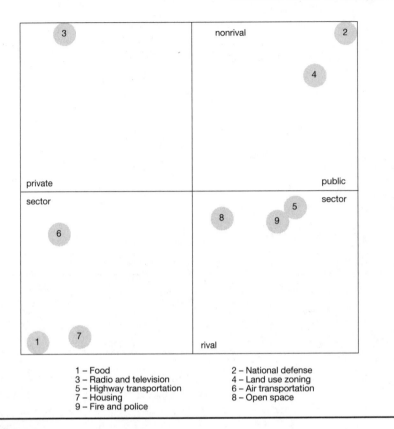

FIGURE 5.1
Two dimensions of "publicness" in goods
(American context)

Public vs. Private, Goods vs. Providers

Figure 5.1 graphs two dimensions of publicness in goods. The provider of goods is represented on the horizontal axis, with public providers shown to the right and private providers to the left. Goods that are provided exclusively by one sector or the other are located at the lateral extremes of this axis, while goods that are provided in some measure by both sectors are located somewhere in the middle, with the exact location depending upon the shares or relative weights attached to public- versus private-sector providers. The vertical axis represents the dimension of rivalry versus nonrivalry in consumption, a concept that we will now explain in more detail. Goods that are purely nonrival in consumption are located at the very top of the axis, whereas those at the very bottom are purely rival. Intermediate locations along the vertical axis represent varying degrees of rivalry.

Most goods exhibit at least some degree of rivalry in consumption: "If you eat it, then there will be less left for me." That is, in the case of pure rivalry, the amount of the good consumed by one person diminishes the stock available for others by precisely the same quantity. Such goods are private goods in the technical sense of the term. Note that it doesn't matter whether the good in question was provided by the market or by the public sector. Rivalry is a quality of the good itself, not of the provider of the good. Nonrivalry is simply the absence of this quality. Radio signals are a perfect example of a nonrival good. One person tuning her radio to her favorite station (and thereby "consuming" the radio signal) in no way diminishes the availability of that signal for other potential listeners. Goods that exhibit nonrivalry in consumption and that are nonexcludable[1] are public goods in the technical sense of the term. Again, this is a quality of the good itself, and is not affected in any way by public versus private provision of the good.

We can specify a location for any good on the graph in figure 5.1 based on these two distinct dimensions of "publicness," and we do so for a range of examples, using the United States as our reference base. Other countries may differ in terms of which sectors provide the specified goods and services, so the location of goods along the horizontal dimension of the graph may depend on which country is used as the reference base. However, placement along the vertical dimension is strictly an aspect of the good itself and is therefore independent of the country context.

The first example, food, is located at the lower left-hand corner of the graph, indicating a good that is perfectly rival in consumption and is provided exclusively by the private sector. This location on the graph is where we would expect to find any service or commodity that conforms to the basic concept of a private good produced and distributed via traditional markets. The next case, national defense, represents the opposite polar extreme as a good that is provided by the public sector and is nonrival in consumption. The defense shield that protects one citizen from foreign invasion or attack applies fairly uniformly across all citizens. There is an implicit assumption in some public discussion of public goods that these two polar extremes are fairly representative of the general distinction between public versus private goods. This presumption holds that private, rival goods are generally provided by the private sector through conventional markets, whereas public, nonrival goods are generally provided by the public sector through nonmarket means. The remaining examples show that the dichotomy is far less clear-cut than might be suggested by these polar extremes, and that in fact many combinations are readily found.

A case in point is radio and television, located near the upper left-hand corner of the graph in figure 5.1. As noted earlier, radio and television broadcast signals are among the best possible examples of a pure nonrival good, where one person's "consumption" of the signal does not in any way diminish what is left over for others. Note that this technical quality of the good is independent also of individual preferences. The fact that you may not have any interest in listening to the same radio station as I do is not germane. In the United States most radio and television is provided by the private sector; hence it is a perfect example of a pure public good in the *technical* sense that is a private good in the *market* sense. Our first three examples have pegged three corners of the graph. What about the fourth, bottom right-hand corner of the graph, which corresponds to pure rival goods that are provided solely by the government sector? It is difficult to think of such examples in the United States context, and only a few die-hard countries remain, run by communist regimes, in which virtually all goods, regardless of whether they are rival or nonrival in consumption, are provided solely by the public sector. However, it is still easy to find examples of countries that do maintain government monopolies on cigarettes, beer, or other goods that are purely rival in consumption.

We have discussed examples representing the four corners of the graph in figure 5.1, thereby mapping out the full range of possibilities. The remaining examples drawn from a planning context are intermediate cases, with some degree of rivalry in consumption and with some public-sector provision. Consider first the case of highways provided for automobile use. In the United States and most other countries these are provided primarily by the public sector, although privately funded tollways are now increasingly available. On balance, though, highways are placed well to the right in terms of the horizontal axis in figure 5.1. One must pause to consider the degree of rivalry exhibited by highways. As discussed in chapter 6, and as we know all too well from daily experience, highways are a congestible good. If traffic volumes are low, there is an absence of rivalry in consumption. However, once traffic volumes increase beyond the design capacity, congestion sets in, and there is a marked rivalry in consumption, where one person's use of the road does diminish another's potential. Based on this reasoning, we have placed highways just below the vertical midpoint in figure 5.1, indicating a good that is slightly more rival than not, on balance.

Air transportation is quite a different case. In the United States context, almost all commercial air transport is provided by the private sector, although the government regulates safety standards closely. This places air transportation well to the left on the chart. There is also significant rivalry in consumption of air transport services, because a particular seat taken by one person is not available for others. One could argue that there is a small element of nonrivalry at a more aggregate scale due to the "lumpiness" of capital. As long as there are empty seats on the plane, one person's status as a passenger does not preclude another person from also being a passenger on that same flight. This example, together with the highway example, shows that a congestible good is best understood as a good that is nonrival for small numbers of consumers but increasingly rival as more consumers participate.

Housing exhibits stronger rivalry characteristics than either of the two preceding examples. My living here precludes your living here. This is partly a social rather than a physical constraint, but the cumulative effect is nonetheless that of a rival good, one that is usually provided in the United States by the private sector. Open space, as another example, is nonrival at lower levels of use, but rivalry increases with congestion through higher rates of use, as any summer visitor to Yosemite National Park knows. The public sector is responsible for most of the open space that is formally set aside for public use, but one should not discount the importance of open space on privately held land. Even if the owners do not permit trespassing, one is often still able to "consume" the vista. Public safety in the form of police and fire protection is another example of a good that is congestible-rival. Particularly with respect to police, their function is largely that of deterring crime that might otherwise affect all or any of us. However, as the number of calls for emergency response increases, the capacity of the force is stretched and rivalry in consumption sets in. If they are busy responding to your call they may not be there to receive mine. Zoning regulation, our final example, is a public good in both senses of the term. Most land use regulations are indeed propagated by the public sector, and its effects on neighborhood character and urban design are "consumed" by all of us simultaneously and without rivalry. (Again, this is true whether or not we are in favor of such regulations—it pertains to a technical aspect of the good rather than to individual preferences.)

The cases reviewed above are suggestive of the variations one finds in the degree of "publicness" exhibited by different kinds of goods. We have seen that variations along the horizontal dimension are specific to particular countries or institutional settings. In most cases it is physically possible for a good to be provided by either sector, although in the United States goods that are highly rival in consumption tend to be provided by the private sector, while goods that are provided by the public sector usually exhibit at least some absence of rivalry. This tendency is evident in the pattern of points in figure 5.1 extending from the bottom left to the top right corners of the graph. The one notable exception to this trend is radio and television, which is nonrival in consumption but almost exclusively provided by the private sector. What makes this good exceptional is the fact that it is an information medium, and there is widespread support in the United States for freedom from government interference in information media.

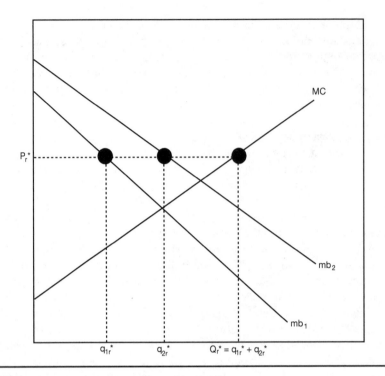

FIGURE 5.2a
Optimal provision of a rival good

Optimal Provision of a Nonrival Good

The market does not support an efficient allocation of goods that are nonrival in consumption. It turns out that the optimal outcome for nonrival goods would require unique prices assigned to each individual consuming the good, while neoclassical markets are characterized most notably by a single price that applies to everyone. This important fact was first established in 1954 by the noted economist Paul Samuelson, who later went on to win the Nobel prize in economics for this and many other contributions. The basic argument advanced by Samuelson is illustrated in figures 5.2a and 5.2b, both of which depict the marginal cost curve for a certain good and the marginal benefit curves for two representative consumers, with quantity registered on the horizontal axis. The principles of marginal analysis as set out in chapter 1 tell us that the maximum net benefit is derived by producing up to the point where marginal benefit just meets marginal cost. This optimality condition, MB = MC, must be met in either case (rival or nonrival good) if

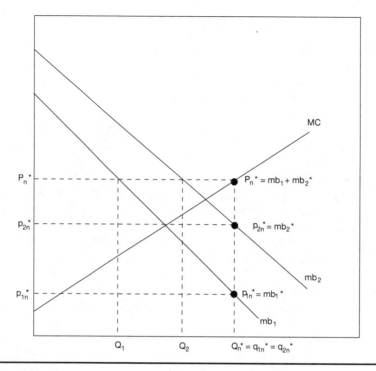

FIGURE 5.2b
Optimal provision of a nonrival good

---

the allocation is to be efficient, but as we shall see, the market will only support this condition in the case of a rival good.

The case of a regular good with pure rivalry is illustrated first in figure 5.2a. Market equilibrium arises at price P_r^*, a price that applies to everyone in the market. By making reference to their demand curves, we see that the two consumers will choose quantities q_{1r}^* and q_{2r}^*, respectively, at the market equilibrium price. The total quantity demanded of the rival good is thus $Q_r^* = q_{1r}^* + q_{2r}^*$, which corresponds precisely to the quantity at which marginal cost equals P_r^*, so Q_r^* is just the amount the producer is willing to supply at this price. This is no accident; it is true by definition of a market equilibrium. If the quantity demanded and supplied were not equal, prices would continue to adjust until equilibrium was restored. The significance of figure 5.2a goes beyond the fact that market demand and supply are in equilibrium at price P_r^*. Even more importantly, from an efficiency standpoint, this market equilibrium condition supports the optimality condition MB = MC. To see that this is true, observe that market equilibrium is obtained when:

$$MB = mb_1 = mb_2 = P_r^* = MC \tag{1}$$

This equation makes three important statements:

- Each consumer is in equilibrium when the marginal benefit he would obtain by consuming one more unit of the good is just offset by the price he must pay ($mb_1 = mb_2 = P_r^*$);
- likewise, the producer supplies the good up to the point that the price she receives just covers the marginal cost of production ($P_r^* = MC$); and
- because the good in question is a rival good, the benefit obtained from the production of one more unit of the good will be enjoyed by one consumer or the other, but not both, and so the aggregate benefit on the margin derived from one more unit of production equals the marginal benefit obtained by whichever individual actually consumes it ($MB = mb_i$).[2]

In sum, this tells us that the cost of producing one more unit of the rival good is just offset by the benefit that *either one* of the consumers would obtain by consuming it.

The demand (marginal benefit) and marginal cost curves in figure 5.2b are identical to those in figure 5.2a, but this time the good in question is perfectly nonrival, which means that everyone can consume the same portion of the good in equal measure. In this case the optimum allocation is at Q_n^*. Because the good depicted in figure 5.2b is a purely nonrival good, both consumers depicted in figure 5.2b are able to consume the good at this quantity, and their corresponding marginal benefits are mb_1^* and mb_2^*, respectively. Notice the important difference between this case and that of the rival good just discussed. In the previous case both consumers adjusted consumption so that their marginal benefits equaled the market price. In this case the level of consumption for both consumers is fixed by the producer, therefore it is the marginal benefits rather than the quantities consumed that vary. So, in the case of a rival good, we have $mb_1 = mb_2 = P_r^*$ with varying quantities, while in the case of a nonrival good we have $q_{1n}^* = q_{2n}^* = Q_n^*$ with varying marginal benefits.

At Q_n^*, which in all likelihood differs from the previous solution Q_r^*, our optimality condition ($MB = MC$) still holds, but under a different guise:

$$MB = mb_1 + mb_2 = MC \tag{2}$$

Note that aggregate marginal benefit in this case is given by the *sum* of the individual marginal benefits for each consumer, unlike the previous case where aggregate marginal benefit was equal to that of *either* individual. The reason is that an extra unit of output in the case of a purely nonrival good can be consumed by all of the consumers simultaneously, so the additional benefits that accrue to each of them must be tallied to obtain the aggregate change in benefit from the production of one more unit of output (i.e., to obtain the aggregate benefit on the margin). In the previous case of a purely rival good, only a single consumer could benefit from a marginal increase in output.

An important consequence of the situation depicted in figure 5.2b is that there is no single market price that supports the desired optimum. In order to persuade the producer to supply an amount Q_n^*, the price should be set at P_n^*, which is just sufficient to cover the marginal cost of producing that amount. Any consumer is in equilibrium when the marginal benefit received just compensates for the price paid. Therefore, to effect a market equilibrium at this allocation, each consumer should be charged an amount corresponding to the marginal benefit they would obtain from that marginal increase in output at Q_n^*. We can see from equation 2 that the sum of those individual marginal benefits is just sufficient to cover the marginal cost of production, so efficiency would be preserved. Unfortunately, conventional markets (at least in their idealized textbook form) have a single price for all consumers and therefore are incapable of discriminating between consumers in this way. This situation precipitates the classic free-rider problem. The free-rider problem arises because consumers are aware that they can all consume a nonexcludable, nonrival good even if it is paid for by someone else. No one wants to be the dupe who actually pays for it without being sure that others are also paying their fair share. The branch of economics known as public choice is concerned with this problem, and much work has been done to devise schemes by which consumers may be induced to divulge how much benefit they receive from an extra unit of the good. With this information it is possible, at least in principle, to set the individual prices that would correspond to the optimum depicted in figure 5.2b. The field of public choice is still relatively young; there is much work to be done in this area. In the meantime, we are left with the problem of how to solve for, supply, and pay for the optimal level of production of nonrival goods.

What happens if we leave it to the market to supply the nonrival good? The quantities Q_1 and Q_2 in figure 5.2b indicate the amount of the good that consumers 1 and 2, respectively, would be willing to purchase on their own at the price P_n^*. These quantities correspond to the levels at which the consumers' marginal benefits just cover the marginal cost of production. In this case consumer 2 has the higher demand, and the pure market outcome is Q_2. At this market equilibrium consumer 2 is just willing to pay for that last little bit of the good, while consumer 1 is unwilling to pay for any more than Q_1. Without additional information about institutional mechanisms in place, one cannot determine what shares would be paid by whom, because so many outcomes are possible. For example, perhaps consumer 1 paid up to Q_1, and consumer 2 paid for the residual, $(Q_2 - Q_1)$. That solution would be consistent with both of their individual demand curves. Or, perhaps consumer 2 paid for the whole bundle, Q_2, while consumer 1 took a free ride. That would also be consistent. There is no uniquely determinable solution, but we can be fairly certain that the market will eventually deliver an amount Q_2 since there is at least one person whose net benefits increase up to that amount, even if he is the only person to pay. And because this is a nonexcludable, nonrival good, everyone can enjoy consuming the good provided by the market at level Q_2 whether they helped to pay for it or not.

Even if those who did pay for the good do not hold resentment over those free-riders who did not, there is another problem with the market outcome. We can see from figure 5.2b that the market will undersupply the good. At Q_2 the sum of the marginal benefits will certainly exceed the marginal cost of providing a bit more of the good; the market outcome in the case of a nonrival good is inefficient and the good is undersupplied. The gap between Q_2 and Q_n^* can be quite large in an economy with many consumers.

So if markets cannot be relied upon to deliver the optimum quantity of a nonrival good, what about the public sector? There are two main problems. First, in the absence of reliable information about the marginal benefit that individuals obtain from an additional bit of output of a nonrival good, it is difficult to know where Q_n^* is. This can be resolved somewhat, albeit imperfectly, through elections, special referenda, or other institutional mechanisms that help the public register their preferences with public-sector decision makers. Once the level of output has been established, the second problem is to find an equitable and efficient way to pay for it. Two principles generally apply: *ability to pay* and *user pays*. Income taxes and property taxes are generally based on the first principle, while user fees, permits, and licenses follow the second principle. Both are used extensively by state or local governments to pay for publicly provided goods.

Tiebout, Local Public Goods, and Neighborhood Quality

One of the most often cited articles in any branch of economics was authored in 1956 by Charles Tiebout in response to the question of how to provide the optimum quantity of a nonrival good. As shown in the previous section of this chapter in reference to figure 5.2b, the market does not offer a price adjustment mechanism that is capable of sorting out different categories of consumers with respect to their demand for nonrival goods. In the case of rival goods, consumers who want more purchase more, while consumers

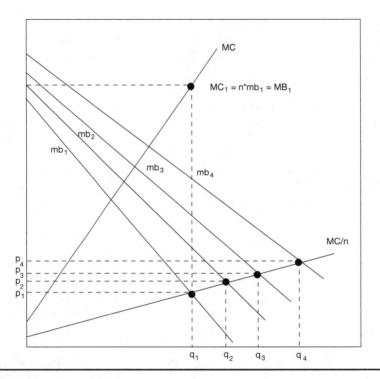

FIGURE 5.3
The Tiebout mechanism with communities of equal size

who want less purchase less. That is not possible in the case of a nonrival good where everyone is supplied the same quantity.

Tiebout pointed to an alternative adjustment mechanism — "voting with one's feet"—which applies in the case of *local* public goods whose nonrival characteristics are confined to specific localities that we may call municipalities. Tiebout envisioned a large number of municipalities, each offering a unique bundle of nonrival goods (that we shall call municipal services) and prices (municipal taxes). In lieu of a market mechanism, each household votes with its feet by selecting the municipality that offers the quantity-price bundle best suited to its own preferences. Tiebout's analysis showed that such an arrangement would in equilibrium satisfy the optimality condition (MB = MC) that Samuelson showed is not met by traditional markets. Tiebout's spatial adjustment mechanism, in effect, solves the problem that traditional markets could not.

Figure 5.3 illustrates the basic principle involved. Here, in an adaptation of figures 5.2a and 5.2b, we have a marginal cost curve (MC) as before and a set of individual marginal benefit curves indicating a range of four distinct preference types. Assume for the sake of argument that there are "n" consumers or households of each type. Figure 5.3 shows how these households will sort themselves into distinct, homogeneous communities via the Tiebout mechanism. Consider what happens when a set of municipalities offers the set of quantity-price bundles found along the curve denoted by MC/n, so that municipality 1 offers the bundle (q_1, p_1), municipality 2 offers (q_2, p_2), and so on. The n households of type 1 who share the demand curve denoted by mb_1 will gravitate to municipality 1 because it offers the only bundle that is compatible with their demand curve. The remaining households will self-select themselves into the remaining municipalities by a similar mechanism. Are the optimality conditions met here? Yes, for each municipality (of type 1) the following condition holds:

$$MC_i = n * P_i = n * mb_i = MB_i \qquad (3)$$

Remember that each of the n households in any municipality consumes the nonrival good available there in full and equal measure, so the marginal benefit enjoyed by any one household for a small increase in quantity supplied must be multiplied n times to obtain the full or aggregate benefit on the margin for that community, as in the equation above.

Thus, by "voting with their feet," households sort themselves according to their preferences regarding the local public good. Based on the same principles of marginal analysis that motivate all consumer behavior in neoclassical economics, each household locates in a municipality that charges an amount for the good that is just equal to the marginal benefit that the household enjoys from the last little bit supplied. Consider households of type 2, for example. The quantity-price bundle offered by municipality 3 lies beyond its reach—we can see from its demand curve that it is unwilling to pay an amount p_3 to obtain the quantity q_3 of this nonrival good. Municipality 1, on the other hand, is well within reach of households of type 2. However, we can see that at price p_1, the marginal benefit obtained by such households exceeds the price, so they will seek to "purchase" more of the good than is available in municipality 1. They can do so by moving to municipality 2. Only municipality 2 offers a quantity-price bundle that leaves households of type 2 in equilibrium. A similar analysis applies to the other household types.

In the analysis above we made the simplifying assumption that there were exactly n households of each type; municipalities formed neatly along the fractional marginal cost line MC/n, as shown in figure 5.3. We can relax this assumption without adding undue complications, as shown in figure 5.4. Here we have a set of individual marginal benefit curves as before, except we now assume that there are a varying number of households of each type, n_1 for

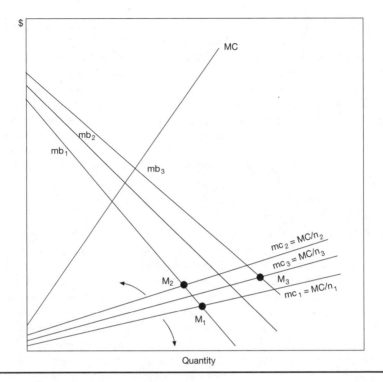

FIGURE 5.4
The Tiebout mechanism with communities of unequal size

type 1, n_2 for type 2, and so on. Likewise, instead of the single fractional marginal cost line MC/n that appeared in figure 5.3, we now have a complete set corresponding to the varying household numbers: MC/n_1, MC/n_2, and so forth. In equilibrium, municipalities will now be located at the intersections of each marginal benefit curve with its corresponding fractional marginal cost curve, as shown in figure 5.4. As before, the quantity-price bundle offered by each municipality satisfies both the marginal benefit requirements of the consumer and the marginal cost requirements of the supplier, and so the optimality condition prevails.

There is one additional complication introduced by the situation depicted in figure 5.4, however. Consider the situation of households residing in municipality 2 compared with their neighbors in municipality 1. Municipality 1 offers its residents more of the nonrival good at a lower price, so residents of municipality 2 have an incentive to move to municipality 1. Evidently the number of consumers of type 2, n_2 is relatively small so the fractional marginal cost curve for the second municipality is relatively steep. There are not enough households of type 2 to support the level of services offered by municipality 2 in a competitive Tiebout-type environment. Thus, the situation depicted in figure 5.4 is not an equilibrium. Note also that as households move from municipality 2 to municipality 1, n_2 falls while n_1 increases, so the situation is exacerbated. As n_2 falls, there are even fewer people to support the level of service provided there. Meanwhile, as n_1 rises, the tax base increases so municipality 1 becomes even more attractive relative to municipality 2. This is a simple yet powerful conceptual device for understanding how a municipality competes to attract a tax base that will support its municipal services and reinforce its attractiveness and competitive standing.

As we have seen, the efficiency conditions that apply to market-supplied rival goods as illustrated in figure 5.2a do not hold for nonrival goods. The Tiebout mechanism provides a partial remedy for this situation by segmenting the market and allowing consumers to "vote with their feet" to select the price–quantity bundle that best suits their circumstances and preferences. While the Tiebout discussion is often framed in terms of a selection of municipalities that offer these local public goods, they might just as well be private-sector developers or entrepreneurs. There is nothing in the Tiebout argument that intrinsically favors the public sector.

The Tiebout model clearly has relevance for planners. This is especially true if we follow Tiebout's lead and consider "neighborhood quality" to be yet another kind of nonrival good. Tiebout himself specifically suggested that household preferences should include other noneconomic variables indicative of neighborhood quality, such as a desire to associate with "nice" people. A branch of economic analysis termed *club theory* conceives of this situation in a rather useful fashion, where municipalities are seen as one example of a general class of economic clubs (Cornes and Sandler 1986). Moving into an exclusive neighborhood is akin to joining an exclusive club. One joins in part to associate with fellow members, and this neighborhood-quality factor is a perfect example of a local nonrival good that is consumed in equal measure by all club members. "Club fees" in the form of real estate prices and property taxes help to maintain the exclusivity of the association. In economics terminology we say that the benefits of club membership are capitalized in the value of property. The only way to join the "club" of, say, Beverly Hills is to live or work there, and people's desire to join is reflected in the value of property there. One has only to visit Chicago, New York, Los Angeles, or any other large metropolitan area in the United States to see the Tiebout mechanism at work in fostering a diverse selection of municipal clubs.

"SEP Goods"

The Tiebout model discussed in the previous section suggests that households tend to sort themselves into relatively homogeneous "clubs" called municipalities. While there is strong evidence of a Tiebout mechanism at work, it is nonetheless true that many municipalities remain quite diverse in terms of income and other club attributes. An interesting dilemma arises in jurisdictions that have a wide range of incomes, and hence different levels of demand for publicly provided goods. Consider, for example, the case of a minority of wealthy households residing in a school district with many poorer families. What is the optimum level of publicly provided schooling from their perspective? Like anyone else, they are keen to receive a high quality of education for their children. And like anyone else, they are less than keen to pay any more taxes than necessary to support those education objectives. If an income or property tax is used to pay for publicly provided education, all households will receive the same level of education, but wealthy households will pay disproportionately. In many cases these households may have an incentive to withdraw their children from public schools in favor of more exclusive private ones.

A simple example illustrates the point. Tables 5.1a through 5.1c depict a jurisdiction with twenty wealthy households and eighty poor ones,[3] with average incomes of $80,000 and $20,000, respectively. The pooled tax base from all households is $3.2 million, which generates school tax revenues of $320,000 using a 10 percent tax rate. This corresponds to a level of support of $3,200 per pupil in the public schools, assuming that there is on average one school-age child per household.

Tables 5.1b and 5.1c consider what happens if the wealthy households use their political influence to lower the tax rate to 5 percent and withdraw their children from public schools in favor of more exclusive private schools. Tax revenues at 5 percent are now only $160,000, or $2,000 per public

TABLE 5.1a

All Households Attend Public Schools; Taxes @ 10%

Category	# of Households	Average Income	Tax Base	# of Public Schoolers	Tax @ 10%
Wealthy	20	$80,000	$1.6 million	20	$160,000
Poor	80	$20,000	$1.6 million	80	$160,000
Total/Average	100	$32,000	$3.2 million	100	$320,000

Revenue Per Public School Pupil: $3,200

TABLE 5.1b

Only Poor Households Attend Public Schools; Taxes @ 5%

Category	# of Households	Average Income	Tax Base	# of Public Schoolers	Tax @ 5%
Wealthy	20	$80,000	$1.6 million	0	$80,000
Poor	80	$20,000	$1.6 million	80	$80,000
Total/Average	100	$32,000	$3.2 million	80	$160,000

Revenue Per Public School Pupil: $2,000

school pupil. Note that wealthy households still pay their share of taxes, even though their children have opted out of public schools.

Private schools are supported through fees rather than taxes. In table 5.1c, we assume that those fees are equivalent to 5 percent of income for wealthy households, or $4,000 per pupil. Poor households do not contribute to the costs of private schools because their children attend public schools.

This example illustrates the incentive wealthy households may have to "opt out" of public schools and use their political influence to maintain lower tax rates. In the first scenario, wealthy and poor households alike were taxed at 10 percent and their children all attended public schools that enjoyed revenues of $3,200 per student. In the second scenario, the financial burden on wealthy incomes is unchanged. They still pay 10 percent toward education, but now 5 percent supports public schools in their area and the other 5 percent is in the form of direct payment of fees for private tuition. While the financial burden has not changed for wealthy households, the quality of education their children receive has improved. The private schools they attend enjoy revenues of $4,000 per pupil, so there is more money to spend on teachers, computers, books, and the other inputs that may contribute toward a higher-quality education. The financial burden on poorer households has eased, as they now pay only 5 percent in taxes rather than 10 percent, but the quality of education in the public schools their children attend has declined commensurately, as public schools now have only $2,000 per pupil to spend on educating their students.

This "opting out" phenomenon bears some similarities to the Tiebout model described in the preceding section, but there are also some important differences. The similarity is that households have a tendency to sort themselves into groups based on incomes and preferences. The difference is that the separation is incomplete in this case; the wealthy households have not withdrawn physically from the jurisdiction. Their income and property still comprise part of the community's tax base. Notice too that the good in

TABLE 5.1c

Only Wealthy Households Attend Private Schools; Fees @ 5%

Category	# of Households	Average Income	Revenue Base	# of Private Schoolers	Fees @ 5%
Wealthy	20	$80,000	$1.6 million	20	$80,000
Poor	80	$20,000	$0	0	$0
Total/Average	100	$32,000	$1.6 million	20	$80,000

Revenue Per Private School Pupil: $4,000

question is an excludable one, as otherwise the privately provided alternative could not cater solely to the upper-income market niche. There are several reasons why wealthy households might "opt out" rather than "vote with their feet" à la Tiebout. First, developers may not have created a complete set of municipal clubs, perhaps because of insufficient population numbers, so the alternatives may be somewhat limited. Second, the very possibility that wealthy households might move can create political pressure to keep tax rates low, thereby lowering the incentive for wealthy households to leave. Third, there may be locational advantages from the jurisdiction in question that are not offered by the alternatives. And finally, moving costs, sentimental attachments, and other factors may pose additional barriers to mobility.

The situation described by the preceding example is one instance of an important phenomenon that has received relatively little attention in the literature on public economics, that of substitutable yet exclusively provided goods, referred to here as SEP goods.[4] This term refers to goods that are provided by both the public and private sectors, but where individuals rely primarily on one source or the other. Education is an obvious example, where the public sector provides the bulk of education services to the public but where there is nonetheless a vigorous market in private schools as well. Health care or hospital services in many countries bear a similar characteristic, where government provides a base level of service but where those who choose to do so may opt for private care instead. In the case of transportation, public transit is typically provided at a nominal charge to the general public, while the bulk of the population opts for private modes. The presence of private security guard services points to a similar phenomenon in the area of police protection. Even the provision of open space bears this characteristic, where spacious private yards constitute a viable private substitute for public parks. SEP goods are characterized further by the near exclusivity of each individual's source of provision. People who own cars seldom ride buses. Children attend either private school or public school, but typically not both. For our purposes, SEP goods are defined as being purely exclusive.

While SEP goods may be provided by either the public or private sector, and while the public and privately provided alternatives are highly substitutable, there are important distinctions between them. First, publicly provided SEP goods are paid for from the public purse so that, at least in the purest case, each person's contribution to the cost of provision is unaffected by his or her individual choice about public versus private provision of the good. In contrast, privately provided SEP goods are supplied and demanded in accordance with market principles and are paid for only by those who choose to consume them. Moreover, there is often a certain inferiority associated with publicly provided as opposed to privately provided SEP goods. Indeed, if this were not true it would be difficult to imagine why anyone would choose the latter, unless the private and public alternatives are relatively weak substitutes. An important consequence of this distinction is that people, through their choices, are divided into two groups corresponding to private and public provision of the good. In general, it is the rich who opt out and the poor who stick with the publicly provided alternative.

The characterization of this dichotomy in terms of economic class raises interesting public-choice questions regarding the provision of the publicly provided SEP good. As we have seen, the rich may have an incentive, to the extent that their political clout allows, to keep the level of publicly provided goods at a minimum so as to reduce their own tax burden. Why pay taxes for a service that will only benefit others? This is in direct contrast to the incentive structure of the poor, who will be more inclined to tax the rich and the poor alike to pay for improved levels of the public services that are utilized primarily by the poor. Of course, there are limits to the tax rate favored by the poor because they also pay taxes, but their expressed preferences will no doubt be influenced by the knowledge that their use of the publicly provided good is in effect subsidized by the rich. Policymakers face the challenge of finding a happy, workable medium somewhere between these two perspectives.

The Privatization Debate

In response to mounting expenditures, declining tax revenues, and the resultant burgeoning account deficits, governments at all levels have looked to privatization as a means of reducing public-sector burdens while enhancing efficiency of production and delivery of services ranging from trash removal to highways. *Privatization* refers to a process whereby the responsibility for delivering services hitherto provided by the public sector is transferred to the private sector. It is useful to review the basic arguments for and against privatization in the context of the lessons learned in this chapter.

The strongest argument in favor of privatization is the efficiency argument. Private-sector firms operating in a competitive market environment have a strong incentive to deliver services up to the point that marginal cost just meets price. Consumers in general are inclined to purchase services up to the point that the marginal benefit is just sufficient to compensate for the price paid. In this way, market price mediates between producers and consumers so that:

$$MB = P \; and \; MC = P \tag{4}$$

and therefore the fundamental efficiency condition (MB = MC) holds.

The public sector does not have the same built-in imperative as the private sector because public-sector decision makers are not directly impacted by negative profitability. There is a very indirect and imperfect feedback mechanism by which voters express disapproval over poor services, high taxes, and large deficits, and by which elected and appointed decision makers within the public sector are held accountable for inefficient resource allocations.

Many of the criticisms leveled at government bureaucracies also apply to large corporate bureaucracies in the private sector. Reduced profitability of a publicly held corporation directly impacts shareholders, those who own shares of the enterprise. When ownership is widely dissipated, with many small owners and no dominant ones, there is little direct oversight by the owners of the decisions made by corporate managers. The latter report directly to a board of directors that is required under corporate law to act in the best interests of shareholders. In many ways this is similar to a municipal corporation, where the city council acts as a board of directors, overseeing operating decisions made by the city manager and other appointed officials. The key difference, of course, between the private and public sectors is the market test that is applied to the private-sector corporation. Poor decision making will reduce the value of the corporation's shares. Existing shareholders will exert more pressure on the board and on management to remedy the situation. The very existence of the corporation may be jeopardized by poor decisions, as the firm faces increased risks of bankruptcy or of corporate takeover. The latter is especially likely where the assets of a corporation are undervalued due to mismanagement, and an outside "raider" determines that it may be profitable to buy up a controlling stake of the undervalued shares, reorganize management, and revitalize the profitability of the firm. This market test is the best assurance shareholders have that management will ultimately act in its interests. The mechanism is not perfect, but history suggests that it is nonetheless a fairly robust and reliable one.

There are parallels in the local government sector to each of these components. Property owners and other stakeholders in a municipality are the public-sector counterparts to the shareholders of a corporation. As a municipality's fiscal situation deteriorates due to poor decision making, property values will decline as property owners seek to unload their "shares." New political coalitions may form to take over city council, with a view to replacing management. While these parallels are encouraging, one must be cognizant of the important differences as well. For one thing, real estate tends not to be actively traded in response to short-term market fluctuations in the same way stocks are. Some people choose to live in their short-term investments, but most homeowners make medium- or long-term investments in the places they choose to live. Main Street is not Wall Street. Another important difference is that there is not the same opportunity for an outside "raider" to purchase outstanding shares of a municipal corporation and to personally realize any gains in net revenue resulting from subsequent management changes. Owning 51 percent of the property in a municipality does not constitute a "controlling share" the same way it does in the corporate sector. Moreover, although municipalities may compete with one another at a distance, they do not compete on the same turf directly. Finally, the decision-making arena in the public sector is in many ways a more complex one, with multiple objectives and no single index of performance. This is in direct contrast to the private sector, where maximizing profits or shareholder value is generally acknowledged, without apology or equivocation, as the overriding purpose of the firm.

On balance, therefore, the imperatives of the market from an efficiency standpoint tend to favor the private sector. There are other considerations, however, that work in favor of some form of public-sector intervention, at least in certain circumstances. These considerations include public goods, externalities, and merit goods. They are all examples of *market failure,* a term that is invoked whenever the market fails to maximize net social benefits, or whenever the following optimality condition fails to hold:

$$MSB = MSC \tag{5}$$

Equation 5 states that production of a good is undertaken until marginal social benefits are just sufficient to compensate for the marginal social costs. It is useful to consider whether and how this differs from equation 4, wherein market equilibrium condition is described. The hope or presumption in equation 4 is that private marginal benefits (MB) and private marginal costs (MC) coincide with their social counterparts. More formally, the market works optimally whenever:

$$MSB = MB = P \ and \ MSC = MC = P \tag{6}$$

So, not only must the condition in equation 4 hold (MB = P = MC) as a result of market operations, the marginal costs and benefits as perceived by individuals in the marketplace must fully reflect society's valuation as well (MSB = MB and MSC = MC). When these conditions do not hold we have market failure. Examples of market failures arise in other chapters dealing with zoning, traffic congestion, cost–benefit analysis, and entitlements. In each of those examples the presence of market failure raises the possibility that a public-sector solution may be desirable, but in no case does it follow automatically, nor is it immediately clear what form or extent of public-sector intervention might be appropriate, if any.

Externalities refer to marginal costs or benefits that are not reflected in market prices so that MC ≠ MSC or MB ≠ MSB. Suppose, for example, that the production of a certain good causes environmental pollution. The marginal cost to society of additional pollution may not be captured in market prices. In this case we get a variation on equations 4 and 6, so that now:

$$P = MB = MSB \; but \; P = MC \neq MSC \tag{7}$$

In this case, consumers still consume up to the point that their marginal benefit is just sufficient to compensate for the price they must pay, so P = MB = MSB. Producers likewise continue to produce to the point where the price they are paid just compensates for *their* marginal costs. However, because of the pollution externality, those costs understate the true costs to society at large, and so MC ≠ MSC. The net result is that MSB ≠ MSC, so the societal optimality condition is not satisfied.

A similar argument applies in the case of merit goods, which are goods that we somehow feel *ought* to be consumed in greater quantities than those generated by market outcomes. For example, one may be of the opinion that highly developed markets in an era of mass consumerism work systematically against the interests of small farmers, so people *ought* to buy more farm-fresh produce than they do. This argument may be expressed as yet another variation on the market failure theme, where this time:

$$P = MC = MSC \; but \; P = MB \neq MSB \tag{8}$$

As before, the market equilibrium condition holds that firms produce up to the point that the price they receive just compensates for the extra costs of production on the margin, and likewise, consumers purchase up to the point that the marginal benefits they receive just compensate for the price paid. In the case of merit goods, however, the argument is that consumers do not fully recognize the benefits derived from purchases of farm-fresh produce supplied by small-scale farmers. There is also a presumption here, one that some will characterize as paternalistic, that consumers are somehow unable to make such assessments on their own and are in need of proper guidance.

Another aspect of the merit goods argument that is not always recognized explicitly is that of *income redistribution*. A social consensus may emerge, for example, that housing, health care, nutrition, education, or transportation are merit goods and that a certain minimum standard is called for. This is another perspective from which to view the issue of separate yet exclusively provided (SEP) goods, as discussed earlier in this chapter. It also bears directly on the issue of entitlements, as reviewed in detail in chapter 9. Consider the case of minimum housing standards. It is difficult to fault a policy or program that has as its premise that every household has a right to basic shelter. There are three logical possibilities to explain why households might fail to meet a specified minimum standard for housing:

- The household has adequate income but chooses not to purchase the minimum standard of housing services;
- the household would like to purchase the minimum standard but is unable to do so because of inadequate income; or
- the household does not have adequate income, but would not choose to purchase the minimum standard in any event.

In the first case, enforcement of a minimum standard would entail a direct overriding of household preferences. There may be justification for this in certain instances. For example, it is generally agreed that a minimum quantity and quality of education is required for all children, regardless of their preferences or those of their parents. In many instances, however, we may be inclined to view the imposition of minimum standards as highly paternalistic meddling. For example, few people would favor public-sector regulations designed to ensure that we floss our teeth or eat green vegetables each day, even if we agree that such practices are meritworthy.

In the second case delineated above, the household would like to purchase the minimum standard of housing but is unable to do so due to inadequate income. In this case, providing housing for the household is equivalent, effectively, to providing additional income, because the presumption is that any additional income would be spent on improved housing; therefore, the imposition of minimum standards is equivalent to an income transfer program. In the third case, however, the household would not choose to purchase the minimum standard of housing even if it were provided with adequate income to do so. Based on its preferences, the household would rather see any additional income spent on other goods and services. In other words, additional income brings households of the third type (as enumerated in the bullet points above) to the same position as households of the first type, so the question once again arises as to whether it is appropriate or justified for the public-sector planner to override the expressed preferences of households that would prefer to increase their consumption of other goods and services before meeting the specified minimum standards. In some cases, as in education standards, most people would agree that the answer is yes. In other cases the answer is clearly no. In large measure the answer depends on one's philosophical orientation regarding the rights and responsibilities of individuals to determine for themselves what is in their best interests.

To the extent that inadequate income is the sole reason for a household's failure to adhere to minimum standards, a direct income transfer is appropriate because, as we have seen, providing the minimum standard is equivalent to providing the income that could be used to acquire it. In many cases, however, declaring a minimum standard is less efficient than an income transfer because it deprives households of the opportunity to optimize expenditures within the implied budget constraint. For some, the indirectness of minimum standards is useful in effecting income transfers that might otherwise run into political opposition. This textbook, however, takes the view that we are not well served by policies that rely on public ignorance to ensure their continuation or popularity. If minimum standards are equivalent to an income transfer, then it is best that the public understands that point when determining the extent of their support.

The setting of minimum standards establishes a set of entitlements, and as discussed in chapter 9, entitlements are a form of wealth. To the extent that these entitlements are perfectly tradeable and transferable, they are no different from an equivalent cash transfer. However, in most cases (food stamps are a good example) the market for such entitlements is at best imperfect or even illegal, so they have full value to the household only if lack of income is the sole reason for its failure to adhere to the minimum standard. In other words, the conditions that would have to exist for the minimum standard entitlements to have full value to the household are the same conditions that make a cash transfer equivalent to entitlements. Therefore, we may conclude that cash transfers are generally more efficient than minimum standard entitlements at delivering value. Exceptions to this general rule are (i) where societal or moral perogatives are deemed to override individual preferences, or (ii) where the transactions costs of effecting cash transfers exceed the efficiency gains.

To conclude, the presence of market failure, in whatever form it arises, does raise the *possibility* of some form of public intervention, but one must consider each case carefully before concluding what kind of intervention, if any, is justified. In general, we may characterize public-sector intervention in the market to correct for market failure as being of two kinds, quantity oriented and price oriented. The latter approach takes the view that markets fail when prices do not reflect marginal costs and benefits, so when this condition arises the best thing to do is to "correct" those prices using taxes, subsidies, or other price-adjusting mechanisms. A quantity-oriented intervention, on the other hand, seeks to specify the quantities at which the optimum conditions are met and then to induce the market through regulations or directives to generate those specified outcomes. Direct public-sector provision of the good in question is not so much a case of market intervention as it is one of supplanting markets through direct public-sector production and distribution in lieu of the private sector. Economists would argue that, wherever feasible, planners should be looking to create and to nurture markets rather than to supplant them.

Notes

1. The issue of excludability (i.e., whether or not someone can be prevented from consuming the good) is important in determining the appropriate institutional response to nonrival goods, and is addressed later in this chapter.

2. It is possible in principle for the two consumers to each consume a share of the marginal output, in which case the aggregate marginal benefit is a weighted average of the individual marginal benefits. For example, if the shares are one-fourth and three-fourths, respectively, then the aggregate marginal benefit is given by $MB = (1^*mb_1 + 3^*mb_2) / 4$. But we already know that in equilibrium $mb_1 = mb_2$, so we quickly recover the original condition $MB = 4^*mb_1 / 4 = mb_1 = mb_2$.

3. The example works out exactly the same if we use 20,000 and 80,000 households, or if we consider the 20 and 80 to denote percentages. It is the proportions rather than the absolute levels that determine the revenue per pupil.

4. The term SEP goods and parts of the discussion for this section are borrowed from E. Heikkila and R. Luo, "Public versus Private Provision of Substitutable Yet Exclusively Provided Goods" (paper presented to the Western Regional Science Association meetings, San Diego, February 1994).

6

The Economics of Traffic Congestion

Introduction

No planning issue seems to rile the local body politic more than traffic congestion. Land use plans are often challenged on the basis of their anticipated transportation impacts. In social settings, when one identifies him or herself as a planner, the first question asked is often, "What are we going to do about the traffic problems in our city?" This chapter focuses on a series of diagrams that facilitate an exploration of four distinct transportation policy alternatives. The base case policy is a "do nothing" policy where no specific action is taken. The diagrams are used to illustrate how this equilibrium solution results in a loss of economic welfare relative to the optimal allocation of trips. The subsequent three cases represent different means of intervening to recapture the dissipated benefits lost to congestion.

We show that the alternative solutions reflect different perceptions of the nature of the underlying problem. From an engineer's perspective the problem is one of insufficient road capacity to accommodate demand; the logical solution from this perspective is to expand capacity. From a community activist's perspective the problem is one of too many cars, and the corre-

This chapter is adapted, with permission, from E. J. Heikkila, "Microeconomics and Planning: Using Simple Diagrams to Illustrate the Economics of Traffic Congestion," *Journal of Planning Education and Research* 14 (1994): 29–41.

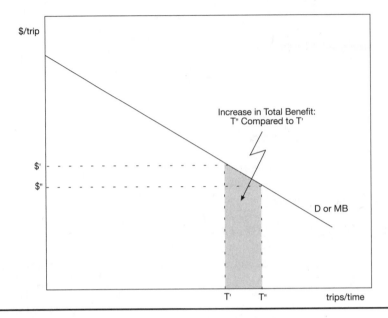

FIGURE 6.1
Demand for, and marginal benefit derived from, trips

sponding solution is to take measures that will restrict demand. The economist's perspective on traffic congestion is one of market failure, whereby the effective price facing individual drivers does not fully reflect marginal costs associated with use of the transportation system. The logical solution from this perspective is to introduce tolls that correct for the flawed price signals associated with the "do nothing" policy. Later sections of this chapter explore the advantages and disadvantages of each alternative, and the final section then evaluates these from the perspective of more traditional planning concerns, including long-run and distributional implications. This is done with the aid of the basic diagrams found throughout the chapter.

The Basic Diagram

The horizontal axis in figure 6.1 measures the flow of throughput volume on a transportation system during a specific time period. The transportation system could be a freeway network, a metro rail system, or an urban street network. The time period might represent a peak period during the daily commute, an entire day, or a full year. The diagram is meant to be interpreted generically. The vertical axis measures costs and benefits per trip. The downward-sloping curve can be interpreted in either of two ways: as a demand curve (D) or as a marginal benefit curve (MB). In the former case, one begins with a given cost (such as $") on the vertical axis and then, with reference to the curve, finds the corresponding point (such as T") on the horizontal axis. Viewed this way, the horizontal axis measures the demand, in trip volume, for a given perceived cost. For example, as the perceived cost rises (from $" to $') the demand for trips falls (from T" to T').

Confusion often arises over the distinction between a shift in the demand curve versus movement along a demand curve. In the preceding example, as costs rise from $" to $', there is a movement along the demand curve resulting in a decrease in trip volumes from T" to T' as more people carpool, travel at off-peak hours, switch to alternative modes, or forgo trips altogether. The position of the demand curve itself may shift due to factors beyond the immediate purview of analysis. For example, the addition of a new transportation alternative may lessen the demand for trips on the system in question and thereby cause the demand curve to shift in. Alternatively, as discussed below, land use policies may affect the demand for trips by altering the overall pattern of mobility within an urban region. If there is a greater (lesser) demand for trips at all cost levels, then the demand curve has shifted out (in). If, on the other hand, there is an increase (decrease) in the demand for trips because of a change in cost, then there is a movement along the demand curve. One must be especially careful to understand this distinction when both effects are taking place simultaneously.

In viewing the curve in figure 6.1 as a *marginal benefit* curve, one begins with a given trip volume (such as T") and, with reference to the curve, then measures the corresponding marginal benefit from the vertical axis ($"). The assumption here is that not all individuals have the same intensity of demand for a trip. The benefits of a trip for any two individuals may well differ substantially in light of different circumstances. Now, imagine that all potential users of the system are arranged in declining order of how beneficial the trip would be to them. Then, for any given trip flow volume (such as T"), marginal benefit refers to the benefit accruing to the most recent or the next individual to enter the system. Thus, for the individual represented by the point T", the height of the curve at T" represents that particular individual's benefit. It is the benefit "on the margin" and hence is known as marginal benefit.

The *total benefit* (as opposed to marginal benefit) associated with a given trip flow volume is simply the aggregation of benefits to each of the individuals using the system. The total benefit at T' is therefore given by the area beneath the marginal benefit curve everywhere to the left of T', as discussed in detail in chapter 1. A similar interpretation holds for T". Thus, the shaded area between T' and T" represents the difference between the total benefit

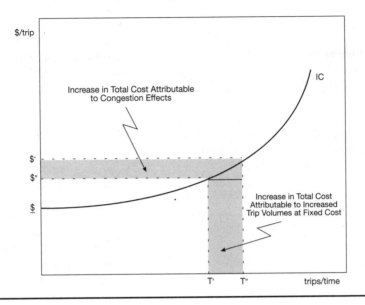

FIGURE 6.2
Individual cost

at T' and the total benefit at T". Notice that total benefit increases with the volume of trips, but at a decreasing rate. Notice too that area is measured in units that represent the product of dollars per trip and trips per unit time. Therefore, total benefit is measured in terms of dollars of benefit per unit time: ($/time) = ($/trip) * (trip/time).

Figure 6.2 depicts the *individual cost* (IC) for different trip volumes. Once demand approaches capacity, individual costs rise with trip volumes, due to congestion-induced delays. Relevant costs include out-of-pocket expenses associated with the trip (gasoline, automobile maintenance and depreciation, and so on) as well as the value of time. To simplify the analysis without loss of generality, we assume that all system users are identical with respect to costs. Notice that the IC curve is depicted as being quite flat at the outset, then begins to rise, first gradually and then more sharply. This pattern of rising costs represents the cumulative effects of *congestion*. When the trip volume is near zero, the individual cost, $, is congestion-free. The value of time spent on a typical trip is still included in this cost, but only the time it would take to get from origin to destination under free-flowing traffic conditions. At very low trip volumes, it is possible to add more drivers or users to the system without contributing to any measurable congestion effect. For example, on a freeway system one can accommodate a certain flow volume before cars begin interfering with one another, so the individual cost curve remains flat for some distance as one moves to the right on the graph. However, once the engineering capacity of the system is reached, additional users become a burden on other users as congestion effects set in. The cumulative effects of this congestion will tend to increase exponentially for reasons we discuss forthwith.

In figure 6.2 the relationship between total costs and the individual cost curve is a "rectangular" one. Total costs are easily calculated by multiplying individual costs by the number of individuals using the system. Consider, for example, the total cost at T'. At T' all users of the transportation system share identical costs of $' per trip. The total cost at T' is therefore given by the product of the two, $' * T', which is represented diagrammatically by the rectangle defined by $', T', and the origin. Now consider what happens as the trip volume increases from T' to T". At T" the total cost is represented by the larger rectangle, $" * T". There are two distinct elements contributing to the increase in total cost as trip volumes increase from T' to T". First, T" represents a higher volume of trips, so total costs would increase even if the individual cost remained fixed at T'. This fixed-price increase in total cost is represented by the vertical rectangle in figure 6.2. However, we know that the individual cost per trip will rise from $' to $" for all users as more traffic enters the system, due to congestion effects. The second component, increase in total costs, is therefore depicted by the horizontal rectangle in figure 6.2, which represents the higher individual costs borne by all system users as a result of increasing congestion.

Marginal Systemwide Costs

Recall from the discussion of figure 6.1 that marginal benefits are defined as the change in total benefits for small changes in T. Similarly, marginal costs for the system as a whole, marginal systemwide costs (MSC), are defined here as the change in total systemwide costs for small changes in T. As discussed in the preceding section, there are two components of change to total cost in this context; one is the increase in total cost attributable to more drivers experiencing a given cost, and the other is a congestion-induced increase in the individual costs experienced by all drivers. These two components summed together yield the marginal or extra cost of an additional trip and are represented by the MSC curve in figure 6.3. Total systemwide cost is simply the aggregation of all marginal systemwide costs. This relationship between total and marginal is perfectly analogous to the relationship between total and marginal benefits discussed earlier. To continue the analogy in visual terms, total systemwide costs at a trip volume such as T' in figure 6.3 are depicted by the area beneath the MSC curve to the left of T'.

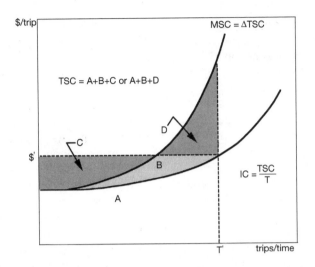

FIGURE 6.3
Marginal systemwide cost, individual cost, and total cost

The astute reader may have noticed that we just introduced a second way of calculating total costs. In figure 6.2, total costs at T' were represented by the rectangle defined by the individual cost (IC) curve at T'. In figure 6.3 the same total cost figure is represented by the entire area beneath the marginal cost (MSC) curve to the left of T'. These two distinct but equivalent views of total cost are reconciled in figure 6.3. With reference to the IC curve, total cost is represented by the combined areas A + B + C. An alternative way of representing that same total cost, this time with respect to the MSC curve, is by the combined areas A + B + D. It follows immediately that the areas C and D are equivalent. An important implication of this fact is that the IC and MSC curves are related to one another indirectly through their relationships to total cost. Specifically, the MSC represents the change in total systemwide costs at any trip volume (i.e., MSC = ΔTSC) whereas the IC curve represents the cost per individual (IC = TSC/T). The two curves coincide exactly, until congestion sets in. Up to this point, the cost associated with an additional trip is just the cost of that single trip viewed in isolation. However, once congestion arises each additional trip not only contributes its own individual cost to the systemwide total, it raises the cost for all of the other users of the transportation system. The MSC curve captures both effects; that is why it always lies above the IC curve after congestion sets in.

In the absence of any congestion effects, both cost curves would remain

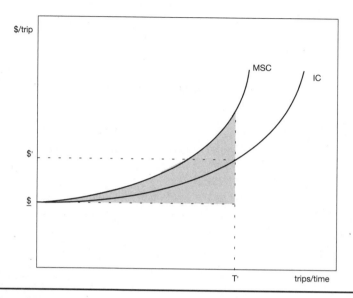

FIGURE 6.4
The cost of congestion

flat regardless of the number of trips. With this in mind, the total cost of congestion can now be depicted in either of two equivalent ways, as illustrated in figure 6.4. Without congestion effects, the total cost of trip volume T' would be represented by the lower rectangle, T'*$. But as we have seen, the true systemwide cost total (with reference to the IC curve) inclusive of congestion effects is given by the larger rectangle, T'*$'. Equivalently, the true systemwide cost total with congestion is given by the area beneath the MSC curve to the left of T'. Therefore the contribution of congestion to the total transportation cost can be represented equivalently by either the rectangle ($' − $) * T' or by the shaded triangle bounded by $ = $, T = T', and the MSC curve. Having identified the cost of congestion, the question remains, what can be done about it? We now turn to four alternative policy responses: do nothing, expand supply, restrict demand, and implement tolls.

Do Nothing

Figure 6.5 puts all the pieces together. The two trip volumes T' and T" now take on special meaning as the volume of trips at which the demand (MB) curve intersects the MSC and IC curves, respectively. For reasons that will soon become clear, we refer to T' and T" as the optimal solution and

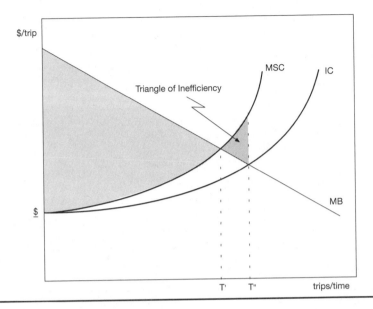

FIGURE 6.5
Do nothing

do-nothing equilibrium, respectively. First, consider what happens in the absence of any policy intervention. Each potential user, in assessing whether to enter the system, will determine whether the benefit he or she derives from a trip will exceed his or her individual cost, as given by the IC curve. So long as the MB curve lies above the IC curve, additional users will continue to enter the system. Recall from our discussion of figure 6.1 that we have arranged (conceptually) all potential users of the system in descending order of their marginal benefits. Beginning with the first entrant (T = 0), we see that marginal benefits are well above perceived costs, so the first user enters the system with pleasure. This condition continues until trip volumes reach T". Conversely, anywhere to the right of T", the individual costs of a trip outweigh the benefits on the margin so the trip volume will decline until it falls to T". By definition, an equilibrium position is one where there is no tendency to change. T" is a stable equilibrium because the trip volumes will always return to T" through the mechanism described above.

The preceding discussion establishes that T" is the equilibrium trip volume for this transportation system, and in the absence of policy intervention, T" will indeed be the volume of trips to which the system gravitates. The process by which this outcome arises is one of individuals making rational evaluations about whether their individual (marginal) benefits outweigh the costs they will incur. On the face of it, this would seem to be a reasonable solution. In a situation where all individuals make trips if and only if their individual benefits exceed their individual costs, surely the aggregation of these costs and benefits will be maximized. Unfortunately, things do not work out so neatly, and that can be attributed directly to congestion. Individuals in this system may be rational with respect to their own costs and benefits, but they fail to perceive (or tend to ignore) the costs they impose on others. Recall that as additional drivers enter the system, they not only contribute to their own costs, but they slow down average trip speeds for everyone else as well. The basic problem is that individual drivers perceive costs on the basis of the IC curve, whereas actual costs for the system as a whole are incurred on the basis of the higher MSC curve.

T' is the trip volume that maximizes benefits net of costs derived from the system. To see this, consider the accumulation of net benefits as trip volume grows from zero. The first driver, or user, contributes a net systemwide benefit measured by the vertical difference between the marginal benefit curve and the marginal systemwide cost (MSC) curve. The same is true for the second driver, but with reference to the height of the curves, "one step to the right" of T = O. As more drivers are added to the system, the corresponding marginal benefits net of costs are added to the total. As long as the marginal benefit curve lies above the marginal systemwide cost (MSC) curve, successive drivers, or users, continue to contribute positively to systemwide benefits net of costs. Notice that, because marginal benefits are gradually decreasing while marginal systemwide costs are steadily rising, the net contribution of additional drivers is positive but diminishes steadily as traffic volumes increase toward T'. Beyond T' the systemwide costs imposed by additional users would outweigh any additional benefits (i.e., MSC > MB); total systemwide benefits net of costs are maximized at T'. Based on the assumption that a transportation planner seeks to maximize net benefits from the existing transportation system, T' is referred to as the optimal solution.

Ironically, the preceding analysis shows that it makes sense to talk about optimum congestion levels. This may sound preposterous on the surface. Surely we cannot be advising planners to purposefully plan for and even advocate congestion, can we? After all, congestion is bad, so how could an optimal solution contain *any* congestion? The answer, of course, lies in the fact that there are both costs and benefits associated with additional trips, where congestion is one component of the cost. The relevant question is whether the benefits derived from additional trips outweigh those costs. The planner's solution identifies the volume of trips at which marginal systemwide costs just begin to exceed marginal benefits, so it is the trip volume at which systemwide benefits net of costs are maximized.

Two additional points emerge from this discussion. First, as we have just seen, systemwide benefits net of costs are maximized at the planner's solution, T'. Second, the system, if left to its own devices, will gravitate to the do-nothing equilibrium, T", where T" > T'. This tells us that lack of appropriate intervention will result in excessive trip volumes—hardly a surprise to those who experience severe traffic congestion on a routine basis. The source of the problem is that individuals make rational decisions about whether to take a trip or not with reference to their individual costs and benefits, whereas the optimal solution focuses instead on systemwide costs and benefits. Systemwide costs include congestion-induced delays for all users of the system, while individual costs do not; thus, the systemwide costs of additional trips are higher than those perceived by the individual.

The loss in economic welfare for the do-nothing equilibrium relative to the planner's solution is given by the *triangle of inefficiency*, as shown in figure 6.5. This is the same triangle of inefficiency that appears in the context of land use zoning, housing, or entitlements in other chapters of this book. Note that as trip volumes rise above T', the marginal cost of each additional trip exceeds the marginal benefit. As a consequence, total systemwide benefits will actually begin to fall as additional users enter the system beyond T'. The darkly shaded triangle represents the total decline in net benefits resulting from a traffic volume increase from T' to T". At the optimal solution, T', total benefits net of costs are given by the lightly shaded area in figure 6.5. At the do-nothing equilibrium, total net benefits are given by the lightly shaded area minus the darkly shaded triangle. The larger this triangle, the heavier the losses due to congestion-induced inefficiencies.

The fact that "do nothing" is suboptimal suggests that perhaps the planner ought to "do something." The next three sections consider alternative modes of intervention designed to eliminate the triangle of inefficiency and restore the transportation system to its maximum effectiveness.

Expand Supply

Congestion arises on a transportation system when usage exceeds the engineering capacity of the system and individual users begin to get in each other's way. One obvious way to cope is to build extra capacity. This is a fairly common solution, as evidenced by continued construction of transportation infrastructure around the country. Figure 6.6 shows the effect of expanding capacity to the point that demand is fully met without incurring any congestion costs. In figure 6.6, individual costs coincide with marginal systemwide costs (i.e., MSC = IC) for all trip volumes up to the equilibrium level. The MSC and IC curves do not diverge until T = T", so the triangle of

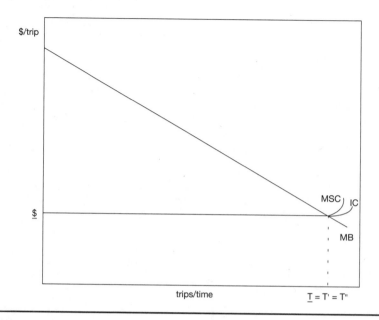

FIGURE 6.6
Expand supply

inefficiency has been eliminated. Moreover, the engineering capacity, the optimal solution, and the system equilibrium all coincide. That is, $T = T' = T''$.

Expanding capacity of the system does not affect the marginal benefit curve. Typically, a trip is not an end in and of itself. Instead, a trip or a commute is a means of getting from A to B. Accordingly, improvements in transportation infrastructure may reduce the cost of a trip but they do not directly affect one's reason for wanting to get from A to B in the first place. For example, the benefit of getting to work on time or of attending an important meeting are unrelated to the condition of the transportation infrastructure. However, the transportation system may have a significant bearing on the costs individuals face as they seek to obtain those benefits.

In figure 6.7 the MSC curves from before and after the system expansion are shown as MSC_0 and MSC_1, respectively. The net benefits for the planner's solution at T_0' are given by the lightly shaded area. After the system capacity is expanded, costs are lowered so benefits net of costs increase by the amount shown in the darker-shaded area. Notice that traffic volumes can increase substantially as a result of lowered costs attributable to the expanded capacity of the transportation system. To some this may seem like a self-defeating or futile exercise, since increased system capacity only seems to stimulate more demand. However, this view ignores two facts: First, travel

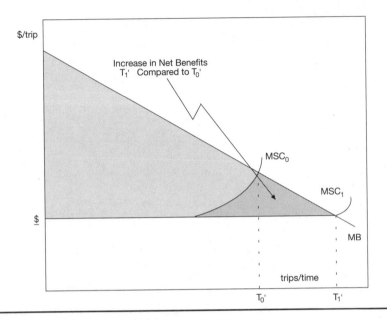

FIGURE 6.7
Net benefits from use of an expanded system

costs are lower for all users under the expanded network, and secondly, total net benefits from use of the system have been increased. The fact that
more people are using the system is a testament to its enhanced value. The
key question is whether the benefits from additional use warrant what are
potentially very large construction costs required to expand the network.

The additional net benefits shown in figure 6.7 are based on benefits and
costs from direct use of the system. Construction costs are not included. For
a proper cost–benefit evaluation of a proposal to expand infrastructure supply, the gain in net use benefits must be weighed against the cost of construction. One must be careful in this situation not to compare oranges and
apples. The net use benefits depicted in figure 6.7 occur on a daily, monthly,
or annual basis, depending upon the unit of time chosen for the horizontal
axis. In contrast, the construction cost represents a lump sum or one-time
expenditure. The proper way to compare the two is through standard
present-value investment analysis whereby the construction cost is treated
as an investment and the net use benefits are treated as returns on this investment. Further discussion of these long-run issues is presented below.

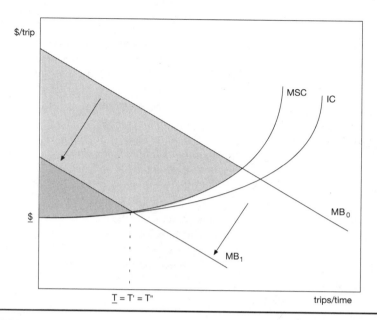

FIGURE 6.8
Restrict demand

Restrict Demand

Another way to deal with the excess of demand for trips relative to supply is to restrict demand. This may look particularly attractive in fully developed urban areas where both congestion levels and land prices (and hence the cost of new construction) are high. Planners have indeed intervened through a variety of mechanisms to restrict trip volumes. In Los Angeles, for example, the South Coast Air Quality Management District's Regulation XV mandated large firms within the region to implement carpooling strategies or face massive fines. Growth controls and other development restrictions are also commonly deployed by planners, often at the behest of the local citizenry, with a view to avoiding mounting traffic congestion.

Figure 6.8 shows two demand curves, MB_1 and MB_0, representing demand levels with and without growth controls, respectively. Growth controls seek to keep the demand curve to the left of (or below) what it would be if controls were not in place. This downward shift of the demand curve relative to the do-nothing solution indicates that there is less demand for trips at any price. As a result of restrictions on land use activities, there are fewer people wanting to travel to work or to shop and fewer destinations to attract these people. The spatial configuration of destinations relative to origins can also affect the overall demand for trips on a transportation system, as implied by jobs–housing balance principles of land use planning. Be careful at this point not to confuse two related effects. Restricting demand in this context refers specifically to a shift in the demand curve relative to where it would be without intervention. This is distinct from actions (such as parking fees, fuel taxes, or tolls) that might raise the cost curves, thereby prompting a movement to the left *along* the demand curve.

The demand restrictions in figure 6.8 are sufficiently strict that congestion has been eliminated and no triangle of inefficiency remains. As was the case with the expansion of supply in figure 6.6, this solution results in a perfect coincidence of the designed engineering capacity, the optimal solution, and the equilibrium level of trips (i.e., $T = T' = T''$). However, in this case the traffic volume has decreased rather than increased, and so too have net benefits. Without growth controls, the flow of net benefits from the transportation system is represented by the two shaded areas in figure 6.8 combined. With growth controls, the net benefits are represented by the dark triangular area alone. Growth controls in this example eliminate congestion without incurring construction costs to expand the capacity of the system, but reduce benefits that might otherwise be derived from the system. The distributional implications of this reduction in benefits are discussed in a later section.

Implement Tolls

The two solutions just discussed, expand supply and restrict demand, emphasize quantity (trip flow volumes) in remedying the imbalance between supply and demand for trips. An alternative approach is to emphasize price or cost (dollars per trip). The latter approach views congestion as a problem of incorrect market signals being sent to individuals who use the system. As explained in previous sections, the cost borne by an individual entering the system is given by the individual cost curve, IC. However, as we have seen, IC systematically underestimates individuals' marginal contributions to total system costs, and so MSC > IC once congestion sets in. As illustrated in figure 6.9, the gap between individual costs (IC) and marginal systemwide costs (MSC) can be plugged by a toll applied to each trip. Once the toll is applied, all individual users of the system face a new, higher cost ($IC_1 = IC_0 + toll$). As before, the equilibrium level of trips is determined by the intersection of the marginal benefit (MB) and individual cost (IC) curves. If the toll is set correctly, the increase in individual costs will be just sufficient to cause the new equilibrium to coincide with the planner's optimum, T'. Notice that this causes a leftward movement along the demand curve. If

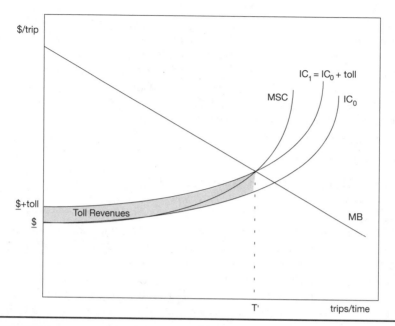

FIGURE 6.9
Implement tolls

the toll is set properly it can bring about a new equilibrium at T', as in figure 6.9. This is the solution most often favored by economists, so figure 6.9 (or some variant thereof) is the one you will find in most urban economics texts. The basic idea here is that a properly set tax on system users ensures that their individual decisions will reflect systemwide valuations of costs and benefits. This idea is not new; turn-of-the-century economist Alfred Pigou proposed taxes or subsidies to correct for externalities, so a toll of this sort is just one more example of a Pigovian tax.

At first glance it may appear that tolls eliminate the triangle of inefficiency, but in doing so reduce net benefits systemwide by the amount of revenue collected. In figure 6.9, toll revenues are represented by the shaded area between the old and new individual cost curves. The toll is an extra cost to individuals who use the system, so it would appear that toll revenues represent a decrease in net benefits. However, the revenues collected through tolls do not evaporate. Toll revenues are a financial resource that can be redistributed via any number of mechanisms. If $100 million is collected in tolls, that sum represents $100 million of potential benefit. The money may be spent on further improvements to the transportation system or, for that matter, any other public expenditure, including direct payments to individuals.

Seen from this perspective, it becomes clear that tolls may be a cost to the individuals who pay them, but they are also a benefit for those who stand to gain by their subsequent disbursement. From a broad cost–benefit perspective, therefore, toll revenues are both a cost and a benefit and so do not diminish net benefits. However, tolls are a real cost from the perspective of users of the system, and that is precisely why the individual cost curve in figure 6.9 shifts upward. The result is a new system equilibrium with fewer trips, as intended.

Comparing the Four Alternatives

Each of the four alternatives discussed above has its unique set of advantages and disadvantages, and each one is an appropriate policy solution for some set of circumstances. The obvious advantage of the do-nothing solution is that it is the easiest to implement. No construction, no growth management plan, and no tollbooths are required. The disadvantage is that the system must continue to bear the inefficiency and aggravation of excess congestion. Do nothing is more likely to be the preferred strategy when the triangle of inefficiency is small, in which case there is not much to be gained by implementing more proactive strategies.

Expanding supply is preferred where the cost of construction and land acquisition is low and where the demand curve is expected to shift out due to urban growth. The attractiveness of this option is also affected by the shape of the demand curve. In figures 6.6 and 6.7 it was shown that an increase in system capacity effectively reduces the marginal system cost associated with additional trips. As congestion costs are diminished, more people will make use of the system, and the shape of the demand curve tells us how responsive trip volumes are to changes in perceived trip costs. The critical question is whether the present value of increased net benefits year after year will outweigh the present value of construction, land acquisition, disruption, and other costs associated with increasing system capacity. Some will argue that jobs associated directly or indirectly with construction activity constitute another benefit. However, it is important to remember that it is virtually impossible not to create jobs with any multibillion-dollar expenditure. The question then becomes whether the number, type, and location of jobs associated with this particular project are preferable to those that might be created through some alternative economic activity undertaken with those same funds, such as housing construction, research and development, or even income redistribution.

Demand restrictions, such as growth controls and other land use regulations, are perhaps the most complicated alternatives to assess from a cost-benefit perspective because of the complex relationship between land use and transportation planning. As noted earlier, transportation is a derived demand; it is not an end in and of itself, but rather a means of getting from A to B. Land use planning addresses the issue of where A and B ought to be, if indeed they should be permitted uses at all. Most economists would agree that, while the issue is by no means clear-cut, growth controls and other forms of land use restrictions generally tend to diminish aggregate welfare through lost economic opportunities. In terms of figure 6.8, one can see that the triangle of inefficiency is eliminated, but net benefits are reduced because access to the system has been restricted.

Tolls are appealing in principle because they address the discrepancy between systemwide costs and individual costs. However, there are a number of problems that must be considered when contemplating the implementation of tolls. First, tolls may be costly to implement, requiring personnel, equipment, and administrative and enforcement overhead. Second, the very act of collecting tolls may itself contribute to further congestion, although technological innovations may, in part, help to remedy this. Electronic scanners similar to those used by libraries or grocery stores could conceivably be set in place so that cars are automatically "read" as they pass through laser sensors, and billings generated automatically by computer. However, this technologically efficient solution raises the Orwellian specter of a large, centrally administered database packed with detailed information on the movements of individual citizens. Another problem concerns the perceived inequity of tolls—a flat toll would appear to impact more heavily upon the poor. As noted earlier, however, it is possible in principle to use toll revenues as a tool for income redistribution.

It may be that the most serious problem faced by those who advocate tolls is that tolls are generally unpopular and misunderstood. Public discussion regarding tolls focuses almost exclusively on their revenue-generating capacity which, while important, tends to neglect their potential as a tool for bridging the gap between individual and systemwide costs. Moreover, tolls may symbolize to many an infringement on freedom of movement, a truly American ideal. Of course, this view overlooks the positive role that tolls can play in reducing the traffic congestion that has already choked off freedom of movement in most major urban settings. Also, the economist's favorable view of tolls is predicated upon an implicit assumption that toll revenues are used benignly to the benefit of the general public. However, there are political and institutional constraints on how toll revenues are allocated. In particular, they are often invested in mass transit projects that are difficult to justify on an economic basis. To the extent that toll revenues are in fact squandered on poor investments, one must consider them a strict loss; this, of course, will adversely affect one's assessment of tolls.

Additional Planning Considerations

The premise of this book is that planners cannot ignore the economic aspects of planning issues if they are to be effective in their jobs. It does not follow from this premise that they should confine themselves to economic rationale alone. Planners often operate within a complex decision-making environment of vaguely defined objectives and constraints and are held accountable by multiple constituencies. Long-range planning goals must be tempered by immediate concerns over political feasibility and distribution implications. It is imperative that any economic analysis be placed within the broader planning context. The graphs can be helpful in this regard.

Consider, for example, figure 6.10, which adapts the earlier graphs to present a long-run view. This can be a useful perspective from which to consider the political debate over how toll revenues ought to be allocated. In our discussion of figure 6.9, we stressed that this revenue is both a cost (as the revenue is raised) and a benefit (as it is spent) and therefore is a wash from a cost/benefit perspective. Moreover, we stressed that toll revenue need not be spent on transportation improvements. In figure 6.9, the motivation for setting a toll was not to raise revenue but rather to correct the discrepancy between individual costs (IC) and marginal systemwide costs (MSC). From this perspective the revenue is a kind of by-product of our pricing policy. The benefits derived from the manner in which toll revenues are spent are independent of the manner in which they were raised. The only expenditure that economists would rule out is a refund of the toll to everyone who paid it; obviously that would defeat the purpose of imposing the toll in the first place.

The fact that benefits from the expenditure of toll revenues are independent of their source is poorly understood by the lay public. What the public does perceive about tolls is that they tend to be regressive, in the sense that the cost of using a facility usually has no bearing on ability to pay. To many, tolls are justified only when they are used to pay for the roadway itself. Figure 6.10 illustrates a long-run situation in which these two views coincide neatly. The new addition in this figure is a horizontal long-run cost (LRC) curve representing the long-run costs of additional trips, including both variable and fixed costs. Variable costs are the costs incurred by drivers themselves, whereas fixed costs represent the regular maintenance, interest, and depreciation costs required to pay for the infrastructure. Notice that the lightly shaded rectangle labeled *total variable cost* in figure 6.10 corresponds precisely to the same total cost rectangle depicted in figure 6.2. As in figure 6.2, the total cost borne by individual drivers is simply given by the cost per individual driver (IC = $') multiplied by the volume of traffic (T = T').

By definition, long-run costs are the total of variable and fixed costs, there-

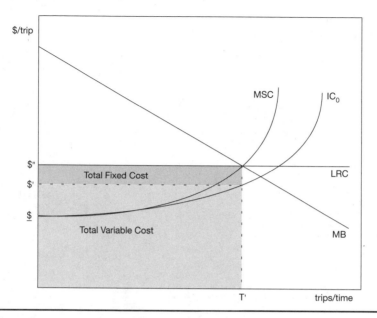

FIGURE 6.10
A long-run view

fore the smaller, darker-shaded rectangle in figure 6.10 must represent total fixed costs. Upon some reflection, you should recognize that total fixed costs in figure 6.10 are equal in value to the toll revenues depicted in figure 6.9. In both cases the dollar amount represented equals the difference between MSC and IC at T' multiplied by the volume of trips at T'. This means that the toll revenues from figure 6.9 are just sufficient to cover the fixed infrastructure costs in figure 6.10. Thus, although most economists would argue that there is no required linkage between toll revenues and infrastructure costs, in this situation there is a fortuitous connection between the two. This may be important from the perspective of planners concerned with the political feasibility of solutions proposed by economists. To the extent that the public is more willing to accept tolls if they see a direct connection between the tolls and infrastructure costs, then the planner may be in a position to advocate a solution that is both politically tractable and economically sensible. However, proponents of mass transit often support congestion tolls as a means of discouraging more automobile use and would therefore be unlikely to support the use of toll revenues to expand the capacity of automobile-based transportation systems.[1]

The astute reader may at this point be wondering why the long-run cost (LRC) curve is horizontal and how it happened to be placed so conveniently

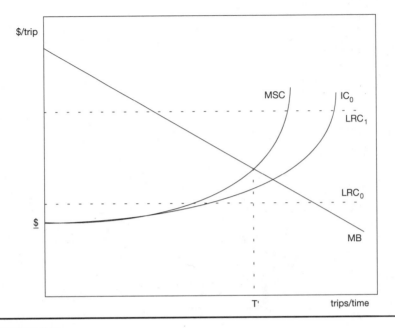

FIGURE 6.11
Alternative LRC curves

at the intersection of the MSC and MB curves. Clearly this is quite critical to the result we just obtained, because otherwise the fixed costs would not fit within the gap between the MSC and MB so precisely, nor would toll revenues just offset fixed costs. There are two parts to the answer. First, a horizontal LRC curve is based on an assumption of constant returns to scale over the long run. This means that long-run costs are assumed to be proportional to trip volumes. This assumption has been subject to some scrutiny and debate by economists,[2] but is probably not too far off the mark. Second, the placement of the LRC curve at the intersection of the MB and MSC curves is predicated upon the nature of a long-run equilibrium and the adjustments that occur to get there. In figure 6.11, two alternative LRC curves are drawn, one above and one below the intersection of MSC and MB. In the first case, that of LRC_0, the marginal benefit of a trip exceeds the long-run cost, so more infrastructure is warranted until the volume of trips has increased to the point that marginal benefits no longer exceed long-run costs. In the second case, just the reverse is true. Thus, we would expect some adjustment to occur whenever the LRC is not situated as it is in figure 6.10, so we must conclude that figure 6.10 does in fact depict the long-run equilibrium placement of the LRC curve relative to the MSC and MB curves.

The distributional implications of policies are another prominent concern among planners. Who gains and who loses may be of more crucial concern than whether aggregate benefits exceed aggregate costs. In the case of the do-nothing strategy depicted in figure 6.5, variable costs are borne equally by all users. The rich and poor alike will be affected by the same traffic conditions. Similarly, if the transportation infrastructure is expanded, as in figure 6.7, then all users will benefit more or less equally. The situation is more complicated on the revenue-raising side because it depends upon how the funds are raised. In practice, highway funds are often paid for by long-term debt (bonds) issued by the public sector, and that debt is paid off through general revenue appropriations. Transit projects are supported as well by sales tax revenues. Local roadways are maintained through revenues raised in large measure by property taxes. Certain excise taxes are often earmarked for state road spending. For example, state gasoline taxes, automobile registration fees, and sales and use taxes on vehicle purchases may be channeled to state highway expenditures or distributed to local governments for spending on local streets. Since the taxes fall on beneficiaries of highways, they are sometimes referred to as benefit taxes, although the link between the amount any one user pays and the benefit that user receives, or the cost that user imposes on the highway system, is tenuous.

The income tax is generally considered to be progressive because those with higher incomes are asked to pay a larger proportion of their income in taxes. This principle is mitigated somewhat in practice, however, when the tax code is modified to include deductions (loopholes) that often favor the wealthy. Sales taxes are more regressive in nature because the poor tend to spend a larger proportion of their net income on taxable commodities, depending upon how the tax code is written in each state. On the surface, property taxes would appear to be more equitable because the tax to be paid is typically proportional to the assessed value of the property. There are two problems here, however. First, there is no clear link between the value of a property and the income or wealth of the owner or tenant. Second, assessed values often bear no relation to property values. An infamous example is California's Proposition 13, which pegged assessed values to 1978 property values and allowed only modest increases subsequent to that unless the property was resold, in which case the assessed value would reflect the current market value of the property. The effect of this policy, intended or otherwise, has been to create a situation where two identical properties may have wildly different assessed values for tax purposes. Thus, the connection between assessed values and ability to pay is doubly tenuous. As we can see, the distributional implications of expanding transportation infrastructure therefore depend quite heavily upon how those revenues are collected. Similarly, the demand curve represents both willingness and ability to pay.

Project evaluations based on the market demand curve may therefore be skewed in favor of those with higher incomes. The best way to deal with this is to examine costs and benefits by income group.

The distributional implications of policies to restrict demand, as per figure 6.8, also depend upon what measures are employed. For example, the demand curve for the highway network may shift to the left if large-scale improvements are made to mass transit. Similarly, growth controls or other forms of land use restrictions may also shift the demand curve in figure 6.8 to the left of what it would otherwise be. The distributional consequences of these two actions are likely to be quite different, however. In the case of improvements to mass transit, one would have to consider the benefits accruing to new and established transit users as well as the costs—and distributional implications—of raising funds to build the transit system. The net gains or losses from this calculation would then have to be weighed against the loss in net aggregate benefits derived from use of the highway system. In the case of land use restrictions, benefits accrue primarily to existing property owners who enjoy increased wealth (capital gains) as their property increases in value. This will tend to work to the disadvantage of younger people and the poor who are not yet in a position to own property and therefore have no defense against increasing rents. In this case, restricting demand works to the double advantage of the wealthier classes who not only enjoy capital gains from increased property values, but also find that their infrastructure is less congested than it otherwise would be. (Note that the relevant comparison here is not "before and after" growth controls, it is "with and without" controls. This distinction is of crucial importance in a growing urban area.)

Notes

1. These and other useful points are made by G. Giuliano, "An Assessment of the Political Acceptability of Congestion Pricing," *Transportation* 19 (1992): 335–358.

2. See E. S. Mills and B. W. Hamilton, *Urban Economics*, 4th edition (Scott, Foresman & Co., Glenview, Illinois, 1989), for a review of this debate.

7

Rethinking
Fiscal Impacts

Introduction

Volumes have been written about fiscal impact methods. Despite this outpouring, a central point has been largely neglected by planners, one that should lie at the heart of any discussion of local government response to urban development. The missing link is the production relation between neighborhood characteristics, local government inputs, and level of service. Real estate development is in essence a transformation of urban space, including its built form and its socioeconomic and demographic composition. The cost of providing a given level of service—be it in education, public safety, mobility, or any other dimension of local government activity—is directly tied to the immediate urban setting. When development occurs, that setting is changed and so too is the cost of maintaining a given level of service, where the latter may be defined quite broadly. This, in essence, is what fiscal cost impacts[1] are all about.

There is a fundamental flaw in the approach that many planners take in evaluating fiscal impacts. Stated simply, current practice uses inputs as a proxy measure of outputs. For example, when the population of a given area

This chapter is adapted, with permission, from E. J. Heikkila and W. Davis, "Rethinking Fiscal Impacts," *Journal of Planning Education and Research* 16(3) (1997): 201–211.

changes, a common response is to measure the "impact" in terms of reduced per capita inputs of, for example, teachers or police personnel. Elaborate methodologies are then devised to calculate, in effect, how many more teachers or police would be required to maintain the original input ratio. It is the impact of urban development on *outputs,* not *inputs,* that is of fundamental concern. Moreover, inputs are often a poor proxy for outputs, so planners are called upon to rethink their traditional approach to fiscal impact analysis.

To do so we must focus more directly on the relationship between inputs and outputs—that relationship is termed a production function in the language of economics. Accordingly, this chapter reviews a wide range of services and considers in some detail: (i) the measurable inputs to the production function, (ii) the measurable outputs, and (iii) a theoretically sound and practically implementable method for modeling the production relationship linking inputs to outputs. This process is initiated in the next section with a review of the current state of the art in both the theory and the practical application of fiscal impact analysis. That review includes an overview of the fiscal impact literature, methods currently prescribed by that literature, and software and organizational practices used to implement those methods.

We then suggest a new approach to the definition of fiscal impacts, one that focuses on the production and cost relationships linking level of service, urban space, and local government inputs. We demonstrate that the current planning methodology can best be understood as a special case of our more general approach, and argue that the conditions that delineate this special case will typically fail to hold. This chapter also reviews a number of practical implementation issues stemming from the proposed method and discusses the emerging potential for geographic information systems to provide a more comprehensive modeling framework in which fiscal impacts can be analyzed and measured. A detailed empirical example is also reviewed.

The penultimate section of this chapter examines how the proposed method can be interpreted and implemented in the context of a range of local government services such as transportation, public safety, and education. Each service must be approached afresh, because the underlying production and cost relationships are quite unique from one service to the next. The concluding section reflects upon lessons learned, particularly with regard to the relationship between fiscal impacts and our ability to model adequately the context in which those impacts occur.

Current State of the Art

Burchell and Listokin's (1978) *Fiscal Impact Handbook* remains the most influential work to date for practitioners in the realm of fiscal impacts. It is an extensive guide for estimating costs and revenues associated with development, proposing six methods for estimating cost impacts: (i) per capita multiplier method, (ii) case study method, (iii) service standard method, (iv) comparable cities method, (v) proportional valuation method, and (vi) employment anticipation method. By and large, these methods satisfy their authors' criteria that fiscal impact models be "conceptually straightforward, clearly detailed and easy to implement and interpret." Three of these methods represent average costing approaches: The per capita multiplier method assumes that the best estimate of future costs is current per capita cost multiplied by the future population increment. The service standard method estimates future cost increases based on average per capita costs for comparably sized cities. The proportional valuation method is an average cost approach applied to nonresidential development. The three remaining techniques represent marginal cost strategies. The case study method relies on interviews with service providers and others to elicit information on the incremental service cost associated with new development. The comparable cities method examines the average expenditures of cities in varying size categories and infers from that an estimate of the marginal cost associated with urban growth. Finally, the employment anticipation method uses multivariate regression analysis to predict the change in municipal expenditures attributable to variations in commercial or industrial employment. Of these six methods, the per capita multiplier is the most straightforward and, not surprisingly, the most often used. Many municipalities rely on software programs and on related consulting services to help calculate impact estimates based on these methods. This chapter argues that the conventional impact measures derived in this fashion can be woefully inadequate.

In recent years the scholarly literature on fiscal impacts has shifted to a focus on fees.[2] Some argue that the rational nexus impact fee is the emerging mainstream approach to calculating impact fees. The widely cited case of *Nollan v. California Coastal Commission* established that all dedications or exactions imposed must relate to the development itself and provide some benefit for that development. In a sense, the literature has gone full circle. Burchell and Listokin (1978) began with a set of methods for measuring impacts. Subsequent publications examined guidelines and techniques for setting fees. The courts have now established that those fees must bear a rational relationship to the underlying impacts, so it is appropriate that we planners now reexamine our conceptual framework for defining what it is that we mean by fiscal impact.

Rethinking Fiscal Impacts

This section introduces a simple conceptual or theoretical framework that will serve to integrate our review of specific services in the subsequent section. The dual cost/production function approach to fiscal impact analysis discussed in this section is a useful example of the relevance of economic methods to planning issues. Noteworthy here is the explicit incorporation of neighborhood attributes into the production (and hence cost) relation linking inputs to outputs. As urban development occurs, those neighborhood attributes undergo change, and therefore so too does the production relation. Thus, it is the explicit incorporation of inputs (including neighborhood attributes) and outputs within an explicit production relationship that gives us the handle we need to define fiscal impacts in terms of the impact that development has on service-level outputs.

Figure 7.1a illustrates the principle underlying our basic approach to fiscal impact analysis. Here, the production relation between local government expenditures on inputs, x, and level of service, s, is represented by the production function $s = f(x,n)$ for some vector of neighborhood characteristics, n. The latter is a symbolic representation of the socioeconomic, physical, and demographic composition of urban space in a specific geographic domain referred to here as a neighborhood. The production function is represented twice in figure 7.1a, once each for two distinct sets of neighborhood attributes, n_0 and n_1, corresponding to an initial ($t = 0$) and subsequent ($t = 1$) configuration, respectively. Movement from n_0 to n_1 describes the change in neighborhood characteristics wrought by urban development.

The production function is defined as the maximum level of service s consistent with an expenditure level x by the local government in the specific neighborhood context described by n. The constraints on production levels may not be merely technological ones, as legal restrictions or other social phenomena are no less pertinent. The nature of the expenditures x on local government inputs will vary from one case to the next depending on how resources are actually configured. For this and other reasons it is convenient to represent these inputs by the dollar amount expended. Likewise, the level-of-service index s will be measured differently for each category of service, as we discuss extensively later on in this chapter.

The change ($\Delta n = n_1 - n_0$) in the vector of neighborhood characteristics is a symbolic representation of the transformation of urban space brought about by the real estate development project in question. In figure 7.1a we have depicted an adverse change in neighborhood characteristics, so that the initial production function $s_0 = f(x,n_0)$ corresponds to a higher level of service for any given level of expenditure x than does the subsequent production function $s_1 = f(x, n_1)$. A positive impact would be represented in

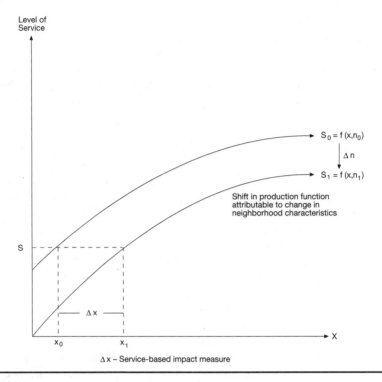

FIGURE 7.1a
Service-based impact measure: a production function view

the reverse direction. It is possible to envision changes to urban space that would cause the initial and subsequent production functions to intersect, producing an ambiguous direction of impact. The issue of which neighborhood attributes appropriately comprise the vector n depends directly upon the production function in question. For example, the age structure of the neighborhood's residents may have little or no bearing on water supply but may be of critical importance to education. These issues are explored below.

If the initial level of local government expenditure on inputs to the production function is x_0, then a direct and obvious measure of impact associated with the transformation Δn is its *physical impact*, defined simply as the change in output Δs resulting from the Δn holding expenditures constant. In terms of figure 7.1a, the physical impact is represented by the vertical distance between the two production functions at x_0. The advantage of using the physical impact in discussions about the effects of development is that it is quite straightforward and direct, and therefore easy to explain to the lay public. For example, the assertion that "average traffic speeds will slow by 5 mph if development occurs unless we undertake to improve street or public transit capacity" is essentially a statement of physical impact. A disadvantage is that the units of impact are tied to our measure of level of service. Traffic impacts may be measured in terms of average speed or some other mobility index, education impacts are based on student achievement scores, policing impacts are calculated in reference to crime rates, and so on. One is quickly confronted with the problem of comparing apples and oranges when relying on physical impacts.

Dollars provide a handy unifying device for measuring impacts. Accordingly, a *service-based impact* is defined here as the minimum cost of restoring service levels to what they were prior to the development in question. Thus, rather than holding x fixed and measuring impacts along the service dimension, this approach holds level of service s fixed and allows the requisite adjustment of local government inputs to serve as a proxy measure of impact. This contrasts with the conventional approach, which, in effect, seeks to hold input ratios rather than service levels constant. In terms of figure 7.1a, the service-based impact is represented by the horizontal distance between the two production functions at the initial service level s_0. It is important to note that the service-based impact measure is a benchmark reference to a production relationship. One need not advocate restoration of service levels in order to make use of this benchmark. As just noted, the most important distinction between the service-based impact measure and the more conventional simple multiplier method is the focus on the production function's outputs versus inputs, respectively. Conventional methods rely on a constant rate of expenditure on a per capita or per household basis— for example, if population grows by 5 percent, so too do expenditures. The change in expenditures required to maintain a constant per capita rate of inputs is the basis for conventional measures of impact. This corresponds to the service-based measure only if the production function exhibits constant returns to scale. Moreover, the conventional measure does not adequately allow for a richly specified model of production, because *there is no formal model production.* It is not possible, therefore, to use conventional methods to discern the differential impacts of individual neighborhood descriptors on service levels.

It is useful at this point to consider a distinction between outputs and effects. Standard treatment conceives of output as work done in the form of units of service or products produced, with emphasis on the viewpoint of the producer. On the other hand, effects are conceived in terms of changes to the consumers or recipients of the service. A public health service may be able to accomplish 200 measles inoculations per day; that's output. Those inoculations may reduce the rate of measles from one level to a lower one,

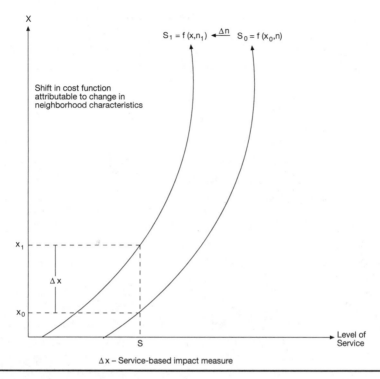

FIGURE 7.1b
Service-based impact measure: a cost function view

or they may not; that's effect. For our purposes the term outputs is used rather broadly to include effects, and the production function is likewise conceived in broad terms to include the nonproducer elements that may contribute to end user effects.

Our interpretation of impact is cost-based, a point that is made clearer by reference to figure 7.1b, which is figure 7.1a rotated counterclockwise 90 degrees and flipped horizontally, a procedure that transforms the production relation in figure 7.1a into the corresponding cost relation in figure 7.1b. This duality between cost and production is well understood in neoclassical microeconomics theory and is enormously useful both theoretically and empirically.[3] The cost function is defined as the minimum expenditure of resources required to attain a given level of service assuming the production technology defined by $f(\ )$. From this perspective, the urban development represented by Δn causes the cost function to shift upward, leading to the increase in cost described by our service-based measure of impact. The service-based impact is perhaps less intuitive than its physical counterpart, but it has the offsetting advantage that the impacts for all services are measured in dollars. While we may have difficulties comparing apples and oranges directly, it is convenient to compare the cost of oranges with the cost of apples.

Welfare-Based Impact

A problem with the service-based impact introduced in the previous section is that it uses restored service levels as the key benchmark, regardless of cost. In some cases this assumption is clearly unwarranted, because it may be prohibitively expensive to restore service levels. For example, it may be physically impossible to recover the same amount of open space per capita in an urban area of fixed size while accommodating population growth.[4] Does this mean that there is an unbounded or infinite impact associated with such growth? The answer is yes if we use a service-based impact using open space per capita as our measure of level of service. A more reasonable approach is to recognize that there is a trade-off between the level of service derived from public services and the level of consumption enjoyed from private goods. For this purpose it is appropriate to use some level of well-being rather than a level of service as our benchmark.

Following this principle, we define the *welfare-based impact* as the minimum cost of restoring welfare levels to what they were prior to the development in question. Welfare is taken here to represent some aggregate measure of societal well-being or quality of life. Thus, in the presence of an adverse change to urban space, the welfare-based impact tells us what dollar amount of compensation to existing residents would be required for them to be as well off as they were initially. Note that the welfare-based impact cannot be larger than its service-based counterpart. The reason is that one always has the option of allocating the entire amount of compensation[5] to a restoration of service. If the two measures differ it is because welfare levels can be restored more efficiently through some other mechanism. In other words, residents may prefer to have the dollars in their own pockets rather than at the disposal of local government service providers.

Comparing Alternative Impact Measures in Practice

One reason that the simple multiplier method has been widely used to date is that it is easy to implement. This raises questions about how practical it would be for practitioners to incorporate service-based or welfare-based impact measures in the course of their work. The short answer is that it takes more effort and more thoughtfulness to calculate these impacts, but that the extra effort is warranted. To measure empirically the service-based impact method, one must estimate the structure of the underlying production relationship. Additionally, the welfare-based impact method requires estimates of the contours of social indifference curves. These requirements are more onerous than those of the simple multiplier method, which focus exclusively on inputs to the production function rather than on outputs.

It is useful at this point to briefly review an empirical example. This example estimates several nested impact measures in increasing order of complexity, including: (i) a simple multiplier method, (ii) a service-based measure, and (iii) a welfare-based measure. The impact model underpinning this example was developed so that each measure could be derived as a special case of the succeeding measure, and was tested empirically using policing and crime data for Vancouver, Canada, for 1981 and 1986. To derive service-based impacts, regression analysis was used to estimate the following production function:

$$\ln s = \beta_0 + \beta_x * \ln x + \Sigma \beta_i * \ln n_i \tag{1}$$

where level-of-service s is measured by (the absence of) crime, x is expenditures on police, and n_i denotes a vector of neighborhood socioeconomic attributes. The observational unit for "neighborhoods" depends critically upon data availability. In this example, data were compiled at the neighborhood planning unit level as defined by the Vancouver Planning Department.

To calculate the welfare-based impact measure, a welfare function was also employed:

$$\ln w = \alpha * \ln s + \gamma * \ln g \tag{2}$$

where w measures welfare and g is a measure of private goods consumption. Equation 2 makes explicit the trade-off between private goods consumption and production of the local government service. Note that welfare w is not observed directly, but is inferred through community-level choices vis-à-vis s and g.

To simulate impacts we employ three distinct scenarios of neighborhood change: (i) a "pure" population change (i.e., with no change in socioeconomic characteristics), (ii) a gentrification scenario, and (iii) family suburbanization. Each scenario was described in terms of a suitable Δn_i where n_i is the same vector of neighborhood characteristics appearing in equation 1, above. The findings are summarized in table 7.1:

TABLE 7.1

Comparison of Estimated Impact Measures

Impact Measure	Pure Population Change	Gentrification	Family Suburbanization
Simple multiplier	$0	($50)	($150)
Service-based impact	$271	($202)	$2,294
Welfare-based impact	$265	($198)	$2,238
Global welfare	$347	($184)	$3,166

These figures are interpreted as the increases (decreases) in per capita income that would just offset the negative (positive) cost impact associated with the corresponding development scenarios. Thus, for example, an increase in per capita income of $2,238 would just offset the negative impacts on crime as measured by the welfare-based measure. The global welfare measure is a more generalized version of the welfare-based impact measure where trade-offs between neighborhoods are also permitted. Where impacts are estimated for two or more service sectors, the comparable figures from each sector would be added together to produce an aggregate estimate of impact.

Several aspects of these results warrant comment. First, the latter three measures bear a high degree of similarity to each other in magnitude and direction, but they are poorly correlated with the conventional simple impact measure. Second, the measures of impact differ significantly from one scenario of neighborhood change to the next, except in the case of the simple multiplier method, which was unable to differentiate adequately between those scenarios. Both findings seriously undermine the validity of the conventional multiplier method as a reliable measure of impact.

Strategies for Estimating Fiscal Impacts

As just noted, one approach to estimating service-based impacts is via traditional regression analysis, whereby production functions are estimated routinely. Output levels for cross-sectional or time-series data are regressed on local government inputs expenditures and on an array of neighborhood attributes. Data on neighborhood attributes are typically maintained by planning departments, but planners must rely on other departments to provide suitable measures of level of service. This can be a delicate process, depending upon interdepartmental relationships and the degree to which other departments are truly supportive of the project. When there is a genuine consensus on the need to estimate the impacts of a development project, the requisite data can usually be gathered without difficulty, because well-managed departments typically maintain reasonably relevant and reliable measures of service levels.

Once the requisite data are in place, running the regression is straightforward from a mechanistic perspective; however, one is unlikely to produce meaningful estimates of impact without the active involvement of someone who is proficient at the design and interpretation of regression equations. All of the usual challenges of regression analysis apply, including model misspecification, multicolinearity, and autocorrelated error structures. Reliable measures of fiscal impact will not be forthcoming from planning departments until and unless they are equipped to deal with these technical and interpretive aspects of regression, either themselves or via consultants. However, we may also expect that as more and more service- or welfare-based impacts are estimated, the procedures for doing so will become increasingly routinized, thereby increasing their overall accessibility and acceptability among planning practitioners.

The preceding discussion pertains to services that can be adequately modeled in a regression analysis framework. Infrastructure-based services in particular do not satisfy this criterion because their production models necessarily incorporate explicit spatial relationships such as "downhill from" that cannot be satisfactorily modeled using regression techniques. Thus, researchers need to develop GIS models of production that are able to capture the spatial dimension of infrastructure-based service delivery. In principle, this approach is compatible empirically and theoretically with other approaches to estimating the service- and welfare-based impact measures. Much more work is required before planning researchers can claim to have successfully developed GIS production models that are consistent with this approach.[6]

Impacts by Sector

Having set out a generic, output-oriented approach to fiscal impacts, we now consider how that general approach may be applied in the context of specific local government services. Table 7.2 summarizes some of the key points considered here for a range of services: (i) policing, (ii) fire protection, (iii) education, (iv) water supply, (v) storm and sanitation sewers, and (vi) transportation. What emerges from the ensuing discussion is a clear sense that the estimation strategy appropriate to one service may not be so for the next. The reason for this, of course, is that the nature of production varies significantly between services. This fact makes it all the more important that a consistent theoretical framework be applied across the board. The key elements that must be considered in each case, as summarized in table 7.2, are:

- appropriate measures for output-oriented level of service (corresponding to s)
- inputs to the production function as provided by local government (x)
- neighborhood characteristics that enter the production function as inputs (n)
- type of model appropriate to the production function in question (s = f [x,n])
- examples from the literature illustrating how such production functions may be applied

Only by linking these specific considerations to each service can we claim to have articulated a theoretically sound methodology that is practically and uniformly applicable throughout. What follows is a sector-by-sector review of how our approach to fiscal impacts can be applied in different settings.

POLICING

Police are a means to an end. The conventional focus on measuring police per capita emphasizes inputs rather than outputs. The reason communities spend money on policing is to enhance public safety. The absence of crime, or some other measure of public safety and security, is therefore the appropriate measure of the level of service provided through policing efforts. Cross-sectional regression analysis provides a suitable modeling framework for the production of public safety, where the effectiveness of expenditures on policing resources is influenced by intervening neighborhood attributes such as income levels, unemployment rates, age structure, and ethnicity. A detailed empirical example drawn from a case study for Vancouver, Canada, was reviewed in an earlier section.

FIRE PROTECTION AND EMERGENCY AID RESPONSE

Like police, local fire departments provide a measure of public safety. This may be best viewed in terms of risk analysis similar to that undertaken by insurance agencies. From this perspective, the allocation of expenditures on fire-fighting resources affects the potential for loss of life and property dam-

TABLE 7.2

Production Functions and Urban Services

Service	Level of Service Index (s)	Government Inputs (x)	Relevant Neighborhood Context (n)	Model Type s = f(x;n)	Examples of Helpful and/or Relevant Literature
Policing	Absence of crime	Police, equipment	Socioeconomic characteristics	Regression models	Craig and Heikkila (1989); Heikkila and Craig (1991)
Fire Protection	Absence of loss of life & property, NBFU grade of service	Firefighters, equipment, water supply	Built form, socio-economic characteristics	GIS simulation model of response time	Brueckner (1981); Chaiken, Ignall and Walker (1975); National Board of Fire Underwriters
Education	Standardized test scores	Teachers, schools, supplies	Socioeconomic characteristics	Regression models	Arnott and Rowse (1987); Dynarski, Schwab and Zampelli (1989)
Water Supply	Water pressure and quality	Water mains, pumping stations	Elevation, land use	GIS simulation models	Ormsbee and Lansey (1994); Clark and Stevie (1981)
Storm and Sanitation Sewers	Environmental quality	Sewer mains, treatment plants	Elevation, land use	GIS simulation models	Attanasio and Danicic (1994); Heikkila (1990)
Transportation	Accessibility, mobility	Roads, transit systems	Socioeconomic characteristics, land use	GIS simulation models	Arentze, Borgers, and Timmermans (1994); Shieh (1995); Moore and Gordon (1990)

age from fire, where that potential may be measured in actuarial terms. Intervening neighborhood attributes would likely include socioeconomic variables as well as aspects of the built form. For example, apartment blocks with wood-frame construction are a source of concern for most fire departments. The geographic placement of fire stations is crucial in determining response times that in turn are fundamental components of the risk equation. Ideally, the decision on how and where to expend additional resources is based on an approach designed to minimize some aggregate measure of risk or response time subject to constraints on variance in response time over all neighborhood units. Models of impact should subsume these same considerations, for it is only by doing so that we can determine what resources would be required to restore service or welfare levels to their initial levels.

A slight complication is introduced here by the joint nature of services delivered by most fire departments. A significant proportion of calls responded to by most major fire departments do not involve fire hazards but relate instead to medical emergencies that fire department personnel are well equipped to deal with. Of course when a unit is responding to a nonfire medical emergency, its capacity to respond to a fire call is diminished, so it is difficult to disentangle the joint production functions of public safety from fire and from nonfire medical emergencies. In both instances, there is likely much to be learned by fiscal impact modelers from risk analyses undertaken by insurance companies compelled to express levels of risk in explicit actuarial terms. The National Board of Fire Underwriters, for example, issues a *Standard Schedule for Grading* cities with respect to their fire defenses and physical conditions. The grade of service provided by a city's fire department is as good a measure of level of service as any, and the underlying methodology used by NBFU is an implicit model of service production.

The joint production of protection from fire hazards and nonfire medical emergency response is a specific example of a more general issue—that of cost accounting for overhead or indirect costs. This is more so in the case of public agencies where there is less of a tradition of cost accounting. A related problem is that of costs that are necessary to accomplish one service but which are almost never assigned to it. For example, the pressure and sustained flow requirements for domestic water supply are much less than those needed to satisfy fire-flow standards, yet the increment is rarely assigned to the fire protection function. Such cost accounting issues are not addressed directly by the modeling approach advocated here, but they do underline the central premise that we need to start modeling the fiscal functioning of services in detail.

EDUCATION

Training and the acquisition of knowledge are the fundamental purposes of education. Thus, standardized test or achievement scores and other results- or output-oriented indexes are the appropriate measures of level of service provided by the education process, whereas student–teacher ratios and other input-oriented indexes clearly are not. Accordingly, the level-of-service index that is used in any fiscal impact study should reflect the stated and measurable goals of the local education community. Research in education has clearly established what most parents know instinctively—that peer effects are fundamental to the process by which students learn. That is, the mix of children in a classroom establishes the framework for internal dialogue and sets the benchmark for levels of performance and, more generally, for attitudes toward the educational process at large. As the neighborhood changes, so too does the composition of its classrooms. These peer effects can profoundly impact levels of service, for better or worse, as measured by standardized test scores or other output-oriented measures of the education process.

Planners seeking to measure such impacts are well advised to begin with studies by education professionals that investigate these effects implicitly. In some jurisdictions, very rich databases are maintained for related purposes. For example, the California State Department of Education regularly publishes data on test scores for all school districts in the state and maintains statistics on the socioeconomic status of district households and other important district attributes in order to assess educational productivity for their own purposes. Dynarski, Schwab, and Zampelli (1989) provide an example of how local characteristics can be incorporated into empirical production models of education. Education offers promising potential for a systematic study of service- and/or welfare-based fiscal impacts. Notwithstanding the abundance of relevant data in this area, any proper fiscal impact analysis would undoubtedly encounter the usual tedium of empirical work, including matching of data records and definition of variables. One may expect controversy over appropriate measures of educational standards and performance, particularly in districts with large proportions of students for whom English is a second language, or where other ethnically or racially charged issues intermingle with educational ones. These emotive issues are likely to be particularly troublesome in education, where peer groups are so important, and in policing, where the relationship between crime, unemployment, race, and policing methods is the subject of highly politicized and emotional debate. To the extent that fiscal impact practitioners seek to incorporate such models in their analyses, they may also be obliged to address these attendant issues.

WATER SUPPLY

Water pressure and water quality are two fundamental dimensions of level of service for water supply. Water pressure depends primarily upon usage, the altitude of the water source relative to the destination, and the availability of pumping stations at strategic points along the water delivery grid. Just as numerous holes punctured in a garden hose can reduce the outflow at the delivery end of the hose, water pressure throughout an urban system may dissipate as urban development results in a proliferation of outlets. Water quality depends primarily upon available sources, where one must go further afield and incur greater expense to bring in additional water supplies at constant quality. As a result, the short-run average cost exhibits sharp increases at key breaking points where new capacity is added; these sharp increases are themselves interspersed by intervals of gradual decrease in average costs as the cost burden is borne by more housing units.

A longer-run view of the average cost function would delineate households in order of their arrival dates relative to each other, but not relative to the arbitrary breaking points that mark new investments and so would be equity-neutral in the sense articulated by Peiser (1988). Clark and Stevie (1981) outline a procedure for estimating these long-run average cost curves. Total cost is then given by the rectangle defined by the average cost curve at any point. The change in total cost as additional units are added defines the corresponding marginal cost curve. This latter curve corresponds most closely to the service-based impact measure because it is the change in expenditure required to maintain initial service levels for the established residents as new ones move in.

The preceding discussion applies to new infrastructure on the extensive margin—that is, as the urban area grows outward. A different situation applies on the intensive margin. As a city increases in density, it may bring about an accelerated obsolescence of the existing infrastructure. The physical life of water mains is typically a century or longer. Having to dig them up and replace them prematurely causes a loss in the residual value of those assets. In figure 7.2, time is depicted on the horizontal axis. Here, the swooping hump-backed curves give the present value of the remaining life of the infrastructure in the absence of redevelopment, where present value is as defined in chapter 1. As redevelopment occurs, the second curve (representing present value for the second life cycle of the infrastructure) is advanced forward in time, thereby truncating the first, resulting in lost-use value as shown in figure 7.2. If the new infrastructure is built to higher capacity than what was originally in place, then rising costs on the extensive margin must be added to those arising from premature obsolescence.

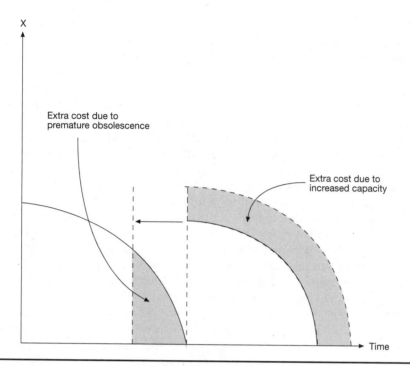

FIGURE 7.2
Increase in infrastructure costs as urban density rises

STORM AND SANITATION SEWERS

Sewer and water services are similar in that they both rely on an underground piping infrastructure to provide a conduit for flows. Moreover, the analysis above regarding infrastructure costs on the extensive and intensive margins of urban development applies to both sewer and water services. However, the fiscal impacts of sewer and water also differ in important respects. In the case of sewers, one must distinguish between storm sewers built as rainfall drainage systems and sanitation sewers built for the discharge of effluent materials. In both cases, level of service is directly related to the quality or cleanliness of water that is finally discharged or recirculated after all treatment and processing has occurred. In the case of storm sewers, the highest concentration of pollutants is found immediately after a heavy rainfall when the accumulation of lead and other toxics on the streets is swept clean by the storm.

Regression analysis is unsuitable for estimating the production relations for infrastructure-based services because it cannot capture the detailed geography that figures so prominently in determining what level of service can be provided to which locations at what cost. Geographic information systems (GIS) will be increasingly useful in allowing planners to model the effects of changing land uses on level of service provided by infrastructure-based systems. For example, GIS allows the planner to relate specific project proposals to changes in storm water runoff coefficients in the catchment area of a particular sewer main and to model the change in outflow (level of service) resulting from the redevelopment. This is perfectly analogous to the production function depicted in figure 7.1a because it relates local government expenditures on sewer infrastructure and neighborhood attributes to level of service. To complete the analogy, one would like to develop estimates of service-based impact measures using this GIS-based model of production. The definition of a service-based impact remains unchanged; it is the minimum cost required to restore service to its initial level. This calculation was accomplished in figures 7.1a and 7.1b by simply inverting the production function to find the dual-cost function, and then by noting the change in cost associated with a recovery of the initial service level. The analogous procedure in the context of a GIS model of production entails the use of expert systems or other decision support software to help evaluate what infrastructure improvements would be required to bring about a restoration of service levels.

Engineers do work with detailed simulation models of sewer and water systems that are appropriate for our proposed fiscal impact methodology. Such models must go a step beyond the common GIS "models" that are really nothing more than a graphical interface linked to a database of existing pipes and related inputs. A production-oriented model must link such inputs to some measure of output. Ormsbee and Lansey (1994) provide an extensive review of optimization techniques that have been developed for water supply pumping systems. These models are analogous to our cost function in figure 7.1b in that they provide estimates of the minimum cost associated with a given service standard, and they do so in a manner that explicitly incorporates the spatial or topological relationships inherent in any water supply system. Similar models are being developed for storm water systems, driven in part by compliance requirements of the National Pollutant Discharge Elimination System (NPDES) permit approval process overseen by the Environmental Protection Agency. Nonetheless, it is clear that there is a great deal of work yet to be done to integrate non-GIS network approaches with vector-based GIS systems.

TRANSPORTATION

No line service provided by local governments is more difficult to evaluate impacts for than transportation. Level of service for transportation is difficult to define and measure. One option is mobility measured in terms of average speeds. A related level of service dimension is congestion, often measured in terms of vehicle/capacity ratios. One problem with these measures is that they focus solely on traffic conditions and not on the length of the trips themselves. For example, if one travels twice as fast over roads that are half as congested but over distances that are twice as long, has level of service improved or not? A more generalized measure of service provided by transportation services is accessibility, typically measured as a weighted sum of destinations, where the weights are in inverse proportion to distance. Destinations are a function of land use, so changes in urban form impact directly on accessibility. Accessibility impacts can be measured using a GIS transportation model in which land uses and the transportation grid are linked through an explicit and recognizable geography.

An additional complication in estimating fiscal impacts for transportation services is found in the combined behavioral and spatial dimensions of the production function. The demand for transportation services is a derived demand. Level of service in transportation is a by-product of innumerable unrelated temporal–locational decisions made by individuals as they organize their daily activities. When urban form is impacted by real estate development the set of possible destinations and origins is altered, as are the attendant transportation logistics. These changes jointly conspire to register an impact on the level of service provided by the local transportation infrastructure. As with each of the other services we have considered, the service-based impact measure for transportation is defined as the minimum cost of restoring service to its initial level. To calculate such an impact measure necessitates a transportation model that can capture the full spatial and behavioral considerations inherent in any transportation planning exercise.

Conclusions

Figure 7.3 is a schematic summary of our definition of fiscal impact. The first line establishes the fact that neighborhood characteristics, n, and local government expenditures, x, act in concert through some mechanism, represented here by a black box, to produce some measure of output or community well-being, s. The representation in figure 7.3 is intended to be as generic as possible, permitting any number of compatible substitutions for n, x, s, or the black box. For example, in the case of policing services,

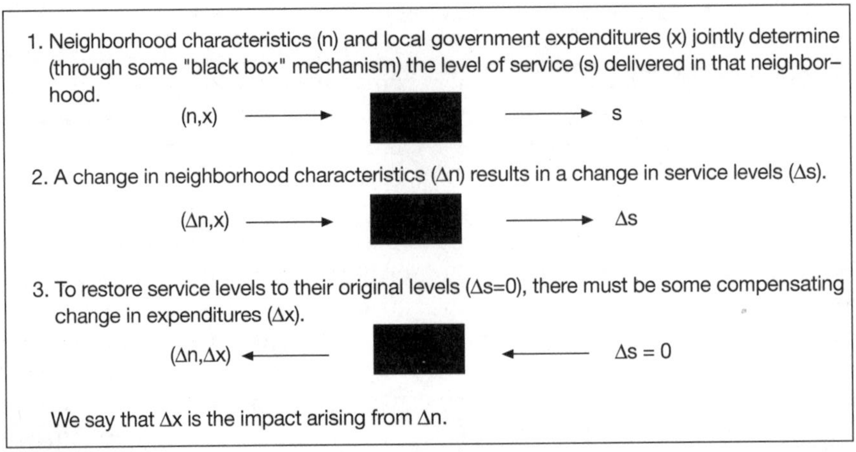

---

1. Neighborhood characteristics (n) and local government expenditures (x) jointly determine (through some "black box" mechanism) the level of service (s) delivered in that neighbor-hood.

$$(n,x) \longrightarrow \blacksquare \longrightarrow s$$

2. A change in neighborhood characteristics (Δn) results in a change in service levels (Δs).

$$(\Delta n, x) \longrightarrow \blacksquare \longrightarrow \Delta s$$

3. To restore service levels to their original levels ($\Delta s=0$), there must be some compensating change in expenditures (Δx).

$$(\Delta n, \Delta x) \longleftarrow \blacksquare \longleftarrow \Delta s = 0$$

We say that Δx is the impact arising from Δn.

FIGURE 7.3
Schematic representation of an impact model

the black box may be a proxy for a specific and detailed regression model that describes how the vector (n,x) is transformed into crime rates. However, in other cases we may be quite limited in our ability to define or measure s or to model the process by which it is produced. For example, quality of life is central to many planning issues regarding the impacts of neighborhood change. It is difficult to define and even more difficult to model explicitly. Nonetheless, it can be accommodated by the representation in figure 7.3, as can environmental quality, heritage value, economic development, and other elusive yet important concepts.

The second and third lines of figure 7.3 articulate our generic definition of impact in the context of this "black box" model of production. As urban form is modified through the development process (or by other means), this will have an impact, for better or worse, on our measure of well-being, Δs. Our measure of impact is the change in local government expenditures Δx on services (or on tax relief) that is just required to compensate for the development—that is, it is the change in expenditures required to restore the initial level of well-being so that $\Delta s=0$. Whether expenditures *actually* change or not has no bearing on this measure of impact. Conventional fiscal impact methods can also be viewed as a special case of this representation where $s = x/n$ so that inputs themselves become the measure of well-being. Thus, if population increases by 5 percent, so too must expenditures on inputs. Inputs are often a poor proxy for outputs, and that is what motivates the use of service- or welfare-based impacts that can delineate inputs from outputs explicitly.

The black box looms large in figure 7.3. It reminds us that our capacity to estimate impacts is limited by our ability or inability to model the process by which vital outputs are produced. One may envision an eventual convergence between fiscal impact analysis and urban modeling per se as the planning profession adopts a more comprehensive view about how impacts should be conceived. GIS models of urban areas ultimately hold great promise in this regard because they have the potential to combine several desirable features. First, they offer an explicit, geographically recognizable representation of real urban areas, and so are much better positioned than conventional urban economic models to provide a framework for evaluating concrete policy alternatives. Second, GIS software is becoming increasingly open to user-generated modifications and add-ons that can simulate service production models in considerable detail. The emerging generation of production simulation models can incorporate neighborhood context quite directly and with great specificity. Third, when supplemented by expert systems or other decision support software, GIS production models can be used to generate estimates of impact that are consistent theoretically with the output-based measures advocated here.

Notes

1. The term fiscal impacts generally applies to both the revenue and cost implications of development. This discussion focuses on costs.
2. Volume 54(1) of the *Journal of the American Planning Association*, published in 1988, has a collection of useful articles on development impact fees.
3. A good introduction to the concept of duality and its applications within the realm of economics is provided by H. Varian, *Microeconomic Analysis*, 3rd edition, W.W. Norton and Co. 1992.
4. This would be true, for example, if "open space per capita" were defined as the inverse of population density.
5. As with the service-based measure, "compensation" in this case refers to the *benchmark* value of the welfare-impact measure and does not necessarily imply that compensation is called for.
6. Two papers that address this issue in more detail are E.J. Heikkila, "Modeling Fiscal Impacts Using Expert GIS: Theory and Strategy," *Computers, Environment and Urban Systems* 14: 25-35 (1991) and E.J. Heikkila, "GIS is Dead; Long Live GIS!", *Journal of the American Planning Association* 64(3): 350-360 (1998).

8

Understanding Cost–Benefit Analysis

Introduction

Cost–benefit analysis (CBA) is a valuation method for projects. A *project*, for our purposes, is any undertaking that alters the world around us in significant ways. Concrete examples typical of traditional cost-benefit analysis include the construction of roads or dams. Likewise, albeit less concretely, projects may consist of regulatory or legislative initiatives (for example, zoning regulations or restricted access zones for vehicles) that effect changes to our environment indirectly by influencing or by regulating the behavior of individuals or groups who interact with that environment. There are four essential steps to a cost-benefit analysis: (i) define the project in question, (ii) determine who (or what) has standing, (iii) catalog the changes to the world around us wrought by that project, and (iv) assess the value associated with those changes. While these steps are straightforward in principle, they are often messy in practice.

For example, with respect to (i) above, it sometimes may be problematic to define where a project begins and ends, particularly for ongoing regulatory endeavors. The issue of standing in (ii) defines the scope of concern for the analysis. While in principle "everybody counts," pragmatic or other considerations may often cause analysts to limit the scope of their inquiry. Regarding (iii), it can be very difficult to assess exactly how the world will differ as a result of the project in question. This is especially true wherever human behavior plays a large role in shaping project outcomes. Most contentious of all are questions regarding whose values are to be used in step (iv) above. As we shall see in this chapter, cost–benefit analysis differs from other project valuation methods in some or all of these categories. In fact, we shall see that cost-effectiveness, profitability, environmental impact, and fiscal impact analyses can all be viewed as special cases of CBA.

A central feature of cost–benefit analysis is its special way of valuing costs and benefits. Specifically, costs are measured in terms of forgone opportunities while benefits are measured in terms of opportunities that one would be willing to forgo. Either way, the notion of *opportunity cost* is intrinsic to the valuation of project impacts in CBA, and the concept of opportunity cost is itself firmly rooted in the same principles of marginal analysis that are a recurring theme throughout this book. A closely related concept is that of the *shadow price* of a resource. Accordingly, this chapter provides a comprehensive overview of CBA, but with emphasis firmly placed on the concept of shadow price and its relationship to the marginal analysis of forgone opportunities.

Project Scope and Issues of Standing

Imagine for the moment that we are able to describe the world around us in a very detailed way by means of an exhaustive catalog of all of its attributes, both before and after the project in question. The list of attributes may include inventories of natural resources or finished goods, distributions of incomes or of consumption levels among representative groups, and any other aspects of our natural or socioeconomic environment that are of legitimate concern. Then, from this perspective, the physical impact of a project may be defined as the net change in such attributes brought about by the specific actions comprising that project, as indicated in table 8.1.

Note that the impacts of a project are based on a comparison of conditions "with" the project to those "without" the project, rather than "before" and "after" the project. The reason for this is illustrated in figure 8.1, which shows a trend line for some attribute x (for example, acres of land devoted to office space) over time. In this example, we see that the rate of growth over time increases once the project is undertaken. If we use the time periods t_0 and t_1 as the basis for comparing "before" and "after," respectively, we see that the before–after comparison would credit the project with too much impact. The true impact at time t_1 is denoted by A in figure 8.1, which is the increase (or decrease) at time t_1 in x attributable to the project alone, net of any increase that would have occurred in any event. In contrast, the

TABLE 8.1

The Physical Impacts of a Project

Attribute	Without Project	With Project	Net Project Impact
x	x_0	x_1	$\Delta x = x_1 - x_0$
y	y_0	y_1	$\Delta y = y_1 - y_0$
...	...	...	...
z	z_0	z_1	$\Delta z = z_1 - z_0$

example:

x—acres of land devoted to office buildings
y—acres of land devoted to open space
z—acres of land devoted to single-family residences

before–after comparison in figure 8.1 would yield an impact estimate of A + B, thereby overstating the project's true impact.

Suppose, for example, that a planning analyst was asked to examine the impact of zoning regulations enacted five years earlier on property values in a certain district. She would be wrong to make a simple before-and-after comparison. Property values would surely have changed over those five years in any event. The real question is, How much of that change in property values is attributable to the zoning regulations? Clearly, such questions are intrinsic to any project-valuation method, and they require a certain degree of conjecturing on the part of the analyst regarding how the world might have evolved under different conditions. This *counterfactual hypothesis* method is often used in the social sciences where it is not possible to set up controlled experiments. For example, urban historians may debate about the impact of the automobile on urban form in North America. In doing so, they are obliged to conjecture about how urban development might have proceeded had the automobile not been so widely available. The validity of one's conclusions in such cases depends critically upon one's understanding of the underlying processes that shape outcomes in either event.

Figure 8.2 illustrates the same point from a different perspective. On the right-hand side, imagine all possible alternative futures. One of these is the future (either observed or conjectured) that corresponds to the project being implemented. Another corresponds to the future (observed or conjectured) that would arise if the project were not implemented at all. The difference between these two is the impact attributable to that project. Clearly, some degree of conjecture is involved, because we cannot observe the world "with" the project and "without" the project simultaneously, so

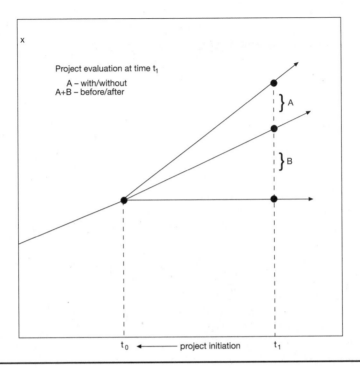

FIGURE 8.1
"Before/after" vs. "with/without"

at least one of these alternatives must be based on counterfactual speculation. The danger, of course, is that there may be a thin line between speculation and fantasy, and we are not likely to have much confidence in a cost-benefit analysis rooted in the latter. The challenge therefore is to establish a credible basis for whatever speculation is required about possible alternative outcomes. Three ways to accomplish this are: (i) to make use of control groups, (ii) to conduct careful statistical analyses, and (iii) to rely on formal models of physical or social processes. We shall briefly discuss each of these methods in turn.

A common method for making with–without comparisons is to make use of "control groups." For example, suppose that our planning analyst is undertaking a cost-benefit analysis of a proposed community policing program in her municipality. One of the first steps is to identify the likely impact on crime rates for that municipality. Ideally, we would want to compare pairs of municipalities that are identical in all respects other than their policing methods. "Controlling" for other factors in this way gives us more confidence that any observable differences in crime rates are attributable to observed

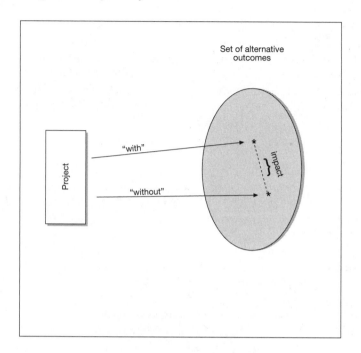

FIGURE 8.2
Discerning the impact of a project

differences in policing methods. Similarly, in an historical context, we might try to gauge the impact of a communist versus a capitalist system on the socioeconomic development of a nation by comparing countries that are largely similar in ways other than their form of government: East versus West Germany (prior to their reunification), or North versus South Korea. Likewise, the reason that human twins are in such demand for controlled experiments regarding human behavior is that identical twins control for biological differences between individuals to the greatest extent possible. And, returning to the example of the impact of zoning on property values, the best basis for assessing a with-without comparison would be to examine property values in two or more municipalities that are similar in all important regards, except with respect to their zoning regulations.

Unfortunately, it is often difficult or impossible to find perfect pairs for purposes of comparisons. Cities, for example, are extraordinarily complex phenomena, and they differ from one another on multiple dimensions. Two cities may be of the same size, but they may differ in terms of ethnic composition, industrial structure, real estate values, proximity to other important urban centers, tax policies, historical development, topography, and numerous other factors that may or may not have a bearing on the impact of a project. Multivariate statistical techniques such as regression analysis can be useful tools for accounting for the contributions of several factors simultaneously, and can help to identify the partial impact associated with one factor by controlling for the simultaneous impact of other factors.[1] The general form of a multiple regression equation is:

$$y = \beta_0 + \beta_1 * x_1 + \beta_2 * x_2 + \bullet \bullet \bullet + \beta_1 * x_1 + \varepsilon$$

where y is a variable whose behavior we wish to explain in terms of an array of explanatory factors, x_1 through x_k, and where ε represents that portion of y whose behavior is left unexplained by the model.[2] So, for example, y may represent the average number of patients per week visiting neighborhood health clinics, which the analyst seeks to explain in terms of various attributes describing the clinics themselves or the catchment areas they serve. In this context, β_i is interpreted as the change in y attributable to a change in the corresponding x_i after controlling for each of the other explanatory variables, x_1 through x_k.

The use of formal models is yet another way we can make with–without comparisons in order to assess the likely impacts of a project. Figure 8.3, which elaborates further on the concept illustrated in figure 8.2, depicts the role of models in this regard by making explicit the processes by which project (or nonproject) outcomes are determined. Typically these processes are represented by models that constitute our formal understanding of the underlying processes or mechanisms that link project implementation to project outcomes. Multivariate statistical models as discussed above are one type of model. Other models may include economic models of market behavior, engineering models of traffic flows, or any other formal representation of relevant processes. Such models need not be in mathematical or computational form, but many modelers do have an affinity for the inherent logic, rigor, and formality of mathematical or of computer-based languages. Notice in figure 8.3 that these models must control for extraneous factors, as discussed above, if they are to give reliable assessments of project impacts.

With this discussion in mind, figure 8.4 provides an overview of the principal elements of cost–benefit analysis. The linkage between a project and its associated impacts as depicted in more detail in figures 8.1 through 8.3 is represented in abbreviated form at the top of figure 8.4. The first list of impacts shown there is a conceptual catalog of all the significant ways[3] in which the world changes as a result of the project in question. Below that, separated by a "standing filter," is a shorter list of those significant impacts that are acknowledged or recognized explicitly. This depiction underlines the importance of *standing* as the determinant of which impacts are actu-

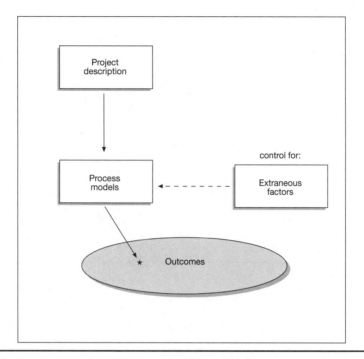

FIGURE 8.3
Modeling project impacts

ally included in a cost–benefit analysis. For example, a planning analyst working for a local government agency may decide to include only those impacts,
positive or negative, from a proposed redevelopment project that are likely
to affect people who live or work within that jurisdiction. Note that impacts
themselves do not have standing. Instead, standing is accorded only to those
individuals or collections of individuals[4] who are in some sense stakeholders and so are themselves materially or otherwise substantively affected by
the impacts of the project. Note that not all stakeholders have standing—
for example, the planning analyst in the preceding example may not accord
standing to individuals from outside the municipality. In principle all stakeholders should have standing in a cost–benefit analysis, but in practice some
may be excluded because:

- the analyst was unaware of their stake in the project outcomes;
- it is not practical to gather information on all parties;
- it is determined a priori by the analyst that such parties have relatively small stakes in the project outcomes; or

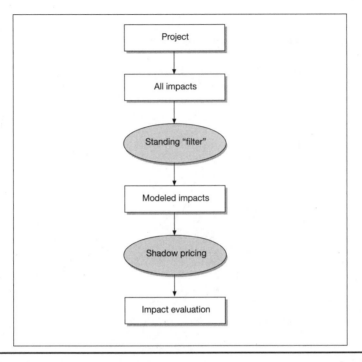

FIGURE 8.4
Overview of cost–benefit analysis

- the motivation for the study is tied to a specific subset of all stake-holders.

These or other considerations may be the reason that some stakeholders are not given standing in a CBA, but to the extent this happens it undermines the legitimacy of the study as a true cost–benefit analysis. Once the issue of standing has been settled it is possible, at least in principle, to establish a list of impacts that are recognized or acknowledged for the purposes of the analysis.

Opportunity Costs and Shadow Prices

The preceding section shows how the question of standing determines which project impacts are formally recognized within the purview of the cost–benefit analysis. The next step shown in figure 8.4 is to assign a shadow price, which is the CBA measure of cost or benefit, to each of these impacts and

TABLE 8.2

Using Shadow Prices to Evaluate Project Impacts

Impact Definition		Shadow Price		Impact Valuation	
Attribute	*Project Impact*	*Benefits*	*Costs*	*Benefits*	*Costs*
x	Δx	v_x	—	$v_x * \Delta x$	—
y	Δy	—	v_y	—	$v_y * \Delta y$
z	Δz	—	v_z	—	$v_z * \Delta z$
total				Σ benefits	Σ costs

to tally them up in order to produce an aggregate assessment of net benefit or cost for the project. In principle this is quite straightforward, as shown in table 8.2, which is itself an extension of table 8.1. Note the notation v (for valuation) to denote shadow price, and to delineate shadow price from market price p.

Table 8.3 provides a concrete illustration of this procedure using a simple example based on a project to provide and maintain wilderness hiking trails for public use. How does the world change as a result of this project? One change is the use of hiking trails at the rate of 10,000 hours of use per year, a benefit valued at $5 per hour for a total benefit of $50,000 per year. On the cost side, land use rights are dedicated to this purpose, and these rights are valued at $200 per acre per year, for a total of $20,000 per year. Finally, the trails must be maintained, and the shadow price of labor is $25 per hour in this example, or $25,000 per year. Based on these calculations, the project would appear to provide a net benefit of $5,000 per year.

It should be evident from this example that the mechanics for evaluating impacts are quite straightforward. Each impact has an associated shadow price. Applying that shadow price to the given impact generates an impact valuation. The sum of these valuations over all costs and benefits yields an estimate of the net benefit (or cost) derived from the project. If the costs and benefits extend over several time periods, then the discounting techniques discussed in chapter 1 are used to express these amounts in present-value terms. The key question, therefore, is where do shadow prices come from?

The concepts of shadow price and opportunity cost are intrinsically linked. Consider first the case of resources such as labor, machinery, or natural resources that are used as inputs to the project being evaluated. The shadow price of a resource measures the opportunity cost associated with its use, so one should ask, "How would this resource be used were it not allocated

TABLE 8.3

Project Valuation Using Shadow Prices: An Example

Impact Definition		Shadow Price		Impact Valuation	
Item	Project Impact	Benefits	Costs	Benefits	Costs
Use of hiking trails	10,000 hours per year	$5 per hour	—	$50,000 per year	—
Land use rights	100 acres dedicated to hiking trails	—	$200 per acre per year	—	$20,000 per year
Labor to maintain trails	1,000 hours per year	—	$25 per hour	—	$25,000 per year
Total				$50,000 per year	$45,000 per year

to this project, and what is the value associated with its use in that alternative setting?" This question is just another way of asking, "What is the opportunity cost of using the resource for this project?" Both ways of framing the question recognize that use of the resource for this project precludes its use in some other capacity. The implied loss is the opportunity cost that is reflected in its shadow price.

Consider, for example, the labor used to maintain hiking trails in the case described in table 8.3. To determine the shadow price of labor we must ask: (i) how that labor would be deployed were it not hired for this project, and (ii) what is the value associated with that alternative use. The answer may vary according to circumstance. To illustrate this point, consider the following different circumstances:

- worker would be employed elsewhere if not used for this project
- worker would be voluntarily unemployed
- worker would be involuntarily unemployed

In each case the relevant question is, "What is the value associated with this alternative activity?" In the first case, the wage rate is an obvious reference point. After all, if a rational employer is willing to pay a certain wage to hire this person, then the value of the employee to that employer must be at least that much. This is the willingness-to-pay principle that we shall have occasion to return to frequently. However, the wage rate is not the sole amount that a typical employer is willing to give up in order to hire an employee. Fringe benefits, payroll taxes, and other costs are often unavoidable. If an employer is willing to pay this amount, then we must presume that this employee is worth that much or more, so a lower bound for the shadow price is an amount equal to the wage plus whatever fringe benefits, taxes, and related expenses are incurred by the employer.

One might ask whether this method is biased toward the single employer who would be willing to pay. What about all the employers who would *not* be willing to pay this amount? The answer is that the highest bidder wins. In other words, even if there is only one employer out of a million who is willing to pay that amount, that is sufficient to establish it as the opportunity cost for this employee. As long as someone is willing to pay, the presumption is that their benefit is at least that amount, so that is the opportunity cost. There is an implicit philosophical stance in cost–benefit analysis that reflects the generally liberal perspective regarding market systems in general. That perspective holds that responsible adults are the best judges of what is good for them and what is valuable to them. Thus, if someone decides they are willing to pay a certain amount (inclusive of taxes, fringe benefits, and so on) in exchange for the services of this employee, so be it. That determines the shadow price for that employee.

What if the employee were to be voluntarily unemployed? That is, if the employee were not hired for this project, what if he decided not to take any employment at all, even though other employment opportunities were readily available? It is important to keep in mind that nonemployment is itself a kind of activity. Perhaps our friend has decided to stay at home to look after the children or to write a book. Perhaps he spends his days playing chess, hiking in the mountains, or all of the above. The real question, from a cost–benefit perspective, is, "What is the value associated with this alternative activity or set of activities?" An important clue here lies in the fact that this person's unemployment status is *voluntary*. From that we may conclude that he was willing to forgo net wages of a certain amount in order to pursue these alternative nonemployment activities. Those forgone wages therefore represent a lower-bound estimate of the value to this person of "buying back his own time." If he were to work on our project, he would lose the opportunity to pursue these other activities, so that is the opportunity cost (and hence the shadow price) of employment for that individual.

The final case we consider is that of involuntary unemployment. This person may have the same set of activities in unemployment as the case considered above: looking after the children, writing books, playing chess, hiking, and so forth. If this is so, shouldn't the opportunity cost of employment be the same for this individual as for the other? The answer is no, and the reason is that unemployment in this case is *involuntary*. From that we may conclude that this person would rather be earning a certain wage, and would gladly give up her current slate of nonemployment activities in order to acquire that wage. Therefore, the net wage that she would receive from employment in this case represents an upper-bound estimate of the value she places on her unemployed status. We see that the critical issue is not what she is doing, but what value she places on that alternative activity. That value is the opportunity cost (and hence the shadow price) associated with employment on our project. The shadow price of an unemployed resource is zero only if no benefit or value at all is derived from that unemployed status.

Notice that in none of these three cases is reference made to the actual payment that would be made to the employees if they were to be hired for this project. This is an important and somewhat surprising point: The shadow price of a resource is *not* based on the actual transaction cost. Instead, it is based on the opportunity cost associated with its use. Notice too that in each of these cases the basic method for calculating the shadow price is the same. First, decide what the "lost opportunity" is. Second, determine what the value of that lost opportunity would have been to whomever might have benefited from it. This is not a difficult algorithm to perform, and common sense should be your guide in implementing it. What can be difficult for some people is to ignore the temptation to use actual payments as a cost basis in lieu of opportunity costs. This underlines an important distinction between cost-benefit analysis and more accounting-oriented methods. The valuation of resources in terms of current use is based on an assessment of their highest and best *alternative* uses. The question that permeates this approach is, "What opportunities might be lost elsewhere as a result of this project?"

The same principle applies to nonhuman resources. Using the same example of a project to dedicate and maintain hiking trails for public use, how does one determine the shadow price of land use rights dedicated for this purpose? Again, the issue is how might those land use rights otherwise be deployed, and what is the net value of their use in that alternative? Would the land be used as a nature reserve? As wilderness? As residential land for vacation homes? It is not always easy to judge what the default alternative is, but in principle the cost-benefit analyst should seek to identify that alternative use that generates the highest benefit or greatest value, as measured by willingess to pay. The term "highest and best use" is often used in real estate to denote the proper method for valuing land. The difference here is that cost-benefit analysis does not assume that the greatest value is necessarily derived from the use that generates the largest *financial* return, although it does not preclude that judgment either. The correspondence between market prices and shadow prices is discussed in more detail below.

Thus far, we have discussed how to determine shadow prices for costs associated with the deployment of natural, human, or physical resources. These are all items that appear in the cost columns of tables 8.2 and 8.3. On the benefit side, the shadow price is typically measured in terms of willingness to pay. In fact, this is not so different from what we have already discussed. The concept of opportunity cost is relevant here as well. In our example, these public hiking trails are presumably of some value to those who set out on them, and that value is best expressed in terms of willingness to pay or willingness to forgo some other opportunity. This is just opportunity cost in reverse. In the case of land or labor resources used by the project, we asked what the value of the opportunity that must be forgone if we are to proceed with the project is. In the case of benefits, we are asking what the value of the opportunity that one would be willing to forgo in order to attain these benefits is. While one is a cost and one is a benefit, the principle by which their corresponding shadow prices are determined is essentially the same in either event: opportunity cost.

Cost–Benefit Analysis and Optimality

Shadow prices have another interpretation, one that reinforces and expands upon the interpretation that we have just reviewed. The concept of shadow pricing has its origins in the field of applied mathematics known as constrained optimization, as reviewed in chapter 1. Here, we establish the link to shadow pricing in the context of cost-benefit analysis.

Figure 8.5 depicts a typical constrained optimization setting. In this example, as in cost-benefit analysis, the objective is to allocate resources so as to maximize net benefits, which in turn are presumed to be some function of a resource input x. It is apparent from the graph that the allocation x^* is the one that yields the highest net benefit, so x^* is the desired level of x. This solution corresponds to a net benefit of $b^* = b(x^*)$. Unfortunately, as is all too often the case, resource constraints limit our ability to attain this objective. In our case, x_0 is the amount of the resource available to us, so we must choose an allocation of x that satisfies the constraint $x \leq x_0$, which in turn corresponds to the shaded area[5] to the left of the vertical constraint line ($x = x_0$). From the drawing it is apparent that the constrained optimum in this case is in fact $x = x_0$, which corresponds to a benefit level of $b_0 = b(x_0)$.

In this context the shadow price v_x of the resource x has a very simple yet powerful interpretation. It is the value of an extra unit of the resource x as measured by the increase in maximum possible benefit that such an increment would provide. And in terms of the graph in figure 8.5, we see that the shadow price corresponds in this case to the slope of the net benefit

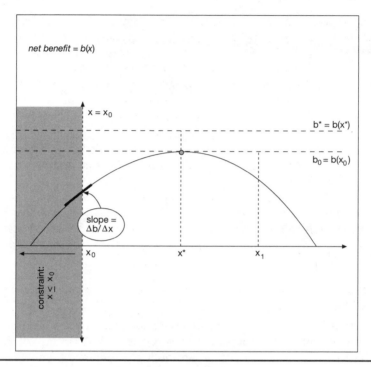

FIGURE 8.5
Graphical interpretation of a shadow price

curve at the point of the constraint. As a bit more x becomes available, we are able to improve net benefit by a certain amount, and that is what is measured by the shadow price of x.

Notice that shadow pricing is rooted in a highly objective-oriented perspective. A resource has no value in and of itself—it only has value by virtue of its ability (or lack of ability) to contribute to the standing objective, whatever that may be. In the case of cost–benefit analysis, the objective is to maximize net benefits, and that gives shadow prices their benefit-oriented interpretation. The shadow price method is a highly purposeful approach to valuation. The advantage of this approach is that the analysis is geared strongly toward the specified objectives, in this case maximization of net benefits. The disadvantage is that the approach can be ruthlessly efficient even in the pursuit of misspecified objectives, so the analyst is obliged to specify her objectives carefully. Further care is required to ensure that the functional relationship (in our case b[x]) between resource inputs and objective outcomes is properly specified.

We have seen that the shadow price of the resource x evaluated at x_0 is positive and corresponds to the slope of the net benefit curve at that point. What about elsewhere? For example, let us consider the shadow price of x evaluated for the constraint $x \leq x^*$. In graphical terms this corresponds to placing the vertical constraint line in figure 8.5 at x^* rather than at x_0. In this case the slope of the net benefit curve is zero, as it has just reached its peak and any further increase in x will actually bring about a decline in net benefits. The shadow price of x evaluated at x^* therefore is zero, so once again the shadow price equals the slope of the net benefit curve. A small increase in x adds nothing to net benefits.

Can the shadow price of a resource be negative? For example, what is the shadow price of x evaluated for the constraint $x \leq x_1$, which is to the right of x^* in "downhill territory" where the slope of the net benefit curve is negative? The answer is that the shadow price will be zero; it is not negative. The reason for this comes back to the interpretation of a shadow price in the context of a constrained optimization problem. The shadow price in our case tells us by how much the *maximum benefit* that we can attain would be increased by an additional unit of x. Remember, the operative constraint in this instance is that x is constrained to be less than or equal to x_1, so we are still free to choose $x = x^*$ and can still attain the level of net benefit b^*. The constraint does not compel us to use all of the resource potentially available to us. However, in terms of our desire to maximize net benefits, the surplus resource (i.e., any quantity of x lying above x^* in figure 8.5) has no value, so its shadow price is zero.

The concept of shadow price that one finds in constrained optimization problems is precisely the same one that is used to evaluate alternative resource allocations in a cost-benefit analysis. Recall our example of the shadow price of labor above. In that example we show that the shadow price depends upon the opportunity cost of labor, which may vary by individual circumstance (employed elsewhere or voluntarily unemployed versus involuntarily unemployed). Regardless of the circumstances, the opportunity cost principle by which the shadow price is derived is the same: Determine the value of that resource in its best alternative use. In figure 8.5 we see that the shadow price is positive at x_0 where more of the resource contributes positively toward our objective of maximizing net benefits, but the shadow price is zero at x^* and at x_1 where we already have all the x we need, so any additional quantities of x are superfluous to our objectives.

Market Failure and Cost–Benefit

In the course of the preceding discussion of shadow prices, one may have paused to question the distinction between shadow prices and market prices.

The short answer is that under perfect market conditions, market prices and shadow prices are the same thing—both measure the marginal benefit derived from one more bit of a good, service, or resource. By definition, markets are "perfect" whenever market prices fully and accurately reflect marginal benefits and costs, and likewise, market failure arises whenever this condition is not met. Thus, *the very use of cost-benefit analysis presumes that markets have failed.*

To appreciate this point, assume the contrary for a moment. That is, assume that markets are perfect so market prices fully and accurately reflect marginal benefits and costs. In this case the shadow prices that should be used for CBA purposes are simply those prices that appear in the market. If that is so, then the condition that benefits exceed costs is equivalent to the market condition that revenues exceed costs, or that positive profits are associated with the project. Now, we all know what happens in perfect markets where there is an opportunity to earn positive profits: Some enterprising entrepreneur will jump right on it. In other words, if it is worth doing, someone will figure that out and will do it. In the same vein, if no one is doing it, it is not worth doing. Thus, under perfect market conditions, cost-benefit analysis is completely redundant, as the market will of its own accord allocate resources in a manner that will wring the maximum benefits from them.

This situation does not hold, however, if we allow for the possibility that market prices do not fully and accurately reflect the marginal benefits and costs associated with resource allocations. In that case, even though markets may still operate with perfect efficiency, they do so with respect to market-based values that differ in some fundamental way from the shadow prices that are obtained from a cost-benefit analysis. This is why cost-benefit analysis is traditionally used for large-scale public works projects such as highways, dams, or airports. The standard competitive conditions do not hold in these instances: We do not find, for example, a host of dam suppliers bidding to provide services to consumers who all "shop around" for the best deal. Instead, these projects typically involve significant economies of scale leading to centralized or single-source provision of services in a highly regulated or public-sector environment. Textbook competitive conditions do not apply, so some other valuation method is needed to assess project benefits and costs.

As mentioned earlier, willingness to pay is a key measure of benefit in cost-benefit analysis. At issue here is to what extent willingness to pay may be constrained by ability to pay. This is the same "wealth effects" concern that arises in the context of the Coase Theorem, as discussed in chapter 9. For example, suppose that we are undertaking a cost-benefit analysis of a flood control project where the chief potential beneficiaries are low-income families living in housing of inferior quality. Their willingness to pay, in prin-

TABLE 8.4

Examples of Double Counting

Benefit	Value
Travel time savings from reduced congestion	x
Increased productivity due to faster deliveries, etc.	y
Faster average travel speeds	z
Direct employment effects (project construction)	a
Indirect employment (multiplier) effects	b
Increased consumer spending due to rising incomes	c

ciple if not in fact,[6] may be constrained by their low incomes. This is a common phenomenon, termed "wealth effect," where a person's marginal valuation of a benefit is colored by his or her wealth or lack thereof. In principle, what a cost-benefit analysis should strive for is a wealth-adjusted assessment of willingness to pay. In other words, how much would this person be willing to pay assuming that he or she had an average level of income or wealth? It is particularly important for the analyst to make this kind of adjustment in shadow prices in cases where the distribution of costs and benefits is highly differentiated by income class or other categories of ability to pay.

Common Mistakes in Cost–Benefit Applications

Sometimes it seems that cost-benefit analysis is misapplied more often than it is employed correctly. Common errors include incorrect shadow pricing, double counting, and confusion over whether work should be treated as a cost or benefit. Shadow pricing is a concept that we have already discussed in considerable detail; it lies at the heart of cost-benefit analysis. As we have seen, the notion of opportunity cost focuses on the value of resources based on how they would be otherwise deployed were the project not to proceed. The idea is not a complicated one, but it is nonetheless often overlooked, forgotten, or misapplied.

Double counting sometimes occurs when the analyst looks at the same costs or benefits from different perspectives and, unwittingly or otherwise, counts both the "heads" and "tails" side of the same coin (figuratively speaking, of course). For example, consider the roster of benefits posted for a hypothetical mass transit project in table 8.4.

The first three items in this example are all measuring the same benefit: the value of time saved. The first item, if done correctly, should already include productivity gains arising from deliveries and other work-related trips. The sequence of questions that leads to the valuation x is, first, how would the time saved be put to use and, second, what is the value of time thus spent? Put another way, if an employee finishes deliveries more quickly, what is the value of the marginal product associated with that time savings? One should be careful in assuming that the employee's wage rate is equal to the value of her marginal product in all cases, although that is in fact the neo-classical equilibrium condition for clearing the labor market. Most people do not sell their time to employers on an hour-by-hour basis. Instead, we frequently find long-term arrangements by which large blocks of time are "sold" to employers who then have authority, within reasonable bounds, to direct and oversee the activities of employees thus engaged. It is not clear whether the wage rate applying to that entire block of time accurately measures the value of the employee's marginal product.

And what about savings in nonwork travel time? The same principle applies. One first asks how that extra time would be put to use, and then asks what the value (using the willingness-to-pay principle) associated with that activity is. Here too the wage rate is likely not the best measure of marginal benefit. How much would the person in question be willing to pay to enjoy an extra hour each evening to pursue hobbies and interests, sit with the family, or simply watch television? Previous travel time studies have assessed the value of leisure activity thus obtained at roughly one-third the wage rate. The third item listed in table 8.4 is the benefit associated with higher travel speeds. Of course, this is quite redundant because it is higher travel speeds that initially gave rise to the time savings whose value has already been (double) counted. To include this item would lead to triple counting of a single benefit, unless one wanted to make the rather dubious argument that the sensation of moving more quickly is itself a substantive benefit.

The next three items in table 8.4 are benefits derived from project-related work. We often see reports in newspapers and other popular media that list employment creation as a benefit associated with a particular project. This raises an important question: In the context of cost–benefit analysis, is work a cost or a benefit? The short answer is that work is a cost, and this point requires careful attention when one is conducting or reviewing a cost-benefit analysis. Let us first examine why work is *not* counted as a benefit in CBA. The opportunity cost argument here is no different from that which applies to any other resource used to implement the project. Labor that is used on this project is necessarily withdrawn from some other activity—even if that alternative activity is staying at home unemployed. The relevant question, as always in CBA, is what the value associated with that lost opportunity is. Let us suppose, for the sake of argument, that the individuals in question place little or no value on their stay-at-home status. In that case, as we have already seen in the discussion of shadow prices, the opportunity cost is very low, so the shadow price of labor would be near zero. This cost must then be weighed against the benefits derived from the project, or more precisely, those marginal benefits associated with the marginal increase in labor. In the context of our example of a transit-related improvement, those benefits have already been captured through the value associated with time savings, as discussed above.

It should be apparent here that it is a serious double-counting error to include project-related wages as an added project benefit. If, as we have assumed, the people in question would otherwise be unemployed, that fact is already fully accounted for by the use of a near-zero shadow price in evaluating the opportunity cost associated with their participation on this project. If, on the other hand, the labor used on this project is being withdrawn from other productive or valued activities, then that fact could also be reflected through the proper choice of shadow prices. In an extreme case, where the value of unemployment is set to zero, and where the marginal product of labor is miniscule but positive, then it is just worthwhile (but barely so) to engage that labor for the purposes of the project. To count wages as an added benefit would seriously distort the cost–benefit assessment.

And what about indirect benefits arising from employment generation? We often read about the multiplier effect on aggregate income that arises when one person's wages translate into increased consumption that in turn counts as another person's wages, and so on ad infinitum. This Keynesian multiplier effect, named after the most famous economist from the first half of the twentieth century, John Maynard Keynes, is good macroeconomics but poor cost–benefit analysis. It is certainly true that there is a multiplier effect associated with an injection of funds into an economy. However, that would be true regardless of whether the funds were spent via the project in question or through any equivalent boost to aggregate demand. As before, the relevant question is how those funds would be deployed otherwise. We can only credit the project with the full multiplier effect if there would be no multiplier effect otherwise, which is unlikely.

A related issue in this regard is that of standing, a topic discussed earlier in this chapter in reference to which costs and benefits are included in the scope of the analysis. Popular discussions about the costs and benefits of large-scale public projects often adopt a relatively narrow perspective on standing, so that benefits that are shifted into one jurisdiction from another are counted accordingly as gains or losses. A more enlightened view seeks to measure the extent of benefits created net of costs, wherever they may occur. We must recognize, however, that the realities of local decision making manifest a certain imperative to restrict standing to the local constituency, thereby creating the conditions for a perpetual game of beggar-thy-neighbor, all under the guise of a pseudoscientific cost–benefit analysis. In the worst case, this leads to a situation where local jurisdictions "take turns" eliciting central government subsidies for local projects that are inefficient overall but which make sense from a local perspective if those subsidies are in place. In the aggregate, of course, everyone loses. This may well say more about the fallibilities of our collective decision processes than about the weaknesses of cost–benefit analysis.

The final item in table 8.4 tallies increased consumer expenditures resulting from rising incomes. This is a blatant case of triple counting. As we have explained, the incomes derived from project-related work are compensation for the benefits derived from the marginal product of labor. Those benefits have already been counted in the form of time savings from reduced congestion and faster trip speeds. Income double counts that benefit. To then take the portion of that income that would be spent on consumption (versus savings) and count it a third time would be a masterful work of duplicity— or triplicity!

Distinguishing Cost–Benefit from Other Project Valuation Methods

Cost–benefit analysis is one of several related methods that are used to evaluate projects. Many—such as cost-effectiveness studies, environmental impact reviews, profitability assessment, and traditional fiscal impact analysis—are best understood as special cases of cost–benefit analysis with certain restrictions applied to questions of standing, to the manner in which shadow prices are established, or to other aspects of the procedure. Table 8.5 summarizes these basic differences.

Cost-effectiveness compares different projects in terms of their ability to deliver a certain benchmark of services or other specified output at lower cost. It is a method for determining the most efficient means to a given end. Unlike cost–benefit analysis, cost-effectiveness does not in and of itself seek to establish whether the end is worthwhile. Likewise, because it relies on a benchmark for comparison purposes, cost-effectiveness is not suitable for choosing between projects that have different kinds of outputs or benefits.

As the name suggests, an environmental impact review (EIR) focuses on impacts that a project may have on the natural or social environment. As such, the issue of standing differs somewhat from a traditional cost–benefit analysis. In an EIR, standing is accorded primarily to those individuals who place value on the environment. One might also argue that EIRs extend standing to the flora and fauna of the environment itself, as in the case of endangered species. There is nothing to prevent one from assigning standing in a

TABLE 8.5

Other Project Evaluation Methods as Special Cases of Cost–Benefit Analysis

	Scope and Standing	*Shadow Prices*	*Other Considerations*
Cost-effectiveness	—	Market prices used in lieu of shadow prices	Benefit or output side constrained to some benchmark level
Environmental	Standing extended to natural domain	Valuation in terms of physical impacts, does not use shadow prices	—
Profitability analysis	Standing confined to the firm in question	Market prices used in lieu of shadow prices	—
Traditional fiscal impact analysis	Standing confined to jurisdiction in question	Market or accounting costs used in lieu of shadow prices	—

similar manner in cost-benefit analysis, but an EIR differs from CBA in that there is a presumed concern with environmental values up front. Another significant difference between an environmental impact review and a cost-benefit analysis is that the former does not make use of shadow prices at all, so there is no explicit mechanism for assessing the relative weight of different costs or benefits. In this regard an EIR is more like an exhaustive catalog of physical impacts, and it is left to the analyst to evaluate the importance of those impacts. As such, the procedures for conducting an EIR are quite compatible with the preliminary steps of a cost-benefit analysis.

Firms in the private sector typically assess projects on the basis of their profitability, which is defined as revenues net of costs evaluated at market prices. By definition, as noted earlier, market prices differ from shadow prices wherever there is market failure, and likewise, market prices and shadow prices coincide wherever markets are free from imperfections. Of course, market imperfections abound in the form of externalities (such as pollution or congestion), economies of scale, public goods, and even taxes (which are part of the consumer's perceived price but do not reflect marginal production costs). From the perspective of a private firm or corporation, it is still the set of market prices that determines profitability, so market imperfections are not of direct concern. From a public-sector perspective, however, it is appropriate to consider these shadow price adjustments, particularly for large-scale projects where the implications of miscalculation either way are potentially significant.

Fiscal impact analysis is discussed at length in chapter 7, so we will not go into detail here. However, it is useful to consider briefly how fiscal impact analysis as it is traditionally applied fits in the context of cost–benefit analysis. Fiscal impact in its traditional form is essentially a cash flow analysis from the perspective of the jurisdiction in question, as taxes and other governmental revenues derived from a project are weighed against the cost of delivering services to that same project. Tax rates, labor costs, and other market or quasi-market costs are used in lieu of shadow prices. Standing is restricted to the perspective of the jurisdiction itself as a corporate entity, and the objective is to determine how a project is likely to impact the cash flow of that agency.

It emerges from this discussion that cost–benefit analysis is a fairly robust general method for evaluating projects. By placing certain restrictions on standing, or by using market prices or cash flow indicators in lieu of shadow prices, one can in effect transform or reduce cost–benefit analysis into any one of several alternative standard project valuation methods. Recognition of this fact can help to put into perspective what those methods do *not* do. Depending upon who is undertaking a project evaluation, and depending upon the purpose and perspective of that evaluation, it may often be the case that a full cost–benefit analysis is not required, and that one of its special cases as enumerated above may suffice. However, whenever it is important to take a fairly broad-based perspective of a project, where standing is inclusively rather than exclusively assigned, and where the principle of opportunity cost as a measure of value is rigorously adhered to, cost–benefit analysis is the method of choice. This is particularly true for large-scale projects for which there is a significant public interest.

While we have shown that cost–benefit analysis encompasses many of its alternatives as special cases, CBA does have its limitations. From a technical perspective, CBA can be quite demanding in terms of data requirements. Moreover, there is always room for doubt about the alternative scenarios that are the basis for any opportunity cost calculations. One practical method for dealing with such problems was suggested by that ultimate pragmatist, Benjamin Franklin.[7] His suggested method for evaluating a project was to take a sheet of paper and list all the "pros" on one side and all the "cons" on the other. Then, instead of calculating shadow prices per se, he advocated crossing out items from either side of the list that are judged to be of equal weight. Or, if appropriate, an item from one side may "equal" two or more items from the other side. This process continues until all of the items from one side are eliminated, in which case the other side "wins." Franklin's method has much to offer. It helps us to remember that the point of CBA is not to develop perfect estimates about the costs or benefits associated with each individual impact, but instead, its goal is to develop a reasonably reliable assessment of whether, on balance, the benefits of a project outweigh the costs.

There may also be room for disagreement with cost–benefit analysis on moral or philosophical grounds. As we have seen, the principle of willingness to pay is the basis for assessing value in cost–benefit analysis. Even if we adjust for ability to pay, one may argue that willingness to pay does not ensure that moral standards—for example, religious or other ethical values—are given proper weight. Thus, CBA is best seen as a project evaluation tool that is broader-based than many traditional alternative methods, but is nonetheless limited in its ability to address the complex ethical dimensions intrinsic to any value-driven project assessment. No algorithm is a substitute for human judgment.

Notes

1. This book provides only the briefest explanation of regression analysis. For a more in-depth explanation the reader is referred to any textbook on multivariate statistics.

2. This is the same approach used with hedonic regression analysis as discussed in chapter 3; in that context the dependent variable y measures housing prices and the variables x_1 through x_k represent housing attributes such as floor space or quality of local schools that might reasonably be expected to explain variations in housing prices.

3. By referring only to significant impacts we are excluding impacts that matter to no one, and so in a sense, we are prejudging that the shadow price on all such excluded impacts is zero or near zero.

4. In some cases analysts may be tempted to extend standing to animals or to inanimate objects, but this is not standard practice. The issue is whether one feels that a homocentric perspective is justified or not. Such a perspective argues that natural resources or environmental assets ultimately derive value from our use or enjoyment of them. CBA can, in principle, accommodate either perspective.

5. Strictly speaking, the constraint $x \leq x_0$ corresponds to that portion of the x axis that cuts through the shaded area in the graph, and not to the shaded area itself. The shaded area denotes all *pairs* (b,x) such that $x \leq x_0$.

6. Remember that benefits in CBA are measured by willingness to pay in principle. No transaction need occur to validate this principle. The point is merely to establish a benchmark of worth, and willingness to pay provides that benchmark.

7. The Benjamin Franklin story is found in A. Boardman, D. Greenberg, A. Vining, and D. Weimer, *Cost–Benefit Analysis: Concepts and Practice* (Prentice-Hall, 1996).

9

The Economics of Entitlements

Introduction

Entitlements are at the core of any society's sense of social order. As the name suggests, an entitlement defines what the holder is permitted to have or to do—what they are *entitled* to. By inference, then, the lack of entitlements denotes an implicit limitation on what one might have or what one might do. Entitlements come in many forms, spanning the spectrum from "inalienable" human rights or constitutionally enshrined rights of free speech, for example, to informal customs or courtesies suggesting that an elderly person is entitled to first priority for an empty seat in a waiting room. Entitlements are often based in law. Social Security retirement benefits or Medicare health care benefits are examples of entitlements that stem from specific legislative acts. Indeed, the public conception of entitlements in recent years has been shaped in large measure by debates over the impact such payments may have on the federal deficit. Many if not most legislative battles or court rulings can be interpreted as efforts to define, interpret, or entrench entitlements rooted in law.

Many other entitlements, however, are the product of social customs, precedents, and culture and so are defined implicitly rather than explicitly. Entitlements can evolve over time, becoming further entrenched or losing force as the societal context changes. The case of smokers' versus nonsmokers' rights in North America offers a good example. Until quite recently, smokers were entitled to light up in restaurants, offices, airplanes, trains, and many other public settings. There was no legislation granting smokers these perogatives, but the entitlements were generally accepted, albeit informally. Over time these informal entitlements began to migrate to the side of non-smokers, many of whom became quite vocal in asserting their claims. "Non-smokers have rights, too" became a rallying cry, along with an assertion of the nonsmoker's "right to clean air." The position of nonsmokers was further entrenched by legislation that formalized many of the entitlements that had already been captured informally through the evolving social consensus.

Obligations may be viewed as a kind of *negative entitlement.* If one is entitled to receive Social Security benefits, one may also be obliged to pay into the Social Security fund. If an elderly person is entitled by custom to a chair, someone else may be obliged to relinquish theirs. In residential settings the obligation that one household has to keep noise levels within certain limits can also be interpreted as the entitlement of neighbors to enjoy peace and quiet. Thus, whether by law or by custom, obligations and entitlements can be viewed as two sides of the same coin. One person's entitlement is someone else's obligation. Later in this chapter we will see that the economic analyses of both entitlements and obligations are virtually identical, with the exception that one carries a "negative sign," mathematically or figuratively.

The notion of entitlements and obligations is central to planning, particularly in the realm of property rights. Master plans, zoning bylaws, land use regulations, due diligence, and public hearings are all planning-related outputs or activities that define or limit property-related entitlements. Developers, landlords, tenants, neighbors, and even passersby may hold some claim to the disposition of a parcel of land. Much of what we call planning entails clarification, interpretation, disentanglement, and oversight of the maze of overlapping or contradictory sets of entitlements and obligations arising from the ownership or use of land. Examples of entitlement-laden planning issues abound. Environmental protection or sustainable development issues are centered on the entitlements of future generations, of numerous contemporary constituencies, and even of natural species (as distinct from the rights of humans to enjoy those species). Likewise, efforts to preserve the "quality of life" in a neighborhood are typically based on claims by long-standing residents that they are entitled to a certain set of day-to-day experiences that are in accord with those to which they have grown accustomed. Although the delineation of these and other entitlements can be quite problematic or even muddled, the battles fought over them are no less vehement because of it.

From the economist's perspective, entitlements are a form of wealth. Small wonder, then, that they are the focus of such contention! *Wealth* in economic terms is a measure of one's capacity to generate or command a stream of income, consumption, or enjoyment. This concept is closely tied to the discussion about stocks and flows in chapter 3, where a unit of housing stock is viewed as an asset that generates a flow of accommodation services. One's wealth portfolio may be composed of many diverse assets. Financial assets include stocks, government bonds, bank accounts, hard currency, and tradeable securities. Capital assets include real estate, factories, machinery, infrastructure, and equipment. Among human assets are intelligence, charm, and good looks. Environmental assets include clean air, mountain vistas, biodiversity, and rain forests. Valued societal assets are social stability, equity, and peace. What each of these assets has in common is the potentiality to produce a stream of income, consumption, enjoyment, or some other form of benefit for those who have a claim on the corresponding assets. As yet another kind of asset, entitlements share this feature, so they too belong in this diverse portfolio of wealth.

This chapter explores from an economics perspective the role that entitlements play in planning. From this view, planning concerns the allocation of wealth, and we pay particular attention to the potential for markets to assist in this process. We begin with a central proposition, the Coase Theorem, that highlights the importance of *transactions costs* and *wealth effects* in determining how, why, to whom, and in what sense the initial allocation of entitlements can be important. The Coase Theorem is useful, therefore, in helping us to better understand how planning, which as we have seen concerns itself in large measure with the allocation of entitlements of one form or the other, is important from an economics perspective. We then turn to a discussion of the two fundamental theorems of welfare economics and show how the Coase Theorem can be viewed as a kind of special case or reinterpretation of these fundamental economic theorems in the context of entitlements. These considerations open the way for a careful treatment of the potential role for markets in assisting planners, and for planners as creators of new markets. In this context we conclude that the emerging nexus between markets and planning is likely to be one of the more significant developments in planning over the next decades.

The Coase Theorem

Ronald H. Coase is a Nobel prize–winning economist whose most influential works examine the role of transactions costs in shaping economic behavior. His work on "The Nature of the Firm" (1937) helped pave the way for the New Institutional Economics that we shall discuss in chapter 10. Another article of major significance, "The Problem of Social Cost" (1960), introduced what has come to be known as the Coase Theorem, which is the focus of this section. More recently, Coase's ideas have been applied by William Fischel (1979) to land use regulation. The significance of the Coase Theorem lies in its clarification of the relationship between an *initial* allocation of entitlements and the *final* allocation of entitlements, as mediated by transactions costs and wealth effects (to be defined below).

Figure 9.1, adapted from Fischel (1979) and from Turvey (1963), helps to illustrate the ideas involved. We will use a simple example based on two college roommates, one of whom enjoys playing her radio at full volume, the other who prefers to have it off altogether in order to concentrate better on his assigned reading (*The Economics of Planning*, of course!). The radio in question has a volume dial that is numbered from zero to ten, where the latter indicates full volume. These volume settings are represented on the horizontal axis and, as we shall see, are the focus of the "struggle" over entitlements for these two students. If the first student has full entitlements, it means that she may play the radio as loud as she likes, and this entitlement position would be shown at the extreme right-hand side of the horizontal axis in figure 9.1. On the other hand, if the second student is granted full entitlements, then he may keep the radio as quiet as he likes, as indicated by the position at the extreme left of the graph. The two sloping curves represent marginal benefit curves for each student, so total benefits are calculated as the area beneath these curves. This relationship between marginal and total is the same as described in chapter 1; it recurs in many other chapters of this text. For the first student, who likes to keep the radio playing at full volume, marginal benefits decrease but total benefits increase with additional volume. Full volume gives full benefit for this student. For the second student, who prefers to study in quiet, the situation is just the opposite, so the marginal benefit curve rises from left to right.

Although our example is the contention between two roommates over entitlements to adjust the radio volume to their preference, the general principle applies much more widely. In Fischel's example the entitlements along the horizontal axis represent the density of development (minimal lot size) permitted on a 300-acre parcel of land just outside the urban fringe. The residents of the surrounding community prefer to see that site remain undeveloped; the landowner hopes to benefit financially from rather extensive redevelopment of the site. Another example could involve the dispute over entitlements between urban beach-goers and inland property owners. The former would like to limit development in the city because of the resulting increase in pollutants that flow into the harbor, whereas landowners naturally prefer to retain full development rights. These two groups may overlap, as some of the landowners may also enjoy going to the beach. That does not pose any problem for the general framework we are introducing. Indeed,

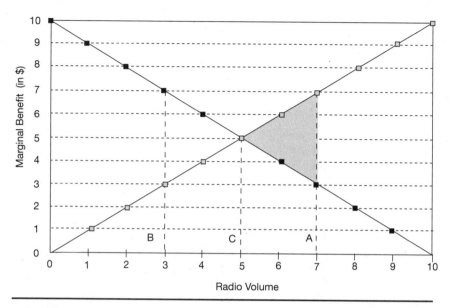

FIGURE 9.1
The basic entitlements diagram

these and virtually any other examples that entail a tug-of-war over entitlements between two or more groups can be accommodated within the framework of this simple model. For now we will continue with the roommate example, because its simple, unadorned nature helps to draw out the issues more sharply. The reader should not lose sight of the framework's broader range of applications, however.

Continuing with our example, we may now begin to run the graph through its paces. In order to simplify the exposition further, we will assume that the marginal benefit curves for both students drop in linear fashion from $10 at their peak to $0 at their base, where the decline is either from left to right or the reverse, depending upon the student in question. To make the example even more concrete, let's assume that each student has $10 in cash on hand. The discussion that follows is simplified by, but in no way depends upon, these assumptions. Now suppose that the initial entitlements are at A, an allocation that permits a volume of "seven" and so favors the first student.[1] We know that this student receives full benefits from full volume, so we might expect her to adjust the volume upward to the fullest extent that the entitlements at A allow, and indeed this is an option for her. However, if the two students are in a position to negotiate, she will be able to improve upon this position. The argument is fully analogous to the land use zoning

TABLE 9.1

Effect of Initial Entitlement Allocation on Final Allocation and Wealth

Initial Allocation	Initial Wealth Student 1	Initial Wealth Student 2	Final Allocation	Final Wealth Student 1	Final Wealth Student 2
A	$10	$10	C	$20	$0
B	$10	$10	C	$0	$20
C	$10	$10	C	$10	$10

example in chapter 2. At the allocation A, the marginal benefit of an extra unit of entitlements is higher for student 2 than for student 1, $7 compared to $3. If the two students were to settle on a price of, say, $5 for every notch on the volume dial, they would quickly agree to set the volume at level five, or allocation C, where total benefits have increased by the amount shown in the shaded triangle. This is yet another appearance of the by now infamous triangle of inefficiency. The mirror image of this story could be recited based on an initial entitlement allocation at B rather than A, where the first student is now willing to purchase entitlements from her roommate in order to play the radio at volume five (allocation C) rather than at volume three (B).

Notice that in both of these cases entitlements are exchanged for cash.[2] We can develop this idea further by constructing a simple table indicating how initial allocations affect final allocations and wealth (table 9.1).

There are two important things to notice about this table of allocations. First, the final allocation is at C regardless of where the initial allocation of entitlements lies. This tells us that it doesn't matter whether student 2 is paying student 1 to turn down the volume, or whether student 1 is paying student 2 to turn it up. Either way (under the conditions set out in this example), the two students will come to an agreement to keep the volume at level five. The second significant aspect of this table of outcomes is that the final allocation of wealth is seen to depend directly upon the initial allocation of entitlements. Thus, entitlements truly are a form of wealth.

In the example just discussed there are no transactions costs and no wealth effects. Transactions costs arise when there are difficulties to overcome in negotiating between the two parties. When transactions costs are high they may overwhelm the potential gains to be made from negotiations between the parties involved. While two roommates may or may not face this problem, it certainly arises in the context of planning issues where the battle over entitlements typically involves many parties, possibly including lawyers, citizen activist groups, real estate agents, and city hall staff. In some cases it may even be difficult to identify or contact the parties involved. For example, how do thousands of property owners make contact and negotiate with innumerable beach-goers in our urban harbor example?

Wealth effects refer to a situation where one's evaluation of the marginal benefit of an entitlement is affected by the level of wealth one enjoys. This is a common, everyday occurrence. If we are wealthy we may be willing to pay a much higher price for one more unit of a good than if we are poor. After all, when we make a purchase we are exchanging money for goods; if we are poor we find that each dollar is more precious, so we are less willing to give one up, even if we have the same consumption preferences as the rich do. As our example makes clear, entitlements are a form of wealth, so wealth effects might influence whether our final allocation is independent of the initial allocation.

So, what *is* the Coase Theorem? In highly simplified form, it states that:

> *If there are no*
> * *transactions costs*
> * *wealth effects*
> *then the final allocation of entitlements is independent of the initial allocation*
>
> *However, most real-world examples are characterized by*
> * *transactions costs*
> * *wealth effects*
> *so the final allocation of entitlements will depend upon the initial allocation*

In our example, it is not difficult to imagine that both transactions costs and wealth effects might figure into the calculus. If the initial allocation of entitlements is at A, the second student may not want to cause ill feelings on the part of his roommate by broaching the subject. That is a kind of transaction-associated cost. The student may judge that the loss of harmony in the relationship exceeds any benefits that might be obtained through a reduction in the radio's volume, so the final allocation of entitlements will remain at A. In this case the students each still have $10 in the final allocation, but the first student is still wealthier—only now she enjoys her extra wealth in the form of a steady consumption of loud music. In the case of wealth effects, the students might place a lower value on entitlements that they are trying to purchase than they might attach to these same entitlements if they were in a position to sell them. (For example, "I'm only willing to pay you $4 to turn the radio volume down from four to three, but it will cost you $6 if you seek permission to turn the volume up from three to four.")

In this example, wealth affects the student's marginal valuation of the asset, and this kind of wealth effect could influence the final allocation of entitlements. Finally, note once again that all of this discussion is predicated on the assumption that the initial allocation of entitlements is well defined. We will discuss this property rights issue more fully in a later section of this chapter.

Two Fundamental Theorems of Welfare Economics

There are two perspectives from which the Coase Theorem might be viewed. On the one hand, we may determine that transactions costs and wealth effects are fundamental to the manner in which entitlements are allocated, so we may concentrate on this point. This is the basic premise of the new institutional economics discussed in chapter 10. A second perspective from which to reflect upon the Coase Theorem focuses on the finding that the optimum allocation of entitlements will be attained regardless of the initial allocation provided that transactions costs and wealth effects are minimized. From this perspective, and with this proviso in mind, the initial allocation is important insofar as it impacts the distribution of wealth, but it does not have any bearing on the efficiency of the final allocation of entitlements. This perspective favors a push to reduce transactions costs wherever possible so as to promote efficient markets. It also favors direct transfers or redistribution of wealth, as opposed to price subsidies or other indirect methods, to address equity issues.[3] This perspective is the sine qua non of the traditional neoclassical microeconomist and has culminated in the two fundamental theorems of welfare economics.

These two fundamental theorems can be stated succinctly as follows:

- *Every competitive equilibrium (CE) is Pareto optimal (PO)*
- *Every Pareto optimum (PO) allocation is supportable by some competitive equilibrium (CE)*

On the face of it these are hardly comprehensible, much less earth-shattering; however, as a pair they point to a strong nexus between markets and efficiency. In fact, these two theorems form the ideological core of market economics. Let us therefore define our terms carefully.

A competitive equilibrium arises in a competitive market economy when, at prevailing market prices, no one has any incentive to change the amount of any goods they are buying, selling, or producing and, further, when the amount that is willingly supplied just equals the amount that is sought at that price. If this condition were *not* met, we would expect prices to adjust until such a time as equilibrium was restored. Note that a competitive economy is defined in terms of price-taking behavior. That is, no individual or firm has sufficient clout to affect market prices, so the latter are purely an expression of aggregate demand and supply. Through repetitive use, this definition has taken on the character of an operative assumption, partly for ideological reasons and partly for mathematical ones.

Pareto optimality (PO), on the other hand, is a basic efficiency condition. In the case of a simple exchange economy,[4] if an allocation of goods or entitlements is not optimal in the sense of Pareto,[5] it means that there is some reallocation of the existing set of goods (or entitlements) that would improve at least one person's welfare without reducing anyone else's. For a production economy, it would mean that resources and activities could be reallocated so as to increase production for at least one firm without diminishing the output of others. To most people, given this definition, it seems only reasonable to strive for Pareto optimality. After all, if we could improve someone's lot without making anyone else worse off, why *wouldn't* we do so? In this way, Pareto optimality has come to be regarded by many economists as a basic measure of efficiency, so any economy that is not Pareto optimal is not making full use of its resources or assets.

Now, let us reconsider the two fundamental theorems more carefully in light of these definitions. The first theorem says that any competitive equilibrium is also a Pareto optimum (CE => PO). A competitive equilibrium is the *result* of a market process, whereas Pareto optimality is a *criterion* by which we judge efficiency. There is no reason a priori for one to correspond perfectly with the other. In the case of the first theorem, the result hinges on the assumption of a competitive economy where everyone faces the same set of prices. Each person is presumed (under the axioms of rational consumer behavior) to adjust their expenditures so that they squeeze out the maximum possible benefit from their budgets in light of these prices. Because each person is doing so with reference to the same prices, they are all making the same kinds of trade-offs on the margin, so all opportunities for gains from trade have been exhausted. Everyone has already traded *indirectly* with everyone else, with market prices serving as intermediaries. Pareto optimality is achieved through indirect trade.

The significance of the first fundamental theorem is that all market outcomes in a perfectly competitive economy will satisfy the Pareto efficiency condition. The second theorem establishes yet another connection between Pareto optima and competitive equilibria. It says that any PO is supportable by *some* CE. This is the "flip side" of the first theorem. If there is an allocation that satisfies the Pareto efficiency condition, then we can conclude that there is some price that would support a market equilibrium for that allocation. That "correct" supporting price is the one that reflects the marginal valuation of goods that is inherent in the Pareto condition. Opportunities for Pareto *improvements* arise whenever two or more people assign different relative values, on the margin, to two or more kinds of goods. Those differing values provide scope for gains from trade. Pareto *optimality* occurs when all such gains from trade have been exhausted, so everyone places the same relative value to goods on the margin. Any set of market prices that adheres to these same relative values will support a competitive equilibrium for the corresponding Pareto optimal allocation.

The significance of this second theorem has to do with the potential for markets to support desirable outcomes. While there are many possible Pareto optima even for a simple exchange economy, not all PO are equally desirable. For example, an allocation that is heavily skewed in favor of one consumer at the expense of the others may be Pareto optimal yet quite unjust. Thus, we can see that Pareto optimality may be a desirable *efficiency* criterion, but it does not in itself guarantee that such outcomes are socially equitable or otherwise desirable. The importance of the second fundamental theorem is that it indicates that any PO is supportable by *some* competitive market equilibrium. Thus, if the CE that arises from one set of initial allocations is undesirable, it does not necessarily follow that the problem is with markets per se. Instead, it may be that the problem is with the initial allocation of wealth or entitlements. The second fundamental theorem points to the possibility of reallocating entitlements to affect a more favorable distribution and then relying on markets to forge an efficient outcome based on the new initial allocation.

Finally, let us reexamine the Coase Theorem from the perspective of these two fundamental theorems of welfare economics. We saw that, in the absence of transactions costs or wealth effects, a voluntary exchange of entitlements as described in table 9.1 would lead both parties to the same final allocation of entitlements regardless of the initial allocation, although the final allocation of wealth is reflective of the initial allocation. We see now that the final allocation point C in figure 9.1 is a Pareto optimum because there is no further possibility for mutual gain through exchange of entitlements. From this neoclassical perspective, one can argue in favor of creating markets for entitlements that—if they are perfectly competitive markets with no transactions costs or wealth effects—will lead to a competitive equilibrium (at C, in figure 9.1) that is Pareto optimal. This corresponds to the first fundamental theorem. Furthermore, if the final allocation of wealth that one attains from this mechanism is too skewed, then the problem could be addressed through a redistribution of entitlements without interfering in the market process. This notion—that redistributional aims can in principle be fostered within a market framework—is at the heart of the second fundamental theorem. Both theorems point to the important potential for markets to assist planners in allocating entitlements. The credo of neoclassical economics that emerges from these theorems is that where markets are weak and ineffectual, they should be improved upon, and where markets are nonexistent, they should be created.

Creating Markets for Entitlements

The issue of property rights lies at the center of any effort to create a market for entitlements. The assignment of property rights in this situation refers to the process by which entitlements are bestowed, or at least clarified. The "rights" in property rights correspond to the entitlements themselves. The "property" aspect of property rights alludes to the idea that the rights embodied in entitlements can in principle be traded or bought and sold much like any other property or wealth that one might have title to. From this perspective any goods transaction also entails a rights transaction—goods without the right to consume or otherwise make use of them are valueless.

As emphasized in the introductory section of this chapter, entitlements and obligations are at the very core of planning. It is useful therefore to explore how and whether markets for entitlements might assist planners in their duties. There are at least two distinct issues involved. One concerns the definition and allocation of entitlements themselves. A second is the creation and oversight of markets within which entitlements might be traded. To clarify these issues, we will begin by considering a specific example, that of pollution entitlements. Numerous other examples could be treated within a similar framework, including school vouchers or fair-share housing.

A market for pollution entitlements is an alternative to traditional forms of quantity-based regulation. In the traditional arrangement, planners act as regulators who determine what quantity of pollution emissions is permitted by which firms. In the market-based alternative, firms trade among themselves to reallocate certificates that entitle the holders to discharge specified quantities of emissions. On the face of it, it may seem absurd for environmental planners to advocate selling the right to pollute. However, neoclassical economic theory suggests that pollution entitlement markets can be useful in obtaining the maximum benefit from a given level of emissions. To see this point, reconsider the simple entitlements diagram in figure 9.1. Instead of two roommates wishing to adjust their radio volume, assume we now have two firms competing for the right to pollute. The marginal benefit curve for each firm measures the increase in the net value of the firm's output resulting from a marginal relaxation of the emissions quota. The basic premise is that pollution is an inevitable by-product of many manufacturing activities. To reduce the level of pollution we must either forgo production (and hence consumption) of these manufactured goods or undertake costly mitigation measures.

In the context of figure 9.1, it is easy to see that an initial allocation of entitlements at either A or B could be improved upon through bartering between these two firms that brings about an eventual reallocation at C. This is a Pareto-improving reallocation, whereby the total amount of pollution emissions has not changed but the aggregate value of output has increased. The basic principle is that firms will bid against each other for these entitlements. The winning bids will tend to come from those firms whose output is highly valued by the consuming public, and for which mitigation measures are costly, difficult, and/or ineffective. Once the market price for pollution entitlements is bid up high enough, other firms will gladly sell their entitlements and use the proceeds to undertake mitigation measures or to explore other business interests entirely. In effect, by purchasing manufactured goods in various markets, the general public is voting *indirectly* on the issue of how to allocate pollution entitlements among competing firms, since the intensity of demand for manufactured outputs is ultimately the basis for firms' demand for inputs, including the right to pollute. Of course some people have more dollars to "vote" with than others, so issues of how wealth is allocated may be relevant.

But what about the general public's interest in clean air and water? How are those interests reconciled within a market framework? These can be accommodated quite easily through purchase and sale of pollution entitlements on the public's behalf. Bear in mind that this is the same public whose demand for manufactured output (directly or indirectly) gives rise to the pollution in the first place. By purchasing or selling pollution entitlements, public agencies concerned with environmental protection can bid for entitlements on an equal footing with everyone else in the market. If the public agency believes that there is too much pollution, it can enter the market and buy up pollution entitlements at the going market rate. By "sitting on" these entitlements the agency effectively removes them from circulation, thereby reducing the amount of emissions allowable. And what if the price of entitlements is too high, so that the public agency cannot afford to purchase them? This indicates that the public would appear to place more value on the margin on an increase in manufactured output than on a decrease in pollution emissions. Otherwise, the public should in principle be willing to accept a reduction in their consumption of goods in order to support an increase in the public agency's environmental budget. The question of enforcement is no less important for a market-based solution than it is for a regulatory framework. The value of an entitlement will be debased seriously if there is no enforcement mechanism to ensure that only those with legal entitlements will in fact pollute.

As we have learned, entitlements are a form of wealth, so the initial allocation of entitlements is quite crucial to determining how equitable the final outcome will be. For example, public agency budgets are critically impacted if the initial allocations are in favor of manufacturing firms, so that public agencies promoting cleaner air are required to purchase entitlements from firms, rather than the reverse. On the one hand, we may like to see the initial entitlements allocated in favor of public agencies so that government budgets (and our taxes!) are not adversely affected. However, if prior to the establishment of an entitlements market, the regulatory regime permits firms to pollute at certain levels, then to grant all the initial market entitlements to the public agency would constitute a form of "taking," and this raises legal and ethical questions. It may be that the most practical approach to creating an entitlements market is to have the initial allocation of entitlements conform as closely as possible to the implicit entitlements existing prior to the introduction of a formal market. In this case there is no traumatic redistribution at the outset, but there is enhanced potential for efficiency gains through the trading of entitlements. Once an entitlements market is in place, it may be that the public is willing to hold out for a handsome sum when selling pollution entitlements to bidding firms, but is only willing to pay a modest amount to buy up entitlements that are already owned by firms. Such a situation is a perfect example of a wealth effect, as discussed earlier in this chapter.

The case of pollution entitlements is but one example of how markets for entitlements may be created to assist planners in effecting more efficient solutions to the problems they encounter. Proposals for school vouchers are based on similar principles. Rather than spending money directly on schools, local governments would issue vouchers redeemable for cash by private schools. These vouchers are a kind of entitlement, because if held in sufficient numbers, they entitle the holder to attend any private school willing to accept them. The emphasis of school voucher proposals is not on the creation of entitlement markets per se. Rather, the intent is to create a mechanism by which education is funded in part by the public sector but provided in large measure by the private sector. Thus, the entitlements in this case would be used to support a more active market for private schools, which in turn would compete on a more equal footing with public schools. The issuance of vouchers is in effect an allocation of entitlements, so it has immediate consequences for the distribution of wealth. Part of the motivation behind many voucher proposals is the wish to make private schools accessible to a wider segment of the population, not just the wealthier classes.

Obligations can be treated within a framework similar to that of entitlements. As an example, consider the problem of fair-share housing that besets many large metropolitan areas in the United States. Housing analysts

recognize that problems of affordability stem largely from restrictions on supply, a point that is also clarified in chapter 3. This problem can be particularly vexing in municipalities that may recognize the need for more housing
opportunities in principle but are resistant to allowing the introduction of
lower-cost housing in practice. Land use regulations such as minimum lot
size can be effective barriers to entry for lower-income households that might
otherwise move into the community and live at higher densities than current regulations allow. Part of the problem is that no single municipality may
be motivated to act unilaterally without assurances that others will also take
on their fair share of affordable housing.

This is an issue that, in principle at least, can be addressed from the same
perspective as entitlements, only now the obligations in question are a kind
of "negative entitlement." Instead of one community paying another in order to acquire *entitlements*, payments (or considerations in kind) might be
made by one community in persuading another to assume *obligations* on
its behalf. Suppose, for example, that ten municipalities or self-governing
communities of roughly equal size agreed that zoning within the region
should be modified so as to accommodate an additional 10,000 units of low-
to moderate-income housing. Negotiation and mediation might lead to some
initial allocation of obligations, say, 1,000 units apiece. These obligations
could then be traded, where some municipalities might be willing to take
on more obligations in return for appropriate compensation.

One might argue that it is unfair or even demeaning to allow a rich community to sidestep its obligations by paying a poorer community to assume
them, and indeed, this is a serious point. On the other hand, there are several relevant considerations here. First, we must presume that any voluntary
agreement reached between two or more parties constitutes a Pareto improvement. After all, if there is no mutual benefit, there is no scope for an
agreement. Second, if there is something objectionable in the notion that a
rich community might persuade another to assume obligations on its behalf
(or equivalently, to purchase entitlements for itself), this objection must surely
be rooted in the unequal distribution of wealth that characterizes these communities in the first place rather than in a process that facilitates Pareto improvements upon that distribution. Third, there is nothing in principle to
prevent one from factoring in the wealth of a community, or any number of
other considerations for that matter, in determining the initial allocation of
obligations or entitlements.

Notes

1. As noted in the introduction to this chapter, the manner in which entitlements are formed and established is a fascinating topic in its own right. For the purposes of this exposition, however, we shall assume that both students agree one way or the other on the allocations discussed in the text.

2. In a less contrived example, we might expect two roommates to resolve a simple matter such as this without resorting to cash payments. The framework applies equally well to "goodwill" payments or benefits.

3. "Equity" is used here in the sense of equality between persons, not in the sense of financial equity as discussed in other contexts.

4. An exchange economy is one where existing goods are exchanged but none are produced.

5. Pareto was an Italian mathematician and economist in the late nineteenth century. He is best known for the concept of Pareto optimality and for a mathematically based measure of inequality.

10

The New Institutional Economics

Introduction

Economics, like any system of thought, evolves over time. Like a great river flowing through the landscape, its multiple tributaries and branches contribute to or diverge from the main stream. In general historical terms, the lay public rightly credits Adam Smith's 1776 classic, *The Wealth of Nations,* as the font for the principle of the "Invisible Hand" of the marketplace that guides self-interested individuals in allocating resources to the ultimate betterment of society's welfare. However, modern neoclassical economics is more closely associated with the work of Alfred Marshall, who introduced the principles of marginal analysis (as described in chapter 1) to the study of economics in a manner that set the course for neoclassical economics in the twentieth century. While Adam Smith's treatise was richly embedded within the historical and institutional context of late-eighteenth-century England and beyond, the Marshallian neoclassical tradition tended to abstract from any specific institutional setting in order to focus more rigorous attention on the development of mathematical models that built on the calculus of marginal analysis (or, more precisely, the principles of marginal analysis derived from calculus).

The emergence and subsequent dominance of *homo economicus* within the study of economic behavior was not without its challengers. From Thorstein Veblen's *Theory of the Leisure Class*[1] to John Kenneth Galbraith's

211

New Industrial State, many authors received widespread popular acclaim for their witty and in many ways devastating depictions of the economist's model of a purely rational consumer whose autonomous preferences, perfect knowledge, and robotlike maximizing behavior seemed outlandishly inhuman and patently unrealistic. Nonetheless, it is fair to say in hindsight that most criticisms by these "institutionalists" were mostly just that—they did not offer a countervailing theory or methodology to match the rigor or appeal of the neoclassical paradigm. The latter, for all its admitted faults, was an extremely powerful device for explaining a wide range of observable behaviors among consumers, firms, employees, and other economic agents. Moreover, the mathematical depictions of microeconomic behavior that exemplify the Marshallian tradition also offered a systematic and theoretically explicit framework for modeling the effect of taxes, regulations, and other interventions or constraints on the optimizing behavior of *homo economicus.* For these and other reasons, the "dismal science," as economics was long regarded (and no doubt still is by many), gradually established its reputation as the "queen of the social sciences" and even attracted the animosity of scholars in other social sciences for its alleged hegemony.

The new institutional economics, or neoinstitutional economics as it is sometimes called, combines elements of Marshallian methodology with a concern for restoring the rightful place of institutions in the analysis of economic behavior. Although it was not until the 1970s that the new institutional economics really began to establish a solid footing as a subdiscipline in the realm of economics, its origins can be readily traced to a seminal 1937 article by Ronald Coase entitled "The Nature of the Firm." As discussed in more detail below, Coase brought the analytical tools of the Marshallian tradition to bear directly on a question that had not been seriously addressed prior to that— why do firms exist at all? The insights introduced by Coase, and subsequently expanded upon by others, evolved into the branch of economics known as the new institutional economics, or NIE for short. In recent decades this approach has been applied fruitfully to the study of organizational behavior, antitrust legislation, regulated industries, economic growth, and the transition from socialist to market economies in Eastern Europe and elsewhere. On the whole, the growth of NIE is a welcome development for planners. It is likely that the growing bond between NIE and planning will enrich the development of both fields in the coming years. In this chapter we explore this symbiosis between the new institutional economics and planning, beginning with an examination of the roots of NIE.

Coase Revisited

The focus of the NIE is on the nexus defined by the intersection of economics, law, and institutions. While its origins lie in Coase's 1937 piece, "The Nature of the Firm," it is also integrally linked to the property rights or entitlements approach advanced by another famous paper authored by Coase, "The Problem of Social Cost," published in 1960. In addition to propelling Coase to the status of a Nobel prize winner, these two papers established the foundation for the new institutional economics. It is useful, therefore, to consider the nature of their contribution and their important implications for the planning profession.

In the previous chapter, we discussed the Coase Theorem at length. To recapitulate very briefly, that theorem states that if there are no wealth effects or transactions costs, then the *initial* assignment of property rights (i.e., entitlements) will not affect the *final* allocation, but it will affect the relative wealth of the parties involved. However, and most importantly, the Coase Theorem observes that the real world is in fact fraught with wealth effects and transactions costs, so the initial assignment of property rights not only affects wealth, it also affects the final allocation of property rights. The importance of this theorem for institutions becomes apparent if we consider that legal systems and markets are, respectively, institutions for assigning and trading property rights.

While seemingly focusing on a different topic, "The Nature of the Firm" also hinges on the concept of transactions costs. In that paper, which did not receive much attention until decades after it was first published, Coase asks a deceptively simple question: If markets are such useful instruments for exchange, why are there any firms at all? Within a firm, the allocation of resources is not directed by markets, but through a hierarchy of command where, for example, my boss gives me direction and I in turn give direction to those under me. The internal operations of firms from this perspective are like cordoned areas where transactions are shielded from or are impervious to direct market influence. Coase asks why, if markets are such efficient mechanisms for resource allocation, rational humans would opt instead for a nonmarket solution. Significantly, Coase does not abandon the economist's reliance on optimizing behavior to explain the existence of firms. Instead, he demonstrates that firms are a logical and rational response to the presence of transactions costs. Or as Coase himself puts it:

> The main reason why it is profitable to establish a firm would seem to be that there is a cost of using the price mechanism . . . a firm will tend to expand until the costs of organising an extra transaction within the firm become equal to the costs of carrying out the same transaction by means of

an exchange on the open market or the costs of organising in another firm.
(Coase, 1937, p. 390, 395)

The costs he refers to are transactions costs. These include the costs of determining relevant market prices, anticipating all possible contingencies associated with a planned market transaction, setting out the terms of market-based contractual agreements, and monitoring and enforcing the terms of that contract. Transactions costs place limits on the extent or effectiveness of the presumed human rationality within a market setting.

Note the Marshallian character of the second part of the quote, where Coase draws on standard marginal analysis to develop the contours of his theory of the firm. This is where Coase differs so dramatically from Institutionalists who would discard the Marshallian analytical tradition because it does not adequately account for the institutional setting of *homo economicus*. Instead, Coase uses Marshallian tools to extend the range of neoclassical economics to include the analysis of institutions. Likewise, NIE does not reject neoclassical economics, but builds upon it. Coase's insights on the nature of the firm have been utilized to develop models and explanations of corporate structure that are widely used in business schools throughout the world.

In both of these seminal papers by Coase, the concept of transactions costs serves as a fulcrum between neoclassical and neoinstitutional economics. In the context of "The Nature of the Firm," if transactions costs are nil, then there really is no reason for firms to exist. The allocation of resources that currently takes place within firms would instead be handled by markets. In the context of "The Problem of Social Cost," if transactions costs (and wealth effects) are nil, then the initial allocation of entitlements does not affect the final allocation. In both cases, the traditional neoclassical depiction of the world is the limiting case as transactions costs disappear. And in both cases, many important real-world phenomena become more explicable as we allow for the presence of transactions costs within the confines of the neoclassical framework. Not only are organizations and institutions incorporated within this framework, they become central to its analysis.

Ernest Alexander (1992) advocates adapting a similar approach to planning, arguing that transactions costs affect political markets just as they do economic markets, and that hierarchical structures of organization for human activity are the default result in either case. From this perspective, the traditional dichotomy of markets versus planning is a false one. Instead, Alexander argues that the real choice is "between more market-like forms of organization and [the resultant] aggregation of collective decisions, or more hierarchical organizations—and the planning that goes with them. This choice can be and is continually made in both the political and economic arenas." No doubt there are numerous stones left unturned by the transactions costs view of how humans organize their economic activity. Nonetheless, the transactions cost view is a significant extension of the neoclassical paradigm of economic behavior that does hold considerable promise as well for applications to planning theory.

A Property Rights Approach to Zoning

In chapter 2 we presented an economic analysis of land use zoning using a traditional neoclassical framework. Land use regulation is an issue that is squarely within the purview of planning. It is instructive, therefore, to compare the neoclassical and neoinstitutional approaches directly. We are aided in this objective by William Fischel (1985), who introduces the neoinstitutional approach to the question of land use controls. It is interesting that this dichotomy between the property rights approach advocated by Fischel and the "externality approach" presented in chapter 2 mirrors a dichotomy between Coase and another famous early economist, A. C. Pigou. Thus, a seemingly arcane debate between two economists now manifests itself under a slightly different guise in the planning field. The property rights approach was clearly articulated by Coase (1960) himself:

> A final reason for the failure to develop a theory adequate to handle the problem of harmful effects stems from a faulty concept of a factor of production . . . We may speak of a person owning land using it as a factor of production but what the land-owner in fact possesses is the *right* to carry out a circumscribed list of actions . . . If factors of production are thought of as rights, it becomes easier to understand that the right to do something which has a harmful effect (such as the creation of smoke, noise, smells, etc.) is also a factor of production. Just as we may use a piece of land in such a way as to prevent someone else from crossing it, or parking his car, or building his house upon it, so we may use it in such a way as to deny him a view or quiet or unpolluted air. (my emphasis)

This statement is fundamental to the property rights perspective, and it is perhaps not surprising that it originates with a scholar who focuses on the intersection between law and economics. From the property rights perspective, ownership of a commodity or of a factor of production is about *rights,* especially the right to dispose of or to make use of that physical "thing" in certain prescribed ways. The concept of ownership is essentially a legal one concerning the allocation of rights pertaining to that property, but the implications of ownership are largely economic. Once a person has established rights to property through legal processes, the economic question becomes one of how to best make use of those rights.

It is useful at this juncture to compare two diagrams we have used in earlier chapters to address issues of land use. The entitlements diagram from chapter 9 follows Fischel, Turvey, and Coase in presenting the property rights perspective. The externalities diagram featured in chapter 2 in the context of land use zoning is best used to convey the Pigovian concept of using taxes or subsidies to "internalize" externalities. This terminology is also convenient because it allows us to use a language similar to Fischel's in describing the difference between the two approaches.

An essential difference between the two diagrams is that the entitlements approach lends itself more readily to a focus on transactions costs which, in the case of land use regulation, are a significant concern. Indeed, as Fischel points out, the exchange of entitlements is prohibited in many circumstances because common sentiment is often quite hostile to the notion of "selling" land use regulations, just as it is to the notion of "selling" health regulations or traffic regulations. Whether sensible or not, this sentiment is a major obstacle to the smooth exchange of entitlements, so it is a significant transaction cost in and of itself. Another significant transaction cost involves the cost of valuation. As we noted above in our discussion of Coase's "The Nature of the Firm" article, obtaining information on relevant market prices (or costs) is a key reason that rational individuals may choose not to conduct their transactions via the marketplace. This is certainly true in the case of land use regulation where it is not always clear a priori what the proper market valuation of these entitlements is or ought to be. The Coase Theorem tells us that, because of these transactions costs, the final allocation of property rights is likely to be highly dependent upon the initial allocation.

The Pigovian strategy of "taxing" externalities carries with it an implicit assignment of property rights or liability. Coase's criticism of this approach is that the Pigovian tradition automatically calls for such a tax, even when alternative social or legal arrangements might be preferable. Coase uses the example of a factory that produces unwanted smoke with harmful effects. He observes that it is possible that the cost of smoke mitigation, or of moving factory production to another location, or of ceasing production altogether may exceed the costs of preventative actions were they to be taken by the affected parties. His argument is that society should strive to make those changes to existing arrangements that yield the greatest total net benefit. Or, as summarized by Coase (1960):

> In choosing between social arrangements within the context of which individual decisions are made, we have to bear in mind that a change in the existing system which will lead to an improvement in some decisions may well lead to a worsening of others. Furthermore, we have to take into account the costs involved in operating the various social arrangements

(whether it be the working of a market or of a government department), as well as the costs involved in moving to a new system. In devising and choosing between social arrangements we should have regard for the total effect. This, above all, is the change in approach which I am advocating.

In terms of our two diagrammatic approaches to the issue of land use zoning, the externalities diagram is useful within the context of a given set of social arrangements. It does not address the question of property rights directly, so it implicitly takes the existing allocation of rights as given. Within that framework, then, the externalities diagram facilitates a Pigovian analysis of how best to correct for externalities. The entitlements approach, in contrast, applies the tools of marginal analysis to questions regarding the redistribution of property rights, recognizing that trade in such rights may be constrained by transactions costs and other institutional factors. Neither diagram is "wrong," nor do they conflict directly. Both, when properly used, can help determine how to derive maximum benefit from a given set of resources or constraints. The difference is largely one of emphasis. As Fischel (1985) explains:

> The importance of the Coase theorem is the approach that it suggests for examining public issues . . . If the defect in zoning is seen to be an incomplete assignment of entitlements, the property rights approach leads one to ask how entitlements ought to be assigned. If the defect is high transactions costs, the approach leads one to ask how to reduce such costs. If the defect is one of fairness, it leads one to ask how entitlements should be distributed or protected so as to promote fairness.

In contrast, the Pigovian approach focuses on instances where market prices do not properly reflect social costs (on the margin), and seeks to correct this deficiency through direct intervention in prices. Thus, in chapter 2 we learned that Pigovian price intervention is an alternative to quantity-based zoning intervention, and in this chapter we see that a Coasian property rights perspective is yet another approach to the issue of land use regulation.

Planning for Developing and Transition Economies

Institutions, in the sense that the term is used by the neoinstitutional economists, are patterns of behavior that regularize interactions between members of human society. Markets, customs, and legal systems are examples of institutions from this broadly defined perspective. The role of institutions is particularly important in the context of economic growth in developing countries, where development may be viewed as an evolving pattern of relationships between societal values, technical change, and institutions. Another Nobel prize-winning economist, Douglass North (1995), whose work has focused primarily on economic development and growth in the United States over the past two centuries, has formulated five propositions that characterize the relationship underlying growth and development:

1. The continuous interaction between institutions and organizations in the economic setting of scarcity, and hence competition, is the key to institutional change.
2. Competition forces organizations to continually invest in skills and knowledge to survive. The kinds of skills and knowledge individuals and their organizations acquire will shape evolving perceptions about opportunities, and hence choices, that will incrementally alter institutions.
3. The institutional framework provides the incentives that dictate the kinds of skills and knowledge perceived to have the maximum payoff.
4. Perceptions are derived from the mental constructs of the players.
5. The economies of scope, complementarities, and network externalities of an institutional matrix make institutional change overwhelmingly incremental and path-dependent.

What North is describing with these propositions is a dynamic process whereby competition drives organizations to invest in skills and knowledge, which in turn shape perceptions, which in turn drive the pattern of individual actions, which in turn reshape institutions, incrementally.

Path dependence (in #5 above) refers to a situation where history carries with it a certain inertia. Consider for a moment the game of chess. The "best move" at any point in the game is strictly a function of what the relative position of the pieces is at that moment in time and in no way depends upon the sequence of moves that came prior.[2] But consider what would happen if the rules of the game evolved as a consequence of prior play. A grand master contemplating a given position would not only need to evaluate the relative positions of the pieces in play, he or she would also have to know the history. That is path dependence. North argues, and it is a view that is fundamental to the neoinstitutional approach, that economic history lurches forward from one "position" to the next in uneasy increments, and the rules (i.e., the institutions) of the game do likewise. This argument has important implications for development planners who seek to foster development through the importation of modern Western institutions such as credit markets, democracy, and private ownership. Path dependence implies that such institutions must evolve in tandem with social values, technology, and economic development and cannot be "implanted" without reference to them.

Path dependence is of crucial importance for transition economies, those formerly socialist states that are attempting to manage transitions from hierarchical, command economies to modern Western-type market-based economies. In attempting to create markets where none existed before, the fundamental problem is one of the creation or reassignment of property rights. In the case of Eastern Europe, for example, many people laid legitimate claim under the old socialist regimes to entitlements that were often specific to those institutional settings. Thus, for many people, particularly the elderly, the transition to a private market economy implies a loss of entitlements and hence a loss of wealth.

We observe the same phenomenon in China, where the central government in Beijing is continuously struggling with decisions over the pace of reform. On the one hand, providing loans and grants to huge, inefficient state enterprises leads directly to enormous government deficits and rampant inflation. On the other hand, exposing these enterprises to the full force of market competition would likely result in the swift expulsion of tens of millions of workers from their jobs. The shock to political, cultural, and economic institutions would be cataclysmic—as it has been in the former Soviet Union—and the Chinese leadership is not willing to risk that. Instead, they are attempting to manage what is, in effect, a revolutionary transition without the chaos that might otherwise ensue. It is the kind of undertaking that is within the legitimate scope of analysis of neoinstitutional economics but that still lies well beyond NIE's capacity to provide assured guidance.

One area in which NIE does offer useful insights is that regarding ownership issues. The governments of many transition economies are under relentless pressure from foreign investment interests to privatize ownership in land and other resources. In China and elsewhere governments have generally retained complete ownership for themselves, and to do otherwise would be wrenching for states that are in many cases still officially communist. To a certain extent it would seem that Westerners have a kind of "hang-up" about ownership and are hesitant to invest in land improvements where they have no title. Recall our quotation from Coase earlier in this chapter regarding property rights. He explains that what we commonly call "ownership" is in fact a circumscribed list of rights with respect to the disposition of that asset. Thus, the issue is not ownership per se; rather, it is the effective enforcement of rights pertaining to the use of that property. Provided those entitlements are well defined, unambiguously assigned, and effectively enforced, there should be no real impediment to investment regardless of who actually "owns" the land. Allowing free and active trading in these entitlements would further enhance their value because they would tend to be bid in favor of their most productive uses.

The problem, of course, is that many developing and/or transition economies lack the institutional framework for accomplishing this task. Potential investors may justifiably lack confidence in the long-term viability of such entitlements and hence may accord them little value. This brings to mind Douglass North's five propositions, above, pointing to the interdependence between institutional settings, general perceptions, and individual actions. These behavioral, cultural, and perceptual characteristics are variables that evolve relatively slowly and retain a great deal of historical "inertia." A narrow approach to economics may tend to discount the importance of these institutional constraints and as a result may tend to prescribe policies that are ill-suited to these contexts. Neoinstitutional economics provides a promising framework for addressing these larger-scale issues more systematically and comprehensively.

Notes

1. One of the best professional puns I've heard, attributed to Professor Martin Wachs, referred to a gathering of academics in a mountain resort setting as the "Leisure of the Theory Class."

2. A possible exception is the case in which the prior move sequence revealed information about the ability of the opposing player who, under the right conditions, might be vulnerable to a "sucker punch." Of course, a sequence of moves by the opposing player suggesting a low level of knowledge might itself be a trap!

Bibliography

Alexander, E. R. 1992. A transaction cost theory of planning. *Journal of the American Planning Association* 58(2): 190-200.

Anderson, J. L. 1987. Modeling trio used for distribution system analysis. *Water/Engineering & Management* 134: 25-28.

Arentze, T. A.; A. W. J. Borgers; and H. J. P. Timmermans. 1994. Geographical information systems and the measurement of accessibility in the context of multipurpose travel: a new approach. *Geographical Systems* 1(2): 87-102.

Arnott, R., and J. Rowse. 1987. Peer group effects and educational attainment. *Journal of Public Economics* 32: 287-305.

Atkinson, A. B., and J. E. Stiglitz. 1980. *Lectures in public economics.* New York: McGraw-Hill.

Attanasio, R., and D. Danicic. 1994. Comparing three stormwater pollutant load models. *Public Works* 125: 51-54.

Auerhahn, E. 1988. Implementing an impact fee system: ten years of experience in Broward County, Florida. *Journal of the American Planning Association* 54(1): 67-70.

Barneby, M. P.; T. MacRostie; G. J. Schoennauer; G. T. Simpson; and J. Winters. 1988. Paying for growth: community approaches to development impact fees. *Journal of the American Planning Association* 54(1): 18-28.

Brueckner, J. K. 1981. Congested public goods: the case of fire protection. *Journal of Public Economics* 15: 45-58.

Burchell, R., and D. Listokin. 1978. *The fiscal impact handbook.* New Brunswick, NJ: Center for Urban Policy Research.

Chaiken, J. M.; E. J. Ignall; and W. E. Walker. 1975. Deployment methodology for fire departments. Santa Monica, CA: The Rand Corporation.

Clark, R. M., and R. G. Stevie. 1981. A water supply cost model incorporating spatial variables. *Land Economics* 57(1): 18-32.

Coase, R. H. 1937. The nature of the firm. *Economica* 4: 386-405.

Coase, R. H. 1960. The problem of social cost. *Journal of Law and Economics* 3: 1-44.

Connerly, C. E. 1988. The social implications of impact fees. *Journal of the American Planning Association* 54(1): 75-78.

Cornes, R., and T. Sandler. 1986. *The theory of externalities, public goods, and club goods.* Cambridge, UK: Cambridge University Press.

Craig, S. G., and E. J. Heikkila. 1989. Urban safety in Vancouver: allocation and production of a congestible public good. *Canadian Journal of Economics* 22(4): 867-884.

Department of Public Works. 1994. *NPDES stormwater discharge program.* Los Angeles County internal memorandum.

Dynarski, M.; R. Schwab; and E. Zampelli. 1989. Local characteristics and public production: the case of education. *Journal of Urban Economics* 26: 250-263.

Fischel, W. A. 1979. Equity and efficiency aspects of zoning reform. *Public Policy* 27(3): 301-331.

Fischel, W. A. 1985. *The economics of zoning laws: a property rights approach.* Baltimore, MD: Johns Hopkins University Press.

Hanson, S., and M. Schwab. 1987. Accessibility and intraurban travel. *Environment and Planning A* 19(6): 735-748.

Heikkila, E. J. 1989. Using simple diagrams to illustrate the economics of land use zoning. *Journal of Planning Education and Research* 8(3) (Summer): 209-214.

Heikkila, E. J. 1994. Microeconomics and planning: using simple diagrams to illustrate the economics of traffic congestion. *Journal of Planning Education and Research* 14: 29-41.

Heikkila, E. 1996. Are municipalities Tieboutian clubs? *Regional Science and Urban Economics* 26: 203-226.

Heikkila, E. J., and S. G. Craig. 1991. Nested fiscal impact measures using the new theory of local public goods. *Journal of Regional Science* 31(1): 65-81.

Heikkila, E. J., and W. Davis. 1997. Rethinking fiscal impacts. *Journal of Planning Education and Research* 16 (3): 201-211.

Heikkila, E. J., and C. Kantiotou. 1992. Calculating fiscal impacts where spatial effects are present. *Regional Science and Urban Economics* 22: 475-490.

Huffman, F. E.; A. C. Nelson; M. T. Smith; and M. A. Stegman. 1988. Who bears the burden of development impact fees? *Journal of the American Planning Association* 54(1): 49-55.

Ladd, H. F. 1994. Fiscal impacts of local population growth: a conceptual and empirical analysis. *Regional Science and Urban Economics* 24: 661-686.

Lillydahl, J. H.; A. C. Nelson; T. V. Ramis; A. Rivasplata; and S. R. Schell. 1988. The need for a standard state impact fee enabling act. *Journal of the American Planning Association* 54(1): 7-17.

Moore, J. E. II, and P. Gordon. 1990. A sequential programming model of urban land development. *Socio-Economic Planning Science* 24(3): 199-216.

Myers, D. 1988. Building knowledge about quality of life for urban planning. *Journal of the American Planning Association* 54(3): 347-359.

Nelson, A. C. 1988. Symposium: development impact fees introduction. *Journal of the American Planning Association* 54(3): 347-359.

Nicholas, J. C. 1988. *The calculation of proportionate-share impact fees.* Chicago, IL: American Planning Association.

Nicholas, J. C., and A. C. Nelson. 1988. Determining the appropriate development impact fee using the rational nexus test. *Journal of the American Planning Association* 54(1): 56-66.

Nicholas, J. C.; A. C. Nelson; and J. C. Juergensmeyer. 1991. *A practitioner's guide to development impact fees.* Chicago, IL: American Planning Association.

North, D. 1995. Five propositions about institutional change. In J. Knight and I. Sened, eds., *Explaining social institutions.* University of Michigan Press.

Ormsbee, L. E., and K. E. Lansey. 1994. Optimal control of water supply pumping systems. *Journal of Water Resources Planning and Management* 120(2): 237-252.

Peiser, R. 1988. Calculating equity-neutral water and sewer impact fees. *Journal of the American Planning Association* 54(1): 38-48.

Peiser, R., and E. Heikkila. 1992. Urban sprawl, density, and accessibility. *Papers in Regional Science: The Journal of the Regional Science Association* 71(4): 153-166.

Rubinfeld, D. L., and P. Shapiro. 1989. Micro-estimation of the demand for schooling. *Regional Science and Urban Economics* 19: 381-398.

Samuelson, P. 1954. The pure theory of public expenditure. *Review of Economics and Statistics* 36: 387-398.

Shieh, J. Y. 1995. Using GIS to measure accessibility impacts of transportation policies: application to Taipei. Doctoral dissertation in progress. School of Urban and Regional Planning, University of Southern California, Los Angeles.

Snyder, T. P., and M. A. Stegman. 1987. *Paying for growth: using development impact fees to finance infrastructure*. Washington, DC: Urban Land Institute.

Stroud, N. 1988. Legal considerations of development impact fees. *Journal of the American Planning Association* 54(1): 29–37.

Tiebout, C. 1956. A pure theory of local expenditures. *Journal of Political Economy* 64: 416–424.

Turvey, R. 1963. On divergences between social and private cost. *Economica* 30: 309–314.

Weibull, J. W. 1980. On the numerical measurement of accessibility. *Environment and Planning A* 12: 53–67.

Index

Note: Italicized page numbers refer to figures and tables.